Praise for *Hiding Out*

"[*Hiding Out*] brims with drunkenness, sexuality and urgency. As a storyteller, Allen is unafraid of the graphic, yet uses those scenes to push forward her narrative. Her gift for holding up the seemingly common to the light, turning it this way and that to unveil gut-punching emotion, is apparent from the first page. . . . Allen's details give heartbeat to every scene. Allen showcases excellent writing skills, packaging grit and grime into glistening prose. Her twisted mystery, family woes of the nastiest kind and multilayered love stories spin together to form a 'can't-put-down' read in *Hiding Out*."

—*Washington Post*

"Bonded by booze and blackmail, the middle-aged Sir John and his barely legal daughter hit bars together, cruising for young men for him and older women for her. Allen's life—once dominated by cruelty and abuse—takes a deep dive into decadence, fueled by cocaine, champagne and Sir John's never-ending supply of mysterious money. *Hiding Out* is about a lot of lies, and some are the ones we tell ourselves."

—*Daily News* (New York)

"[Tina Alexis Allen] doesn't hold back in her memoir *Hiding Out*."

—*Teen Vogue*

"Tina Alexis Allen was tired of living in the shadows. . . . She is hoping [*Hiding Out*] will encourage others to come forward and speak out against being abused."

—FoxNews.com

"*Hiding Out* is a whiplash read for its drama and intrigue, but it's also an openhearted exploration of history, hypocrisy, and the fact that we may never know the answers to the questions that have shaped our lives."

—Shondaland.com

"I read [*Hiding Out*] cover to cover. The writing was excellent, and [I] was completely engrossed; the story is incredibly compelling."

—Megyn Kelly, *Megyn Kelly Today*

"This is not a book for the faint of heart. Tina scrubs her soul clean within its pages, uncovering and exposing the web of lies her young adulthood had become. . . . [She] succeeds on all levels with this memoir you definitely will not forget."

—Talk Nerdy With Us

"Scandalous, resonant, and refreshingly free of self-justification, *Hiding Out* is a compelling tale of sin and service, concealment and disclosure, hedonism and righteousness. At its heart is the troubled love between a papal knight worthy of the pen of Evelyn Waugh, and a daughter who might have stepped from the pages of Anaïs Nin. More than a memoir of Catholic family dysfunction, and more than a journey into addiction and recovery, it's an in-the-moment dose of the exhilarating tragedy of being alive."

—Mark Riebling, author of *Church of Spies*

"Brutally honest and shamelessly truthful, Allen discovers that deceit is not an individual act, and learns how, unless interrupted by sunshine, exploitation endlessly engenders exploitation. Throughout the memoir, however, Allen's strong sense of self guides her away from shadow and unerringly towards real family love. For the author, the very act of writing this book—of declaring the truth after years and layers of lies—*is* her transformative path. And so we, as readers, in receiving these secrets, act as agents of her transformation."

—Father Richard Rohr, author of *Falling Upward*

"A writer candidly confronts her personal truth in her quest for transformation, transcendence, and redemption."

—*Kirkus Reviews*

"Deeply felt."

—*Booklist*

Hiding Out

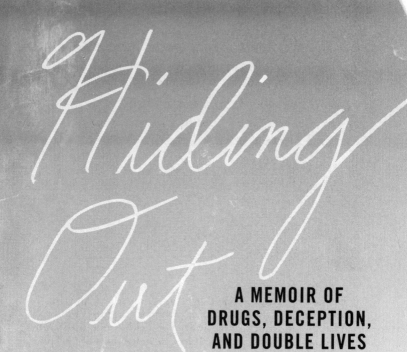

Hiding Out

A MEMOIR OF DRUGS, DECEPTION, AND DOUBLE LIVES

TINA ALEXIS ALLEN

DEY ST.

An Imprint of WILLIAM MORROW

This is a work of nonfiction. The events and experiences I describe are all true and have been faithfully rendered as I have remembered them, to the best of my ability. I have changed the names of the members of my family and those closest to me in order to protect their privacy. Though conversations come from my keen recollection of them, they are not written to represent word-for-word accounts; rather, I've retold them in a way that reveals the meaning of what was said and the spirit of the moment.

DEY ST.

HarperCollins books may be purchased for educational, business, or sales promotional use. For information, please email the Special Markets Department at SPsales@harpercollins.com.

A hardcover edition of this book was published in 2018 by Dey Street, an imprint of William Morrow.

FIRST DEY STREET PAPERBACK EDITION PUBLISHED 2018.

Designed by Paula Russell Szafranski

Lettering by Owen Corrigan

Library of Congress Cataloging-in-Publication Data has been applied for.

ISBN 978-0-06-256568-6

18 19 20 21 22 LSC 10 9 8 7 6 5 4 3 2 1

For everyone who hasn't yet spoken up,

written it out, or quietly embraced their story

Contents

Prologue

To whom it may concern: I'm okay. I survived. So, it's all good. Well, that's probably an overstatement. But I am good. I don't do what I used to do; I almost never even want to. That's progress. I'm proud of that. This is starting to sound like a disclaimer, or a warning. Maybe it is. Please be forewarned: if you worry for the girl I was—the one you are about to meet— just know the woman I am is a fierce, mostly well-adjusted warrior, who cares for her well-being and yours, too—even though we don't know each other.

I also care about my freedom. I take it very, very seriously. It's what I live for. Constantly testing myself to take off another layer of my armor, another layer of shame and guilt, and be bold, be honest. Get naked. Fall. Cry. Hate. Love. I imagine it's why I became an actress. Although, as wise as I think I might be, it took an outsider to explain, after reading this book, that I have always been an actress. There was no way I was going to be anything else—no matter how many careers I may have had before. She's right. I've been acting my whole life. It's how I got through it all.

After years of recklessness, I'm very careful about how I spend my time these days, who I share myself with. It might be hard to believe when you read about the girl I once was, but I'm coming up on twenty-five years of a loving partnership. She is my chosen family and the foundation for the work I do in all other areas of my life. When my partner and I have those occasional conversations about the blood and guts of our long-term commitment, I am still amazed how good it feels to risk it all in the name of honesty. I'm not interested in lying to her or to you. Pretending that I'm completely recovered from all of it. But I aim to be.

To be transparent, I'm not sober in the AA sense of the word, but I have chosen not to drink, as a way of making amends to myself. Mostly because, when I decided to become an actor at nearly thirty, I knew I had a lot of catching up to do. I learned very quickly in my first acting classes that I couldn't fully access my emotions if I had consumed even a couple glasses of wine the night before. And so I stopped, because having an acting career that involved a full expression of my feelings trumped bold, rich, expensive Cabernet. My life improved once I decided to put my drama on stage and screen, instead of off.

Seven years ago, I decided that the next right step in my career and my healing—they have never been separate—would be to write and perform a solo show playing my deceased father. Like, literally, to put on a suit and tie, hair slicked, Dad's English American accent operating, and to be him, no holds barred. My intention was to understand Dad more deeply. He had passed in 2005—five years before I embarked on the show. And I had long forgiven him for the things he did that you'll soon read, so the hard part was over.

For many reasons, I do not believe telling the truth about Dad's secrets is blasphemy, betrayal, unkind, or disrespectful. I don't judge him. And there is much to learn from history. So,

I took on his shame, his guilt, his poor decisions, his charm, and his goodness in front of a live audience. Daughter into father, transformed, I was him. I wasn't acting Dad. I really felt I became him. In so doing, I finally understood him, his anger, his pain, his darkness, his love. The experience was a healing salve for my relationship with him. It was also one of the scariest things I have done, and that was before some of my siblings began sending e-mails. They said I was wrong, heartless, careless, thoughtless, and generally a bad person for telling the truth in a public forum. How dare I? And the fact that my tagline for the show was sardonic and funny proved their point.

There can be problems when you insist on telling the truth in a gigantic family that was raised in a culture of secrecy. I imagine that's probably true even in small families. The challenge to tell it like it is can be overwhelming, as if you were swimming the English Channel with weights on your ankles. You might drown or you might find a strength you didn't know you had. You might give up your people pleasing, disrobe from the keep-the-peace coat of armor you've spent much of your life wearing. You might come to terms with the fact that everyone in your family has their own wounds, their own version of the story, and their own sense of right and wrong.

I decided not to do polling about what should or shouldn't be included in this book. To me there is no shame in telling the truth, but ironically, I think shame is usually the reason people don't. Why do we keep secrets? Who are we protecting? And why? I find the whole truth invaluable. Worth the risk. Why would I want to pretend my father was just this holy man without telling the whole story? For me, his amazing life is a wealth of opportunity for teaching moments. There's much to learn from him, and I'm interested in that journey. Not protecting his false image. Or mine.

I've had enough pretending; it consumed my childhood. Adults have asked me to keep their secrets since well before I was ten. I'm done. Not out of revenge, but out of a deep-seated belief that it's the secret that causes the pain, the disease, the bondage, more so than the thing you are keeping secret. Maybe it's true that the world will judge me, and Dad, label us sinners, horrible people, from a disgraceful family of so-called Catholics. It's highly possible. But I say better that than to live a half truth, buried in secrets.

My third-to-last therapist used to say, "Tina, tell your family that you are not changing any of the names in order to protect the innocent." She was a very progressive woman who knew that we are only as sick as our secrets—there's never been a truer cliché, as far as I'm concerned. That said, I have changed names and descriptions of people and places, because I've come far enough to know that there's only one voice to listen to when it comes to secrets and lies and telling your side of the story: your own.

So everything you are about to read is my truth. Well, to be clear, my younger self's truth. I decided to write this story in the first person, sans the older, therapized me who might have been tempted to overanalyze, explain, justify, or hold your hand through this period of my life. More than anything, I didn't want to mess with the purity of her experience. She—younger me—never felt safe to tell anyone what was going on. So this decision to let her lead was simply me wanting to stay out of her way. And honor her. I didn't want to inaccurately portray her feelings and actions by planting my adult self between you and her. This is her story. So, I don't claim to speak for anyone else's experience. I know there are as many different stories and interpretations as there are human beings. I am one. And this is mine. And only mine. Take what you like and leave the rest. But when you are done, I hope you will come back to one thought that I really want you to remember: I'm happy. I'm good. Really.

1

Congregation

Even though she's married and doesn't live here anymore, my big sister Frances climbs the creaky stairs to the girls' floor practically singing, "Tina, you're dead." Ever since I was a kid Frances has seemed to enjoy tormenting me. Once she woke me from a sound sleep by holding smelling salts under my nose, and when I was eleven she kicked my leg repeatedly while I read the four questions at our paschal meal. The only thing stranger than my not wanting to get Frances in trouble for torturing me over bitter herbs and haroseth is the fact that my devoutly Catholic family even celebrates Passover. Dad insists on observing everything involving Jesus.

The polished veneer of Frances's burgundy gown and cropped velvet blazer can't smooth out the bite in her attitude as she warns, "Dad's asking where the hell you are."

"Why me? Magdalene and Rebecca aren't ready, either."

Her laughter is acid. "Well, he hates you."

I push into the steamy girls' bathroom with a sudden stomach-ache, wishing she wasn't right. He does seem to hate me.

"Please shut the door," sweet Rebecca says from the shower.

While rolling my long hair in hot curlers, I kick the warped door shut. "You better hurry up, Dad's pissed that we're late," I say to Rebecca.

The door swings back open, and Kate pops her head in. "Hey, Tina, do you have a hair ribbon I can borrow?"

"I don't wear them anymore, I'm not into preppy."

"There's nothing wrong with preppy," she insists, looking as pretty and conservative as a Kennedy.

Magdalene rushes in, grabs Kate's wineglass. Chardonnay sloshes up the side as she eagerly tilts it toward her lips.

"Would someone PLEASE shut the darn door? It's freezing," Rebecca begs.

Magdalene peers through my panty hose. "Are those my lace underwear?"

She bumps me, pushing for center stage in our toothpaste-sprayed mirror.

"Give me a break, I wouldn't touch your disgusting underwear."

"I swear to God, those better not be mine!"

I give Magdalene the finger and walk out. Even though I admire her, we've always been competitive, probably since we are the two most athletic girls in our family. After sharing a bathroom with seven sisters for most of my eighteen years, it should be easier now that the last of us is in college. But having so many back home for the holidays reminds me how sick and tired I am of sharing—except when I don't have clean underwear.

Careful not to smudge my freshly painted fingernails, I throw on a nightie, walk down the creaky steps, and slip along the dark-paneled second-floor hallway, past the boys' bedrooms and the second-floor bathroom. The sounds of Christmas Eve at 5 East Irving Street rise up from the first floor: a blender swirling, the gurgle of baby talk from my nephews and nieces, the hard laughter of my five brothers, all coated by Johnny Mathis's falsetto.

The heavy mahogany door to my parents' room is open as I approach. A pile of unwrapped gifts and thirteen empty stockings are strewn across the floor.

"Is that one of my lovely daughters?" Mom calls out, her face lighting up as she sees me. "Ahhh, there's my baby . . . just in time to help your mother with this." Mom nods at the diamond and emerald necklace next to her on the bed. I kiss her soft cheek and breathe in the familiar smell of perfume and hair spray.

She is shaving a corn from her pinky toe with a straight razor blade. I glance at her purple ankles and calves—raw and veiny—and a lump forms in my throat.

"May I borrow a nail clipper?" I ask, tamping down my emotion.

"Sure, sweetie, in my side drawer." She gestures to the cluttered bedside table that is spilling over with ripped coupons, a spool of thread, Scotch tape, and Christmas bows, spread among her rosary beads, a worn Bible, and a can of diet soda.

Mom moans as she sticks a Dr. Scholl's corn pad between her toes and begins repositioning her two-hundred-plus pounds in order to get her feet into the support stockings, which are the thickness and color of an Ace bandage. She yelps as she pulls the hose over the four inches of redness between her ankle and calf, then pushes herself off the sagging bed. With a half bend, she tugs the hose over her wrestler-size thigh and attaches it to her white garter.

Dad flies into the room, holding an empty ice tray.

"What the bloody hell is taking so long?!"

I flinch at the vicious clip of his British accent and without thinking I'm standing in front of Mom—my sweaty hands fiddling with her necklace, my mouth dry.

"What do you need?" Mom asks kindly, stepping out from behind me.

Dad's clean-shaven face is flushed with rage as he scans the mound of unwrapped presents. A dish towel, stained pink from the whiskey sours he's been blending, is thrown over the shoulder of his ruby smoking jacket.

"What do I need? What do I need?! Well, for starters, I need someone to fill up the bloody ice trays around here! How the hell am I supposed to make sours for forty people with no ice?" he says, waving the tray in front of Mom's soft blue eyes.

"Dear, the boys picked up bags of ice. I'm sure they put them in the basement freezer."

"I don't damn well care about bags of ice, what I care about is common courtesy!" His moist face turns toward mine, his large nose close enough for me to see his pores. "When you finish using a goddamn ice tray, fill it up!" he yells.

"Dad, I'll go get the ice," I blurt defensively.

He steps closer. I jerk away, expecting a slap, but am hit only by his cold, hateful stare. Dad only slapped me across the face once. I was eleven, in the kitchen with Mom, when he began to verbally attack her.

"Leave her the hell alone!" I yelled, as if I were David standing up to Goliath.

Too bad I didn't have a sword. Now, Dad expresses his anger silently, those small green eyes oozing disdain at me, and his narrow lips turn down in disgust at my curlers, stockinged feet, and general lack of readiness.

"GET THE HELL OUT OF MY ROOM! You're late! You girls will be late to your own funeral!"

It's no secret that if it were up to Dad, he would have had thirteen sons and zero daughters. He was hoping to have at least enough boys to name after the twelve apostles. Sounds funny, but it's no joke.

I stare down at the clean crease of his tuxedo pants, at the shine on his long black dress shoes, at the pale carpet.

"I just need to help Mom with her necklace," I murmur defiantly, giving him my backside, refusing to leave.

Mom reaches for the flowy peach gown that hangs atop her closet door; her white slip rises, revealing her mounds of dimpled flesh.

"Oh, for God's sake, woman, you really need to lose some of that weight," Dad says, his nostrils flaring as a look of repulsion sweeps over his face. Mom drops her head like an abused stray. I want to strangle him, but before I do anything he swivels toward the door and kicks a pile of gifts: flannel pajamas fly out of a white box; bags of stocking stuffers spill; a record album sails across the room and into Mom's bare, raw leg. A whimper escapes her lips.

"How many bloody gifts does this family need? There are children starving all over this world!" And with that, he marches out.

"John, I'll be right down," she calls meekly, swallowing the humiliation like a communion wafer.

We silently check for broken skin, only finding a small indentation in the center of her shin. I look away. Dad's immaculate bedside table is set like a church altar: satin runner, wooden rosary beads, a pocket Bible, Italian lire lying in a fine china dish engraved with an image of St. Peter's Basilica, prayer cards stacked as neat as a casino deck.

"Tina, zip me up, please," Mom gently commands while running rose lipstick over her mouth.

"Sure," I whisper.

"I must be shrinking or you're still growing. Heavens, I used to be five foot six," she muses.

I look at us standing in the mirror. At sixty, she must be shrinking, because I'm definitely five foot six—same as I've been since I was twelve, and I'm probably not going to have another growth spurt. Not even my University of Maryland basketball coach can scream more height out of me. I drape the jewels across her throat, staring at our reflections.

My body is like Dad's—narrow hips, long legs—but my face is Mom's—almond-shaped blue eyes, strong thin nose, delicate lips, and pale skin.

"Now, hurry and get dressed, sweetie. Let's not upset your father any more."

†

In the corner of the foyer, a ten-foot Douglas fir dazzles with colored lights; candy canes; my favorite ornament that I always hang: an elf holding a basketball; and perfect crisp gingham bows that preppy Kate pressed and tied before draping the tinsel one strand at a time. A sea of presents swells out from under its branches—six feet deep and four feet high. With the noise rising, my body tightens as if bracing for a cresting storm wave.

I inhale the pine, perfume and cologne, roast beef, Yorkshire pudding, and Dad's infamous Cabernet-soaked gravy; slowly, the tight spot in the middle of my chest eases.

"Farrah Fawcett, watch out! The baby of this family is all grown up!" My brother-in-law Chip whistles as I descend the staircase, the last to arrive at our Christmas Eve celebration.

"Nice of you to join us," my brother Simon says dryly, then sucks on his whiskey sour and eyes my dress over the lip of his crystal glass.

"Shut up," I murmur without meeting his gaze.

"Excuse me, what did you say?" He feigns aggression.

Simon's wife, Becky, rushes out of the packed living room toward us.

"Tina, don't you think that dress is more appropriate for New Year's Eve than Christmas Eve?" She gives me a tight smile.

It is as noisy as a henhouse where the rest of my family has gathered around the hors d'oeuvres in the living room. Not even the wall-to-wall carpet can mute the sound.

Kneeling in front of the decommissioned fireplace that

houses the Nativity scene, Rebecca gently points out the various players to a few of the children. Above them hang portraits of Mom and Dad wearing their Knights of the Holy Sepulchre robes embossed with the crusader cross on their hearts. My parents are so devoted to the Catholic Church that they have been knighted—Sir John and Lady Anne Worthington—by Pope Pius XII.

Hanging between the paintings is a three-foot crucifix—a reminder that your troubles are irrelevant in the grand scheme of all Jesus endured.

"Hey, kid," my sister Margaret calls while blowing her cigarette smoke toward the high ceiling.

Then a swarm of beautifully dressed creatures converges on me, tossing comments like rice at a wedding: "Oh, you look pretty, Tina." "Neat dress!" "Hey, baby sister." "It's about time." "Diego, look at her figure: holy moly, I should play basketball!" "How's the season going, Tina?" "You dating anyone?" "Hey, hot dog, how's the jump shot?" "Go Terrapins!"

"Hi . . . Thanks . . . Hi . . . Good . . . I like your dress, too . . . Shut up . . . The season's going great . . . No, not dating anyone," I fire back at them—mostly lies. Keeping secrets in a big family is easier than one might think, because with so many people, there's no chance for a real discussion. It's all one big constant interruption. When questions get too personal, I just turn my head to another conversation.

Margaret's husband, Diego, puts his thin arm around me.

"You look almost as good as I do tonight," he teases.

Even I can see that his fitted black suit and movie star looks could cause girls to throw their panties. Rowdy laughter and high fives erupt from the corner where three of my brothers in their boxy suits—Luke, Matthew, and Paul—are shaking their heads in our direction.

"Where'd you get that suit, fag?" Luke japes.

"You expecting a flood on Christmas Eve?" Matthew points at Diego's tapered pant leg.

"Yeah, I am," Diego banters.

"Okay, but Sammy Davis Jr. wants his suit back, faggot," Paul cracks.

Dad staggers up to Diego and me, but I refuse to acknowledge him.

"Christine, you finally decided to join us," my father slurs, handing me a whiskey sour. His black bow tie pinches the blotchy skin of his neck.

"I was late because I had basketball practice," I answer brusquely, sipping my drink.

Dad nods approvingly at Diego's suit. "Young man, there are more sours in the blender, don't stand there with an empty glass."

"Tina, you want a refill?"

"No, I'm good—"

"Her name is Christine! I never understand why you people must bastardize a saint's name." Dad squeezes the back of Diego's neck, sending him on his way.

Gazing up at the crucifix, Dad reaches inside his velvet jacket, resting his hand on his heart as tears form in his eyes.

"Christine, please . . . take a moment to see . . . look there." He points his index finger toward Jesus on the cross, his massive ruby ring distracting my glance.

"How dare we complain?" my father says softly, wiping a tear away. He assesses the crèche. Each year Dad gets down on his knees to set up the Nativity scene. For these hours, he is a stranger to me, acting gentle with his wooden flock, but it's too short a time for me to let my guard down with him or expect his love will shine my way. Dad's main squeeze seems to be Jesus—whether the baby in the manger or Jesus the man, who's plastered on the cross throughout our house in every art form: statues, sculptures, prints, and paintings. Dad never gets wrapped up in our birthdays the way he does Christ's. In fact, he doesn't know our birthdays, only our feast days—the birthdays of the saints we are named after. The closest he ever gets to fatherly behavior is when he lays out straw, props up camels, and steadies the wise men bearing gifts. His final ritual for setting up the Nativity is kissing baby Jesus and then covering the little guy with one of his crisp white handkerchiefs, to remain in place until Christmas Eve.

"Christine, our most gracious and gentle Savior was born and then died for your sins. This . . . you must never forget."

I look for an exit strategy and gulp my drink. An electrifying freeze spreads through my brain just as Mom enters the room carrying a plate of stuffed mushrooms. She transforms into a beauty on Christmas Eve, a rare occasion when she takes a little time for herself, wearing makeup, jewels, and a gown from Lane Bryant. My siblings swarm her, and she beams, as happy as she's been all year, in the midst of her children.

"Mom, do you need help?"

"Sit, Mom, you have to try Gloria's spinach dip."

"What can I do?"

"You look lovely, Mom."

"Mom, why don't you put your feet up and let me take over?"

She drinks in all the attention. Dad watches, polishing off his sour.

"Your mother is a saint," he says with envy, knowing none of us love him half as much as we love her. He then takes a plastic bottle of holy water from the mantel.

"Shall we bless the tree? Children! Mother!" He waves his large hands as if leading one of his pilgrimages, and there's a rush of velvet, satin, chiffon, and fine wool into the foyer. Someone shuts off the music, and the excited and tipsy adults surround the magnificent tree, the little ones pushing to the front, practically eye to eye with the mountain of gifts. The lights are dimmed as Dad begins to sing.

" 'O come, O come, Emmanuel, and ransom captive Israel that mourns in lonely exile here.' " Dad's beautiful tenor— perfected during years in a prestigious London boys' choir—

ignites a longing within me. Perhaps I want to bask in some of the attention he gives Christ.

Helen, the oldest girl and my godmother, wraps her arm around my waist, reminding me how lucky I am to have big sisters. The boys are huddled together, belting through their chuckles. Mom croons next to Dad, hands folded, eyes glistening as she gazes at her brood.

I feel a powerful rush of love and pride in my family; it takes my breath away. I wish this moment could last and utter a prayer that Dad's temper will remain softened by whiskey. As we continue caroling, he douses the tree with the holy water, then passes the bottle to Mom to hold as he picks up a linen scroll.

"Family, we have received a special apostolic blessing from the Holy Father," Dad announces, unrolling the paper. He reads slowly, exaggerating his accent: "His Holiness, John Paul II, cordially imparts his apostolic blessing to the Worthington family and invokes an abundance of divine grace."

The singing starts again, and I finally find my voice when the gang roars, "Five golden rings!" in a laughter-filled rendition of "The Twelve Days of Christmas." Then Dad herds his Trapp Family Singers back into the living room to bless the manger.

"Owww!" I cry out, feeling a sharp pinch under my arm.

Dad glares at me; Simon snickers. I'd like to shove him into the tree, let the pine needles do my dirty work, but repress my fury instead. Dad makes a grand sign of the cross over the Nativity and the family follows. I join the ritual out of obligation. Dad reads from a small black prayer book. "An angel of the Lord appeared to them, and the glory of the Lord shone around them, and they were terrified. But the angel said to them, 'Do not be afraid. I bring you good news that will cause great joy for all the people. Today in the town of David a Savior has been born to you; he is the Messiah, the Lord. This will be a sign to you: you will find a baby wrapped in cloths and lying in a manger.'"

Dad hands Mom the prayer book as he gets down on one knee, bowing his head with great reverence and tenderly removing the handkerchief. Christ is born. He tucks the handkerchief inside his jacket, rises, and offers a final blessing: "In the name of the Father and of the Son and of the Holy Spirit. Now, who wants a whiskey sour?!"

†

As soon as dinner is over, I stealthily slip away and into the front hall.

"Where the hell do you think you're going?" Simon demands as I wrap a black cashmere scarf around my shoulders.

"Out," I say, trying to act casual while searching for Mom's car keys near the front door. He steps closer, his over six feet of height dominating me, even in my heels.

"Yeah, smart-ass, I figured that. Where? Midnight mass starts in a half hour. I'm sure Dad wouldn't appreciate you leaving in the middle of dessert."

There are a million things I could probably scream at him right now, but there's no bridge from the shoreline of my feelings to the depths of the words.

"I need to get Mom some stocking stuffers at the drugstore, okay?" I lie effortlessly, hoping he won't be a dick and draw attention to my exit.

"I'll save a seat for you at mass," he says, softening, and heads into the loud dining room.

Grabbing the Chevy key chain from next to a commemorative tiara of Pope John Paul, I slip out the front door. Sneaking off the wraparound porch, happily away from that game of secrets I play when around my family, I want to giggle, to dance and swing my arms like a schoolgirl. Despite the frosty night blowing through my dress I glide down the front steps. The massive elm trees dusted with an early Maryland snowfall spread their arms wide, as if celebrating with me.

I breathe easily into the night and cross the frozen lawn to the end of our long driveway. Thrilled to drive—soul music blasting—to my girlfriend Nic's house for a quick Christmas make-out under the mistletoe among her gay friends, who are too old to worry about sneaking out.

"God damn it," I yell. Three people have parked behind my getaway car.

I peer through icy windows for keys left in the ignition. Nothing. Inside Simon's Honda, I spot my favorite basketball—an expensive leather game ball I stole last year from my high school equipment room—on the vinyl seat. The asshole is still taking my shit without asking.

Toes numb, my slight buzz now sour, I climb back onto the porch and peer through the bay window. In the dining room, the oval teak table is packed elbow to elbow. A separate kids' table is elegantly set for the overflow. Fat silver candelabras cast a glow over the china and burgundy wine. The ocher mission jar—a staple in the center of the table for as long as I can recall—has been moved to the end of the buffet tonight. Still, Dad expects us to drop at least a penny a day into it so that the kids from the Home of Peace orphanage in Jerusalem can have food on their table and get a decent first communion outfit.

My chair is taken by my eight-year-old niece, who is singing for two of my brothers. At the far end of the dining room table, Dad shakes his head—a look of disgust covers his ruddy face, nostrils wide in a huff. Nose pressed against the frosted front window, I watch Dad's rage build.

He slams his hand down, turning a silver breadbasket upside down. French rolls go flying. The chaos halts. Grown-ups become childlike, with wide eyes and tight mouths, as Mom bows her head. Dad's muffled yelling reaches the porch as he stands up and throws down his cloth napkin. Sheepish faces watch him leave the room as he screams, waving his hands in a rage.

I wish he'd leave for Rome right now, instead of tomorrow.

2
Blessings

When it comes to older women, I'm a barnacle. The slightest bit of intimacy, and I'm no longer eighteen, I'm struck, stuck, needing to be fed like a hungry toddler. Even Coach Norris noticed something between me and Shawn—one of the assistant coaches at Bergen State—our opponent tonight. Coach hovered around our quick postgame conversation as the rest of my teammates boarded the Greyhound for our three-hour ride back to campus.

"Tina!" Coach Norris calls, standing at the door of the bus, a slight smirk across her handsome face.

I climb onto the bus and find an empty seat in the front—normally, the quieter section where those players who want to study sit. The back is noisy; a boom box plays Chaka Khan. The bus grinds away from the small college gymnasium.

"You okay?" Norris whispers, leaning on the upholstered seat next to me, holding a stack of small white envelopes. Unintentionally, I catch her eyes—they seem to be assuring me that whatever I say won't be held against me. Just a secret between her and her freshman player.

"Yeah, I'm okay." I act cool, pretending she didn't just watch me flirting away with an opposing coach.

"You want to talk about it?" She smiles.

I fake a smile back, shaking my head, afraid that she might tell Nic—her friend, my girlfriend—whatever I say. No way I want to deal with that fallout. Keeping secrets is a second skin I wear, even with people I know are gay, like Coach Norris. She stares at me, probably hoping her authority will break my silence, but this is lightweight compared to most of the things I've hidden.

"Here you go." She hands me an envelope with my per diem and walks down the aisle to pass out the rest. After a short distance on I-95, I see the golden arches of McDonald's in the distance. Our husky driver exits the New Jersey turnpike, cruising around the off-ramp, toward our pit stop. Full with longing, I'm not hungry.

I remember the special Friday nights when Mom didn't feel like cooking and broke the rules—good Catholics shouldn't eat meat on Fridays—by feeding us McDonald's when Dad was overseas, which was most of the time. We'd have to call ahead to have them specially prepare our order: twenty-six hamburgers—most of us got two—fourteen large french fries, plus apple pies and milk shakes. Only Mom would remain reverent, ordering a Filet-O-Fish. I always went along to pick up the food, so I didn't get stuck with one of the french fry containers that had been ransacked. Being the youngest of thirteen makes you crafty, keeps you on your toes, and trains you to run like hell when you hear "DINNER!" so you can get a place in the front of the chow line.

My teammates pile off the bus as I feign serious involvement with my political science textbook. I stretch out across two seats and open the per diem envelope. A crisp ten-dollar bill seems puny compared to the spending money Dad would give us. Maybe to make up for his lousy childhood in London during World War I, which included rationing and air raids;

a stepfather who beat him with a belt, according to Mom; or worse, being a bastard child. In 1920, Dad's mother and her husband, Mr. Worthington, left London for Alberta, Canada, with their infant son, Ed, to find work. While working on a ranch, Dad's mother had an affair with the horse trainer. Eventually, pregnant with his child, she left in disgrace back to England, her marriage to Mr. Worthington over. Dad was born in London, his mother pretending Mr. Worthington was the father, when, in fact, Dad's father was secretly the horse trainer. When Dad was thirty, he tracked down Mr. Worthington and learned the truth: Worthington wasn't his old man. And despite further attempts, he never found his father. Dad's real last name—our real last name—will never be known.

Soon after Dad was born, his mother left him and his older brother with her mother, who had thirteen kids of her own, while she went cavorting around London. A few years later Dad's mother retrieved her sons to live with her new husband, Mr. Hall, the stepfather who beat Dad frequently. Maybe that's why Dad yells and screams so much.

In order to escape his stepfather's fist, Dad lied about his age and joined the British Merchant Navy at sixteen. During World War II, while serving with the British Army in Palestine, Dad seriously considered joining the priesthood. On a brief leave, he was in Jerusalem at the same time as Anne Allen. She was a nurse in the American army on leave from Africa, visiting the Holy Land for the first time. She became our mother.

On Good Friday 1944, Dad, practically a scholar of Catholicism, offered to give Anne Allen a guided tour of the Stations of the Cross. Not a romantic date, but it makes sense when you consider how much both of my parents adore Jesus. In the photo of them walking the cobblestone Via Dolorosa—the path that Christ took to his crucifixion—they are sporting their military uniforms. Dad looks beefier than the skinny man I've always known and a bit nerdy with his thick black glasses—blind as a bat even then; and Mom, big boned but not yet fat, looking kinda butch with her short hair, sturdy shoes, purposeful stride, and striking New England looks. Sometimes I wonder how long it took my father's sharp tongue to wear down that strong woman, who proudly served her country and who stands even more erect than he does in the photo.

My mother has always been very patriotic, enlisting in World War II not because she has an aggressive bone in her body but because she felt it was her duty, since no one else in her family could. Her eyes get watery as quickly during "God Bless America" as they do when she talks about losing her father when she was nine or reminisces about Winnie, her sister, who at age twenty-seven died of tuberculosis, when Mom was just twenty-two. When Winnie was bedridden she wrote a poem to Mom: "Day after day bed-fast I lie, gazing lastingly at the sky. / How oft comes the sweet memory of my dear sister Anne and me. / At sunset, before the nightfall, to my dear Anne I would call, / come with me and watch by my side at the beautiful clouds as they ride." Not Wordsworth or Tennyson, but full of undying, sweet, corny, sisterly love.

Sometimes I'm not sure if it's Mom's Depression-era upbringing as the youngest of five children, or all the loss, that makes her warm chubby face unable to mask the droop of sadness. Yet, melancholy as she often seems, I've only seen her cry once.

My nana—whom I never met—was a devout Catholic, kind and selfless like Mom, but looked as serious in photos as the lady in *American Gothic*. During the Great Depression, and despite the frigid New England winters, Nana Allen, a jobless widow, waited until her children got home from school to light the coal stove. They were so poor, the nuns at Mom's Catholic school gave her an old uniform to wear. It must have felt good for Mom to be able to buy all of us brand-new school uniforms and saddle shoes every year. Mom talks much less about her dad, an Irish bar owner, who I'm pretty sure served himself a drink as often as he served his customers. Mom doesn't remember a lot about him, since she was so young when he died, but she does recall that Nana used to say, "Little girls shouldn't sit on their father's lap." Why would she say such a weird thing? I have always wondered if Grandpa Allen bothered Mom, or was Nana just warning her because of something that happened to Nana when she was a little girl?

My parents' four-year courtship happened mostly via airmail between London and Boston. During that time, Dad's mother died and Mr. Hall got remarried, leaving Dad with stepparents. Eager to marry Mom, he begged his commanding officer in the London War Office for a transfer to the War Office in the U.S.—located in Washington, D.C. Their small wedding took place in Massachusetts, the honeymoon a simple weekend in New York City while on their way down to D.C. and their new life together in the nation's capital. Mom, already twenty-eight, immediately became a baby factory—pop, pop, pop—having thirteen kids in fifteen years. After a few years, with five kids and more on the way, Dad started a travel agency, Holy Pilgrimages. I can't deny it, Dad has balls.

Travel runs in our veins. Our first family trip to New York City, in 1968, was to celebrate my parents' twentieth wedding anniversary, and we were showstoppers. Manhattanites were so enthralled with us, a well-mannered clan ranging in age from five to twenty, some asked if we were part of an orphanage. On a lark, we were invited to the stage during a weekly radio show featuring Vincent Lopez and his orchestra and sang "Edelweiss." We began a family tradition as the American version of the Trapp Family Singers, performing the song regularly at weddings or anywhere they'd have us. Even though my parents wanted more kids, they stopped after me—Mom says I'm her "lucky thirteen." That may be true, but I'm pretty sure her uterus finally cried uncle. The thing that my parents and a lot of devout Catholic families seem to miss is that the rhythm method doesn't work if you always got rhythm.

Now, despite the smell of french fries wafting through the open bus door, I don't feel like moving. You'd think I'd played the entire game instead of the meager final one minute and six seconds, after our team already had the game in the bag. I slip the ten-spot into my black dress pants, the crease still crisp, if uneven, from a solid hour of pressing last night at Nic's. Her face scrunched when I asked for the iron; she knows I never iron. I suck at it.

"Don't you have a maid who does this for you?" Nic joked as she handed me the can of starch.

It's true, Erie Frye, our longtime housekeeper, eventually got too old for waxing floors and scrubbing toilets, but Mom knew Erie needed the money, so she kept her on just to do our ironing. On Tuesdays, she'd press everything from linen napkins to Dad's custom-made shirts from Bangkok to our Catholic school uniforms. By the end of the day, the dining room looked like a religious laundry, with perfectly pressed garments hanging on the mahogany ledge that runs around the room, among Dad's vast collection of religious icons.

†

It still seems impossible—dreamlike, a comedy really—that a Greyhound bus arrived right outside our home to pick up my family, the back tires appearing mammoth compared to the wheels on our neighbors'—the Dorans'—shiny Cadillac. I watched the scene unfold out of a narrow third-floor window. The puff of dark smoke floated across the street toward the Ellermans' elegant porch, the dignified white pillars bright against the dirty exhaust. The towering vehicle seemed as awkward idling in front of 5 East Irving Street as me without a basketball on my hip. A sea of rowdy travelers descended across our front lawn—patches of grass missing from the wear and tear of a ginormous family taking frequent shortcuts—past hastily trimmed hedges, dragging suitcases and carry-on bags toward the bus. The redbrick sidewalk quickly transformed into an unruly queue spilling in multiple directions, with my ecstatic, waist-high nephews shoving and bumping their way to be first. My heart raced as I watched out Magdalene's bedroom window, ready to grab my suitcase and make a run for it, hoping I still had a shot at getting a window seat for our three-hour ride from the Maryland Beltway, up I-95, to JFK Airport. Being the youngest, I was used to fighting for a good seat. Even at four years old, I knew enough to clutch an apple while I took my nap to be sure no one ate it while I was sleeping.

I've always loved traveling. My first trip overseas, at barely ten years old, was filled with adrenaline-rushing anticipation. I was breathless for months over the concept that I would travel first class from New York to London—on an ocean liner that my siblings explained was longer than our suburban street and taller than our three-story house. How could a ship be longer than East Irving Street? It seemed as absurd as the old lady who lived in a shoe, who had so many kids she didn't know what to do.

Although that Greyhound bus was not nearly as long as the SS *France*, it did grab the attention of our neighbors, the elderly, well-groomed Dorans and the even older Mr. Shields—a former White House speechwriter. They stood on their tidy lawns and hosed sidewalks in their conservative apparel, watching another wild Worthington happening.

Our neighbors seemed to accept the chaos pouring out of 5 East Irving Street, since they too had raised large families, attending the same Catholic school and church right around the corner—Blessed Sacrament. In fact, B.S., as it's known, is so close to our house, we can walk out the front door five minutes before mass starts and still be early. Chevy Chase had loads of large families who belonged to Blessed Sacrament

Parish—the Smarts had sixteen children, the Shaughnessys thirteen, the Harringtons fourteen, the Crosbys ten, and on and on. When I was a baby, 7-Up sponsored an annual picnic at Rock Creek Park for families in the neighborhood with seven or more kids. The place was packed—good luck trying to get a turn on the swing set or the sliding board.

Dad said chartering a Greyhound was the most logical means of transportation to get twenty-five of us to New York's Kennedy Airport for our flight to Rome. Owning a travel agency, he'd know. I have no idea how, but Dad paid for the whole trip. Twenty-seven people—Dad even invited his stepparents, the Halls—ten days, first-class hotel, plus the chartered Greyhound. No one else seemed to know where all the money came from, either, but it never stopped any of us kids from enjoying Dad's generous offerings. He usually sent us a few at a time, or one by one, but that year, 1975, was a Catholic holy year, so Dad invited everyone—in-laws, grand-kids, even a few girlfriends and boyfriends. No sooner had we pulled away from 5 East Irving Street and turned right onto Connecticut Avenue, passing the exclusive Chevy Chase Country Club, with its stately stone wall—no Jews, blacks, or Italians allowed—than Dad started calling out our names from oldest to youngest, his formal roll call reminiscent of Sunday mornings, when he'd shout our names from the second-floor landing—not moving on until he got a rousing response—to be sure his children were awake for mass. One by one, we marched, still obedient, to the front of the bus—ranging in ages from twenty-eight to thirteen—to retrieve our white envelope from Dad. "Philip!" "Helen!" "Gloria!" "Luke!" "Margaret!" "Simon!" "Matthew!" "Kate!" "Frances!" "Magdalene!" "Paul!" "Rebecca!" "Christine!"—Dad refuses to call me Tina, like everyone else. We all settled back into our seats, politely opening our white envelope to find a crisp hundred-dollar bill tucked inside the itinerary—spending money, courtesy of Dad.

There had always been money for private schools, frequent trips on the Cunard ocean liners, summer beach house rentals, and expensive dinners at D.C.'s finest restaurants, although Mom still cut coupons from the Sunday paper. Over the years, we had a few panic-inducing conversations around the dinner table when Mom announced that Holy Pilgrimages might go bankrupt. Like most dramas in our family, it was a huge deal at the time, and then it just seemed to disappear. Before we knew it, Mom was off on another trip to Paris, or somebody was going to visit the Greek islands, or Dad decided to put in a swimming pool. I can't ever recall a time when Dad's wallet wasn't packed with fresh hundreds, and our trip to Italy that year was no exception.

My family loved seeing the sights of Rome from our own private bus—like the Partridge Family without the instruments. One day the bus got stuck on a narrow street—a small car blocking the way—so my five very athletic brothers hopped out along with my brothers-in-law, picked the car up, and moved it. Throughout Rome, Dad seemed to have access to everything and everyone—even Pope Paul VI, whom we had an audience with. One of the most powerful Catholics at the Vatican—the papal nuncio of Italy, Archbishop Magni—celebrated a private mass for our family. I watched afterward as he and Dad had a hush-hush conversation in a corner of the hotel lobby that seemed as serious as a troublemaker's teacher-parent conference.

Everything was lush: We were treated to a lavish dinner hosted by the head of Alitalia airlines; took over a small hotel on the island of Ischia; toured the Vatican, the basilicas, the catacombs, and Naples, all courtesy of Dad, including lots of wine.

The lobby of our five-star hotel in Rome was coated in gold leaf, with a giant marble staircase and grand pillars throughout; the ceiling reached as high as a basketball gymnasium. Rebecca and I shared a suite with old-style European windows that opened outward; the drapes were long enough to make play clothes for a large family, the bathtub as big as a fountain. Mom says Rebecca and I are just like Winnie and her: opposites but very close. Whenever we traveled, Rebecca and I shared a room—same as we did at home—and we'd been going to school together every day since kindergarten, but just because we were close doesn't mean I told her my secrets. I didn't. I didn't tell anyone my secrets. I even bullied Rebecca at times— even though she's eighteen months older. Once I peed on her bed. Once I decided that we each had to stay on our own sides of the room, never, ever crossing the designated line—but of course, my side had the door. In third grade, when I started getting in trouble at school for the first time, my teacher would summon Rebecca to my classroom and, in front of the entire class, tell my sister that when we went home, she was to tell Mom what a bad, misbehaved child I was. Of course, like a true sister, she never did.

According to Mom, I was a very good girl through second grade, but something suddenly changed when I was nine. What happened? I've never told even Rebecca about what two of our brothers started doing to me then. It started with the confusing horror of Simon, nineteen, coming into my bedroom in the middle of the night. Then Luke, twenty, began putting his hands on me or telling me he wanted to show me something in his room or the basement. Neither of them seemed to know that the other one was also hav- ing sexual encounters with me. Their size, and age, and of course the fact that they were the "boys," gave them all the power. Even the swimming pool wasn't safe. They grabbed whatever they wanted, the way bank robbers do. Dad always favored the boys. Mom, too, with her own old-fashioned ways. Girls are supposed to clean and cook and serve. The boys take out the trash once in a while and play sports. Dad's constant eye rolling and scoffing at his daughters seemed to deliver a collection basket full of negative labels: girls are always late, we're frivolous, wasting time applying makeup, curling our hair, shopping for God knows what, and yapping. Lots of yapping. Wouldn't he be surprised to know some of the behaviors of his favored heirs.

It could have been weekly, monthly, I'm not certain, but the sexual abuse by my brothers became regular over the course of a few years, until Simon and Luke finally stopped when they got married. Both had girlfriends during the entire time. I wonder sometimes whether someone had abused them, and whether they did to anyone else what they did to me.

After some time my mind ignored the disgust, because my body started to like the way it felt. It was confusing, because when my brothers weren't violating me, they gave me extra attention: coming to my basketball games, letting me play in their all-male pickup games. In an odd way, I was one of the boys when we weren't in the dark. This is when I started breaking empty soda bottles against the school walls, smoking, kissing boys behind the auditorium curtain, and being mean to Rebecca. Although I'm away at college, whenever I'm around Simon or Luke I feel a surge of anger that never seems to release, as if my feelings are pinned in a mousetrap. It is the gnawing in my gut that I live with every day—even though I try to ignore or numb the ache.

Dad's stepparents only came to Rome from London for a few days, since Granddad Hall was confined to a wheelchair, having had a stroke years before. Dad and his stepparents are polite but distant with each other—not at all affectionate like our family. I'm not sure if it's because they're English, or because there's not an ounce of blood between them, but the Halls seem as chilly as our deep freezer. If Dad is mad at Mr. Hall for beating him, he never lets it show. Instead, he is exceedingly kind and generous—giving them money and helping Granddad in and out of his wheelchair.

"Can I get you a tea, Dad?"

"How about you sit in this chair, Mother? It's most comfortable."

Behaving like a fretting nurse.

It's typical of my dad to be much nicer to people who are handicapped, poor, old, or ill. Sometimes I wonder why he takes out all his anger on us instead of the man who beat him. All I know is no one talks about what's really going on in our family or how they truly feel about stuff, including me.

Pulling through the campus entrance, past the University of Maryland sign, our bus stops to let everyone off. My dormitory stands in the distance, cold and unfamiliar, because I've only spent a night there since arriving at college six months ago. The bus idles in the parking lot, and I gather my belongings slowly so that my teammates and coaches will get off first. I know Nic will be waiting as usual across the parking lot, hidden, motor and lights off, until the coast is clear for me to sneak into her van and head to her house. I hop off and linger in the parking lot, pretending to wait for a ride. A few players are talking trash, goofing off as the bus leaves, a blast of heavy exhaust filling the air. I keep my distance, pretending that I don't see Nic waiting a few rows of cars away.

"Who you waitin' for, rookie?" our team captain asks, seeing me alone, off to the side. The other girls turn, hands jammed into their winter coats, waiting for my response.

"My mom . . . I'm staying at my parents' house tonight."

"Bitch is homesick already!" another teammate jokes.

High fives all around. I laugh, pretending I think it's funny, and wait until they finally get tired of standing in the cold. I may not be able to outjump a single one of them, but I sure as hell can outwait anyone. Once they are long gone, I make a run for it, sprinting down the long row of cars, keeping my head low and body crouched, hiding. My secret is safe for another night.

3
Ascension

Nic pushes through the front door of her house, carrying take-out from the local Chinese restaurant. A black Adidas tracksuit hangs easily on her toned body. As usual, she discreetly watched my basketball practice today from a dark corner of the University of Maryland's coliseum. Even though I love Nic's attention, it also makes me nervous that my teammates might find out about our relationship, or become suspicious that Nic's friendship with Coach Norris could give me preferential treatment. Wishful thinking. Fact is, on the court, Norris treats me like any other freshman on a full basketball scholarship. Riding my ass in practice, while I've been riding the bench all season. On weekends, Coach hangs out at Nic's rental, a modest brick rambler in working-class Wheaton. Just a bunch of women in their thirties drinking Bud Light and passing the bong in between competitive rounds of horseshoes. I get tongue-tied and never know what to call her at these parties—Coach? Eileen? Miss Norris? I guess I just feel more confident, and safer, when I'm alone with Nic.

My biweekly coach/player meetings in Norris's office are always official until Coach tells her secretary to hold any calls and closes the door. "How's Nic?" She winks, all teeth. I hate that we barely talk about my lack of playing time.

A March gust blows in behind Nic, and I tighten her blue men's robe around my naked body. I rarely shower in the locker room after practice, preferring her power-head nozzle and nice shampoo to the cheap shit the athletic department offers. No one knows that I've only slept in my freshman dorm room once this year, wanting the comfort of Nic—whom I've been in a relationship with for two years, since I was sixteen—and her queen-size waterbed.

Nic switches on the hanging brass lamp, illuminating the faux fur sofa and matching armchair that hulk in the living room like a brown bear and her cub. A few patchouli-scented candles, cheap softball trophies from her women's summer league, and a bag of weed lie on top of the redbrick fireplace.

"Did you remember chopsticks?" I ask, collapsing into the fur.

"Oops. Sorry." She cracks up, dropping a roach into an ashtray. Her bloodshot eyes gaze over me as she leans in and gives me a long kiss. She tastes like pot and spearmint gum.

"I may want you before the mu shu," she teases, her speech at half speed.

I wish I could get high, too, but basketball and bongs don't mix.

"You were hot stuff on the court today," she comments on her way to the kitchen.

"Same as every practice. Norris better fucking play me tomorrow," I gripe, discovering a fresh blister on the ball of my foot.

"Let's call her up and tell her that."

"You call her, she's your friend!"

I click on the television to Dan Rather's nightly report—a habit from growing up in the nation's capital, with a father who watches the six thirty news as religiously as he attends morning mass.

"Family coming to the game tomorrow?" Nic says too loudly.

"Maybe. Definitely Mom."

"It's Parents' Night . . . no Dad?"

"Nah. He's busy with some archbishop from the Vatican. Like I give a shit."

"For a travel agent, he sure has some friends in high places," Nic speculates, entering the room.

"For an asshole, he's sure lucky to have any friends," I say.

Nic laughs, handing me a paper plate piled high with rice, mu shu pork, chicken and broccoli, and egg rolls. Since Nic's the grown-up with the job, she always treats me to dinner.

"Thanks." I kiss her full, soft lips.

"Any of your old high school girls coming?" she says with a bite that even a joint can't mellow.

"NO! Stop it. I don't talk to her anymore."

"HER? Which her? Last I remember, there were many hers," she says sarcastically, plopping onto the couch next to me.

I sigh deeply and head to the kitchen for duck sauce and, hopefully, an end to this topic. Older women don't let anything slide, especially if you make a mistake—like sleeping with your classmate during Senior Beach Week. When Nic came to join me partway through the trip, we took a moon-lit walk along Chesapeake Bay, and I confessed to bedding a willing Catholic girl. Nic collapsed into the sand in tears. I felt numb, but powerful, too. A rush of confidence filled me; she would never leave me.

That is unlike my first lover—and former teacher—Miss Lange, who after my eighth-grade graduation from Blessed Sacrament decided it was time to be with someone her own age. For three years, Miss Lange and I were having sex on Saturdays while the rest of Chevy Chase was pruning azalea bushes around their stately homes or attending Georgetown Prep lacrosse games. Our fifteen-year age difference, and the fact that I was eleven when we started our affair, made it all taboo. "No one would ever understand, and no one can EVER know," Miss Lange would drill me. But she too got jealous, especially when I'd go to junior high parties and the boys would ask me to slow dance. "Did you feel them get hard?" she would ask. I could never tell if she wanted me to say yes or no, so to be safe I would just shake my head and change the subject.

Having an affair as a kid has its downsides: you can't drive, you can't pick up the tab, you have to be home before ten, and you can never spend the night without creating the world's best lie. Then again, being the secret object of a grown-up's lust made me feel like Wonder Woman. Still does. Bursting out at the seams with power, confidence, and maturity—way beyond my eighteen years. It's not that I don't get jealous, too, but I guess I'm usually the one causing the jealousy. On purpose sometimes. Like on the court, when I put my defender on their heels so they can't recover. Offense is the best defense.

"Do you want anything?" I shout to Nic from her cramped dark kitchen.

"Iced tea, and for you to apologize," she says, unsatisfied with a year of "I'm sorrys."

Inside the avocado-colored refrigerator, the tea-stained plastic pitcher sits among bottles of condiments and a can of whipped cream. I fill up her favorite Redskins glass, dumping in ice cubes. Sashaying back into the small living area, I deliver the beverage, hiding the whipped cream behind my back.

"Well?" she presses.

I pose in front of her, pushing my bare leg out of the loosening robe.

"Don't do that, I know what you're doing," she scolds, lighting up the roach.

"Yeah? Well, I know what you're doing," I whisper, running

my long fingers through her chestnut hair. She cracks a smile as she holds her deep inhale.

"Close your eyes," I say quietly.

"No."

She takes a final hit, dropping the tiny ember.

"You're going to be very, very glad you did," I assure her. "Close them."

She shuts her eyes, laughing. Her pretty face is relaxed; smooth olive skin with light peach fuzz highlighted by the glow of the lamp.

I drop the robe.

"Keep them closed," I insist.

I squirt the whipped cream across my bare chest, then straddle her, offering my small breasts to her mouth. She opens her eyes and moans, then begins licking the cream. Her hand grabs between my legs.

"You like that, don't you?" she demands, rage simmering.

"Yeah . . . I do . . ." I pant softly.

"It's mine. Only mine, got it?" she growls, throwing me onto my back and climbing on top.

†

My jaw tightens when I see my father's blotchy red face and lurching body cross the middle of the basketball court with just under three minutes left in the first half. Wasted, he lets his lower lip roll in and out like low tide. For sure, he's feeling his liquid lunch with the archbishop. Somehow his dark Italian suit and silk tie still hang beautifully, but there is an ill-fitting cowboy hat perched on his head, and the sight of it makes me queasy.

One of my teammates steals the ball from North Carolina State's point guard. Her breakaway layup sends a wave of cheers through the stands. Hundreds of hands clapping awaken Dad and he scurries off the court.

The backs of my knees are sweaty from sitting on the bench for the first half. All season, I've discouraged my family from coming to my games, preferring not to feel a gang of sympathetic eyes on their benchwarming baby sister. Dad hasn't needed any dissuasion, as his reason is always "I'm working."

"Hey, John Wayne, park your pony!" Nic shouts from a few rows up.

She has no clue that the man is my father. A few of my teammates burst into laughter, high fiving and kicking their feet against the bench like wild horses. I force a chuckle, so they won't suspect this zigzagging guy shares my DNA, while keeping my eyes down, so they also won't know the woman doing the heckling is my girlfriend.

"Focus!" Coach Norris's tight mouth narrows, her big eyes glaring at the bench.

As Dad begins his wobbly climb up the steps of the coliseum, I could give a shit about our six-point lead, and instead, rubberneck to follow the train wreck. A few rows up, Mom gets his attention with a reserved wave, head low. Her mannerisms scream modesty, a woman who doesn't like to draw attention to herself or stand out in a crowd. Mom squirms in the red metal seat and pushes herself up, using the narrow armrests as leverage. Dad stumbles over the legs of a few fans, and I can see him, smiling, and charming, and probably mouthing, "Pardon me, pardon me, pardon me." The charm evaporates by the time he reaches Mom. Standing like a traffic cop with his outstretched arm, he insists that she sit down. She squeezes herself back into her seat while he looks away, head shaking.

High-tops screech on the hardwood, and then the horn blows, signaling the end of the first half. Our bench empties into the locker room.

After we win the game, Maryland's mascot, the Terrapin—a goofy round turtle—is bouncing around the plush carpet of the banquet room, giving high fives and low fives to Tasha Ricketts, the game's high scorer. Coach Norris and her staff stand in a corner, sipping celebratory beers with a few fathers who dissect the game while proudly holding commemorative Parents' Night T-shirts. I slipped mine into my mother's purse when we entered the party, wanting to hide any reminder of another game where I rode the bench.

The University of Maryland has over thirty thousand students. The women's basketball program recruits from all over the world. My teammates are Olympians and high school All-Americans; we have a staff of athletic trainers; and Adidas gives us free sneakers. I'm as far as I can be from my high school days, as a big fish in a little pond.

Most of my teammates pile man-size portions of food onto their plates, talk with their mouths full, wipe mustard with the back of their hands, and burp loudly under the adoring gaze of their parents. I spend long stretches of time in the ladies' room, avoiding reality and Dad, but finally find myself standing alone at the ravaged banquet table, the silver platters, which had been piled with thick slices of rare roast beef and turkey, now wiped clean. I stare at sprigs of parsley lying wilted on trays and condiment stains of yellow, cream, and red on the white tablecloth.

I discreetly watch my father, supported by the massive trophy case, slowly twirling his wineglass stem between his manicured fingers. Whenever Dad drinks, he gets drunk. He drinks often. A few feet away, Mom sits alone in a winged armchair, eating her third helping of potato salad. She drops her head with each forkful, as if too ashamed to chew in public. Watching them in their own worlds, I'm flooded by an urge to overturn the buffet tables. Dad catches me looking his way and starts toward me. I turn my back, praying he's coming for the pinot grigio instead.

"Dear . . . you . . . play . . . PLAYED . . . marvelous," he slurs.

He takes my hand in his large clammy one. Inches from my face, sweaty beads tap-dance on his forehead; blood vessels crawl up his face, infesting his nose and overtaking his otherwise good skin.

"I didn't play, Dad."

He pulls mouth spray from his breast pocket, struggles to remove the cap, then squirts it onto his tongue.

"A partridge in a . . . ?" Dad quizzes, sliding the spray back into his jacket. I fake interest in a bowl of cherry tomatoes.

"A . . . partridge . . . in . . . a . . . ?" he repeats.

"A pear tree," I shoot the answer at him, searching for something to grab on the table so I don't grab his neck.

"You played . . . very well . . . my . . . Mary, Queen of Scots . . . now . . . who was the . . . actress . . . in the movie about Mary?" he says, cross-eyed.

"Katharine Hepburn," I say without looking at him. He takes out his thick wallet and removes a fresh hundred-dollar bill, forcing it into my clenched fist.

"Correct you are, my basket . . . ball staaar."

"I didn't even play, Dad," I snap.

He seems genuinely confused and places his shaking hand on the tablecloth, landing in a glob of mayo.

"God writes straight with crooked lines," he says, reaching for a bottle of wine.

It's empty, but I don't say anything. He clumsily turns the wine bottle, clipping the lip of his glass and knocking it onto the table. I grab it one-handed and flip it upright, in one fierce motion.

"Chris-tine, dear . . . you look tired . . . from your . . . scholarship, your studies . . . a vacation . . . my dear . . . this . . . is . . . a must," he rambles, eyes rolling back.

Dad reaches for another wine bottle. I snatch it from him.

"They're all empty, Dad! Let's go."

I'm captain of the family team now. A position he lets me take only when he's too drunk to remember where he put his rage; too drunk to do anything but battle his eyelids for control. I walk away, he follows. His hand lands heavily on my shoulder. I slow down, allowing Dad to hang on to me as we make our way toward Mom, who is sweeping the last bit of potato salad off her plate with a finger.

"Greece . . . yes . . . Greece . . . a few days in Athens . . . then . . . off to one of the islands," he suggests.

My jaw lets go of its lockdown, as if I've inherited my mother's patience. I look at him, unafraid. His offer softens me. Tears surprise my eyes. He's showered the older ones with trips to Greece, the Holy Land, and Lourdes to help push wheelchairs on his Pilgrimage for the Disabled, but this is the first time he's offered me such a trip.

"Dad, can I bring a friend?"

His face lights up, stopping and staring at me as if I was just born. A flash of sobriety washes over him. His smile spreads, as broad as a clown's.

"Yes, my little Kate Hepburn, of course, you may bring a friend along."

4

Revelation

Last week, after completing my final exams, I pulled my clothes out of Nic's cedar closet, preparing to leave the comfort of her safe, mellow haven, where I don't have to keep any secrets or listen to my dad ranting at my mom, and return to my third-floor bedroom at 5 East Irving Street for the summer. I finally broke the news to Nic that Dad wanted to have dinner at the University Club with me and my "Greece counterpart" to discuss our itinerary. Despite being excited about the potential of her first trip abroad, she paced in her galley kitchen, repeatedly adjusting her bathrobe, and then rolled a joint as she spewed her concerns: "We have to act really cool. Does he know I was your softball coach? If he asks, should I say I'm thirty or lie? How old should I say I am?"

Tonight, when I hopped into Nic's idling brown van outside my house—she never comes to the door—her joint was down to a roach. I lean my face out the window and inhale freshly cut grass as we round Chevy Chase Circle, wrapped in a ring of white tulips. In the center of it all, a grand fountain blasts water toward the fading orange sky.

"If Shirley Chisholm, Geraldine Ferraro, or Bella Abzug wanted to be a member at the University Club or just drop in for some crab cakes, they'd be denied," I grumble, dabbing my mouth with fuchsia lip gloss in the visor mirror.

The formal dining room is the only place in the University Club where women are permitted, but only when a male member accompanies them.

Nic shakes her head as she turns her van off D.C.'s elegant Embassy Row and into the cobblestone circular driveway of the University Club. We roll up to the valet, and even though Nic detailed the tires and vacuumed the tan carpeting in her gas-guzzling love shack, I wish I had asked to borrow Mom's Impala. The back of the van is wall-to-wall shag rug—floor, walls, and ceiling—with a single mattress covered with a brown paisley sleeping bag. A brand-new air freshener dangles on the rearview mirror, its pine scent mingling with Nic's musky men's cologne.

My palms feel moist as she throws the van into park. Two uniformed black men in bright white tuxedos open our doors. The outstretched hand before me is like a magic wand that turns me into a girly girl. I giggle, offering a limp wrist. As I slide out of the passenger seat—sundress riding up to meet my light gray panties—the attendant eyes my bare thighs. I enjoy the moment.

"I got it! I got it!" Nic barks at the other valet who's escorting her by the elbow toward the massive iron doors. She glances back at me, and her mouth twitches with jealousy until I release my attendant's arm. Slightly bowlegged, Nic walks hurriedly along the red carpet and up the marble steps. The silk wrap dress and white espadrilles I lent her cannot hide her athletic bounce. From a distance, I check out her perfectly proportioned, smooth tan legs.

"Wait up," I call, catching her. I casually touch Nic's arm—soft enough to count as an "I love you," but fast enough to not raise suspicion. She pulls away.

"Did anyone tell the University Club we got the right to vote?" I quip, offering my humor as a peace pipe.

"You're a handful, you know that?"

"I know." I smile at her as we pass another uniformed man holding a door for us.

Nic takes a deep breath, and her hooded eyes widen as she peers down the grand staircase into the formal dining room. Mom was right, this place *is* fancy schmancy. Nic descends the immaculately polished steps, holding the brass rail, her face expressionless, her legs shaky.

I scan the meticulously set round tables for Sir John—the name he prefers we use in public. Neither tall nor muscular, my father would not have made the cut in the Middle Ages, when the first Knights of the Holy Sepulchre were the protectors of Jesus's tomb during the First Crusade, but in modern times he passes.

"Christine, dear!" Dad waves like a passenger on the deck of a departing cruise ship. He wears his loose I've-been-drinking smirk. Sir John's always the first one to arrive at a place that serves alcohol. On the table there is an empty aperitif glass and a smudged wine goblet—a drop away from being completely drained.

"Oh God, here we go," Nic mumbles as we pass table after table of gray-haired men in Capitol Hill wardrobes, eyeing us.

"You look lovely, my dear." Dad kisses my lips and I flinch at the unexpected affection. Intoxicating citrus cologne lingers in the air and I step back, surprisingly proud of his sleek navy suit, Pierre Cardin tie, and immaculately shaven face.

"Hello, Mr. Worthington," Nic says, offering her nervous hand.

Dad takes her face in his palms, kissing her on both cheeks. She blushes.

"Well, well, another beauty. Aren't I the lucky one?" he boasts.

A blond waiter—head-to-toe in black tuxedo with tails—stands nearby, hands behind his back.

"Michael, have you forgotten something?" Dad winks.

The tall server sails over to pull out our cream-colored chairs and bows apologetically.

"What may I get you, Sir John?"

"A partridge in a pear tree." Dad grins.

Michael tosses his weight from side to side, laughing, eager to please.

"And a bottle of Dom Pérignon, *s'il vous plaît,*" Dad adds.

As Michael walks away, Dad's lazy left eye follows him, then quickly returns to Nic and me. His lower lip slips out and he nods vigorously.

"I noticed . . . the two of you," he slurs.

Nic reaches for her water, smiling at Dad. Across the crowded room, Michael picks up a silver wine bucket and our chilled Dom takes center stage, like a victorious prizefighter being carried to our table.

"Thank you, Michael. Michael the archangel." Dad leans back in his chair, watching our waiter's soft hands open the champagne. I paw at my empty glass, twirling it from the stem.

"Christine! Stop fidgeting." Dad shakes his head disapprovingly.

I want to smack his droopy lip back into place. As Michael fills our glasses, my fluttering hands remain neatly folded in my lap, waiting for everyone to be served.

"Pour mine all the way to the rim, our archangel," Dad directs.

"As you wish, Sir John." Michael bows his head, giving Dad the royal treatment.

Raising his glass to Nic and me, Dad smiles openly, awaiting Michael's departure.

"Here's to the Greek gods. Tonight we will not save any libations for them." His flute taps ours and we drink.

Bubbles tickle my nose; the champagne is smooth, warming my chest.

"I think . . . I should join the two of you . . . in Athens."

My head spins as I steal a glimpse of Nic swallowing hard. Not bothering to look for Michael, Dad takes the bottle out of its icy home and refills our glasses. There is only the sound of the bottle clinking against our glasses and the bass of men in conversation around us.

"That would be nice," Nic suggests unconvincingly.

Since I trade in secrets and lies, I step up to the plate. "Yeah, that would be . . ." My voice rises.

"My ladies, I noticed . . . as you stood at the top of the staircase . . . and then descended . . ."

He takes a long pause, smiling and nodding at us, then continues, "I am . . . it was very . . . well, yes."

"What, Dad? What?!" The words fly out of me.

Nic pushes her knee into my thigh.

"Dear, I have eyes. I noticed as you two walked down the stairs. Yes, I knew immediately. I know young lovers when I see them."

Dad takes our hands to his lips and kisses them. A quick glance darts between us girls, releasing uneasy laughter. *How could he know?* Dad joins Nic's hand with mine and raises his Dom. I'm light-headed and terrified at being so exposed, shaking from the inside at the thought of my whole family knowing. Head down, I pause, stunned and frozen as a statue, holding Nic's hand in mine. *This is crazy.* I let go and grab my champagne glass, unable to look at Dad.

" 'Love is a many-splendored thing, it's the April rose, that only grows in early spring,' " he croons, pitch-perfect.

Nic stares at him, enchanted.

Dad raises his flute to me and my dry throat locks. I have no words, my secrets laid out.

"And you may be interested to know . . ." His voice drops lower. His eyes glide across the dining room like a spy assessing the enemy, and he covers the right side of his mouth. "I buried my lover in the war," he confesses.

"What?" I mumble.

"'Pardon me,' Christine, not 'what,'" he corrects my ungracious language.

"Pardon me?" I ask properly, unable to look at anything but my distorted image in the monogrammed dinner plate.

"I said, I buried my lover in the war . . . His name was Omar."

†

"Did you order the crab cakes?" Mom asks as she pushes her saucer-size eyeglasses up her nose. As she stands at the kitchen stove, her arms hang out of her sleeveless muumuu like flabby wings.

"No. I had chateaubriand," I say, plopping myself—still a little drunk—at our Formica kitchen counter. Nowadays, the three wrought-iron chairs are mostly empty at breakfast, since Rebecca got married and Magdalene moved to Austin to be with her boyfriend. I like having my own bathroom, but everywhere else, there's just too much space. A week has passed since I secretly moved out of Nic's house, hung my ACC Championship plaque on my bedroom wall, and slipped photos of us under the mattress.

I catch myself in an alcohol daze, staring at my red Maryland shorts and untied high-tops, wondering if the whole Omar thing was a mirage. This morning, I rolled out of my floral duvet cover sweating liquor but determined to conquer any sign of flat-footedness and my weak left hand before heading back to basketball training with the team in September. I may have been a benchwarmer last year, but I promise myself next season—sophomore year—I'm going to be a starter. Even after a first-round cut at last year's East Coast Olympic trials, my eyes are still set on the 1984 Games. I keep reminding myself that I was the youngest player at the tryouts—just seventeen—and I will get better each year.

"Well, you missed out, Miss Fancy Pants. It's not every day you get to eat at the University Club. You'll just have to take my word for it—those crab cakes are yummy," Mom says, popping an English muffin up out of the toaster. I consider peeling my sweaty legs off the vinyl cushion, stumbling over to the back door, and making my way into the deep end of our pool before this conversation goes any further.

"I used to love chateaubriand for two, but it's not much good when your father's stomach can't tolerate it," she muses.

The removal of most of Dad's stomach—a by-product of ulcers—when I was a baby suddenly takes on new meaning when I consider his secret. On the one hand, I know he must have wanted to be a father, but maybe in another way, he couldn't stomach not being able to express his true nature. Then again, maybe the guilt of living a lie gnawed at his gut. A wave of nausea crashes through my bloated middle. I want to shake Mom. Tell her everything. Then give her a hug and never let her go.

"Did your father have a lot to drink?" she asks, pinching off burnt scrapple from the edge of her worn spatula. She sucks the black morsels from her fingertips.

"Not that much," I lie, tallying the two bottles of Dom, two bottles of Châteauneuf-du-Pape, and God knows how many rounds of Frangelico. My head spins with all the things I do not tell her—that he's planning to meet Nic and me for a few days in Athens. That he's already made another reservation for three at the University Club the night after we get back from Santorini. How do I tell Mom that Dad was screwing a Palestinian soldier before Mom and Dad's first date—that blistering day in Jerusalem when they walked the Stations of the Cross along the Via Dolorosa?

"How did your friend . . . Nic? Is that her name?"

"Yeah, Mom, short for Nicole," I remind her for the twentieth time.

"That's a strange nickname for a teacher . . . coach . . . Well, how did Nic enjoy the chateaubriand and everything?" She's been fishing ever since Nic and I started spending time together after she became my junior year softball coach, often suggesting that I hang around friends my own age.

A plate of scrambled eggs, scrapple, and a perfectly toasted English muffin are served to me with a loving smile, and I forgive her for wanting to know more than I will ever tell her. About Dad or me. She sits down next to me at the counter. Her big legs spread out and her pale blue slippers seek support on the bottom rail of the chair. I feel as heavy as she looks, overwhelmed by what I learned last night. Lying to Mom about myself is one thing—I've been doing it since I was eleven—but Dad, he's, well, my father, and her husband. Her gay husband, or whatever he is. Holy shit.

"It's very generous of your father to pay for her trip. She really lucked out," Mom adds, shaking her head.

"Where's your breakfast?" I try changing the subject.

"I'll get it, you just enjoy yours. It's not often I get to see my baby—at least off the basketball court." Mom smiles, patting my bare knee. She sips her coffee, looking to the screen door, becoming still. "Oh, Tina, listen to those birds singing. We have our own personal choir."

I lean over and kiss her fleshy cheek, hoping someday soon, Dad will stop criticizing her for everything she's not and just treat her to some crab cakes.

†

I just can't wrap my head around this. I spent hours in my room this afternoon, going over last night's confession. My case against Dad—the mean SOB I've hated for as long as I can remember—has now done an about-face. With this revelation staring me down, I realize that it's entirely possible that I loathed him all these years because he hated me first. Clearly, I never knew him. Not fully.

Since Dad arrived home from work tonight—promptly at 6 P.M.—every word out of his mouth seems to have a double meaning, or maybe I'm just hearing everything that way now. My nervousness amps up the moment Mom, Dad, and I take our seats at Dad's end of our ten-foot table. Our threesome seems so tiny compared to the endless empty dining chairs— all twelve of them. Dad looks over at me as Mom puts her napkin on her lap. His long stare locks my limbs—always a sure sign I've done something wrong, and in a blink I pull my elbows off the table and sit up straight.

"Would you like to say grace, Christine?" he asks with a smile.

"Dad, why don't you do the honors?" I respond way too formally.

Mom chuckles at our odd exchange. We all make the sign of the cross and bow our heads.

"In the name of the Father and the Son and the Holy Spirit. Bless us, O Lord, and these thy gifts which we are about to receive from thy bounty through Christ, our Lord, Amen." Dad finishes grace with a squeeze of my sweaty hand, served with a side of smirk. I glance at Mom, glad she missed his show of affection toward me—too busy buttering her slice of pumpernickel.

"We've got Christine's itinerary all planned out," Dad boasts as Mom gets busy with a barbecue chicken thigh.

I happily grilled the meat tonight, taking advantage of any reason to escape into the backyard, poolside, and breathe easier, even if the air was laced with lighter fluid and charcoal.

"Yes, I heard. Some people have all the luck," Mom says.

"I will try to join them in Athens for a few days, if possible, on my way to the Holy Land," Dad explains with a forced air of parental responsibility. Knowing the whole truth underneath the fact is both exhilarating and scary as hell. I am all too familiar with this game of cover-up. "I'm going to Nic's," or "I'm going out to a party," while avoiding the details that actually create my world. This connection is unnerving. My full-time juggling act has become second nature. But I don't know what to do with his.

"Why don't you take some time off, dear? It would be nice for you to have some time with your youngest." Mom's voice is as kind and gentle as a kindergarten teacher's.

"It would be nice. I haven't taken a vacation since . . . I don't even know the last time," Dad throws out.

It's the familiar tone he takes when he's describing the traveling. Part victim, part braggart. I recall a hundred nights sitting at this table listening to Dad go over and over his detailed itinerary before officially posting it up on the bulletin board the day before he departed for two, three, or four weeks at a time. As I sneak a piece of gristle out of my mouth, now I wonder: Did he really need to travel that much? Did he have other motives? The way he explained it last night at the University Club made it sound as if he had much more to tell. "We have all the time in the world to discuss this, Christine." The gleam in his eyes made it clear that the Palestinian, Omar, was just the first chapter.

"You're awfully quiet tonight, Miss Basketball Star." Dad nudges my elbow playfully. "What's wrong, you only slept until noon?" he teases.

"No, I was up pretty early," I lie.

"I wish I had known you were up *early*, we could have gone to six thirty mass together." He laughs.

As I roll my corn in the puddles of butter on my dinner plate, Dad hums a few bars of some Gregorian chant, tapping his long fingers on the bare wood. His fingernails are immaculate, as usual. If I didn't occasionally catch him in the first-floor bathroom clipping them, I'd think they were the product of a manicure. Not a hangnail in sight. After last night's bombshell, his impeccable hygiene is about more than a former British Army officer being tidy. His obsession with not having a single hair growing from his ear comes back to me. For some reason, my sister Kate was the go-to gal for the plucking, poor thing. I nearly choke when I recall catching Dad getting dressed years ago, wearing his boxers and clearly putting deodorant on his balls.

"I need to use the bathroom, excuse me," I say, trying to shake off the sensory overload.

"Will you bring me another Tab, sweetie, while you're up?"

"Sure, Mom." I slip behind Dad's chair and pass by Mom, stopping to kiss her head.

I walk beside the long marble buffet, letting my hand glide across its cold, smooth surface. Once out of the dining room, I let out a sigh and head for the bathroom, closing the door and locking it. I rest my face against the lightweight wood. I feel the urge to vomit.

Over by the sink, on the white counter, is Dad's giant bottle of Listerine, his contact lens solution—he's never worn glasses. Too vain? I examine the scrub brush for his crystal clear nails and the small round plastic brush that he uses regularly on his scalp despite having a flattop. Creams, aftershave lotions, and multiple pairs of tweezers. *Jesus Christ. Look at all of this. No straight man would use all of this.*

I sit on the toilet, biding my time, my hungover head in my hands. Truth is, I'm relieved that someone in the family knows my secret and loves me even more because of it. I just wish I could go back to dinner feeling calmer. It's not like I don't appreciate him not hating me, I just need a little time to get used to our new secret language.

5
Covenant

Entering the Lost and Found, a rowdy men's bar, I strut a few steps behind a tanned Nic in her capri pants and Dad in his white linen suit, adjusting the floppy straw hat I bought myself on our Greek vacation. I'm jittery. Jesus, never thought I'd be at a gay bar with my dad. I've been going to these clubs since I was sixteen, when Nic took me to Crazy Eights, across from the projects in Baltimore—a neighborhood so dangerous, you had to knock on the door to get buzzed in. Once inside, I put on such an act of cool and confidence that no one even carded me. Nic said I behaved like I owned the place.

"I've got it, love." My father waves off Nic's billfold as he pulls a crisp hundred-dollar bill off the top of a thick wad of fresh notes. Dad stares lustfully at the leather-clad bouncer's bulging crotch and I catch the hunk returning the look. Nic catches my eye.

"Is your dad gay or bisexual?" she whispers.

"Hell if I know," I snap.

"Well, he's one heck of a charmer," she says admiringly.

"Let's get a drink, my ladies," Dad shouts over Bowie's "Let's Dance." His arm extends, insisting we lead the way through the afternoon tea dance. No chance that he'll lose us in this sea of muscle and neatly trimmed mustaches. I couldn't stand out any more if I were Mary Magdalene belly dancing at the Last Supper. Hairy arms swipe mine, leaving patches of wet and earthy smells on my ivory gauze blouse, overpowering my mother's Joy perfume that I pumped off her vanity. The dated, *Saturday Night Fever*–like dance floor is packed. There are the Village People cops with batons, cowboys in chaps showing off big packages wrapped in soft leather, and drag queens wearing vibrant boas and wide-shouldered *Dynasty* gowns with exaggerated makeup and false eyelashes. I bounce my narrow hips to the booming music as I scope the dance floor. The bar is three deep for drinks, but Dad is happy to wait, surrounded by a small clique of slight young guys, as well as the burly muscle types.

A cherub-faced preppy guy taps Dad's back and then quickly says he's sorry while eyeing my father's snug trousers. I feel myself flush. For years Dad's enormous penis, which is always visibly tucked down his left pant leg, was nothing more than a shared joke with my brothers and sisters.

One dinner when Dad was away on some holy trip, Kate sprayed a mouthful of red wine across the white tablecloth.

"Kate, what in the world . . . ?" Mom demanded.

With a straight face she said, "Frances was wondering if Dad gets his left pant leg tailored a bit larger, so he can fit 'Sergeant Pepper' in there." The table fell silent. My heart raced, hoping we hadn't embarrassed Mom, while my own face heated up.

"Well, your father wears . . . boxers," my mother said, blushing, a silent laugh jiggling her round belly. The gang erupted into howls.

"No, no, children." She covered her mouth with her hand, stifling a laugh. "European men have a different . . ." but before she could finish, the room hit a fever pitch. Tears rolled down my face, and Kate ran helplessly toward the bathroom.

My father's smirk at the country-club hustler flitting around him turns my stomach. Flirting at the University Club with Michael is one thing, but there's no buffer here. No line in the sand.

My father slips a hundred-dollar bill into my palm, and with a quick nod like a CIA operative, he murmurs, "Keep an eye on things." I watch the hustler cross the dance floor—his swaying ass leading my father to the men's room.

"Three white wines and a shot of tequila, please," I shout to the shirtless bartender.

"That must be weird for you, huh?" Nic whispers in my ear.

I shrug and kick back the burning tequila, not bothering to chase it, and walk away. I step in my four-inch Candies onto the dance floor and feel the same rush as when I step onto the basketball court. The bass-heavy music sets off a string of moves, quick and connected, as Isaac Hayes groans, "Don't let it go, don't let it go." A gorgeous, sequin-gowned drag queen is fanning her flawless Lena Horne skin as a few bulky men dance around her adoringly. I move in, pivoting toward her, and grab her small waist. A whistle blows, tambourines shake, and the circle of men are left flat-footed. The sequined beauty queen puts her hand inside my gauzy shirt. A thrill rushes between my legs as she holds my breast, her long press-on nails scratching my bare skin lightly. I feel her sigh and lean up to her mouth, losing my breath, insides dropping as if I'm speeding down a roller coaster.

"No, no, little one, no kissing on the mouth," she says in a smoky voice.

I kiss her cheek softly, smelling L'Air du Temps in her long wig—the same perfume Miss Lange wore. She touches her face and looks at me wide-eyed, like she's a mime pretending to be flattered. I lean in again, hoping she's changed her mind. She lets me move closer this time. Men are chanting us on. Sharp fingernails dig into my upper arm as Nic spins me around to face her.

"What the hell are you doing?" she demands, yanking me off the dance floor.

Caught but blinded by glamour, I look back as the beauty queen blows me a kiss.

"I'm so over that!" Nic yells, shoving me toward the bar.

"She's just a drag queen," I play it off.

"How would you feel?"

"I wouldn't care," I lie, glancing toward the men's room. No sign of Dad. My stomach starts to ache, worry trumping any remorse.

Three fresh shots of tequila are lined up in front of our wineglasses. I pick up a shot, pour it down my throat, then kick back another.

"Tina, I can't do this anymore."

I hand Nic the last shot of tequila, wanting this conversation to go away, so I can focus on chasing down Sir John. She sets it on the bar and faces me, her gentle brown eyes needing something—something I can't give.

"What am I supposed to do?! I have to find my dad!" I cry, leaving for the men's room.

In the dim bathroom, my heart drumming, I slip past men's backs as they point themselves into the urinals. At the four stalls I whisper, "Dad? Dad?" and look under doors. Under the third door I discover leather slip-ons that look like Dad's entwined with deck shoes. Staring at their hairy calves, I hear a moan. Suddenly outraged, I shout in a low gruff voice, as I bang on the door, "Get the fuck out, there's a line!" and then haul ass out of the bathroom.

Trembling, I'm suddenly desperate to find Nic, like a little girl lost in the grocery store. I search the steamy, packed club with mounting panic. Finally, I spot her pushing her way out of the club as if she's clearing a path with a machete. I run like hell, apologizing as I knock drinks and bang elbows, catching her in the alleyway just outside.

"Nic, wait!"

She turns, tears in her eyes.

"I'm really sorry, really," I say, afraid this time I've finally gone too far.

"I need to go, I can't . . . I just need some space," Nic says without looking at me.

I watch her walk toward a cab. A wave of dizziness follows—my body heats up in a panic, and a fear of being left alone swallows me. Refusing to look at the departing cab, my eyes stay down.

"Baby cakes, you runnin' out on Miss Darla?" the drag queen purrs, holding the door open as she flicks her cigarette into the gutter.

†

After another round of drinks, Dad and I walk across the potholed street to his red convertible, holding hands. Lightheaded and nauseous, I can't stomach any more partying. "Mom's alone at home and has a lot of preparing for tomorrow's barbecue. Maybe I should go home and help her—skip the University Club tonight," I say softly, hoping to guilt-trip him but not get him mad.

"They are expecting us, dear," he insists, as if they really give a shit.

While carefully driving Dad's car from the rough streets of Southeast D.C. to the dignified Northwest neighborhood, I lose my buzz, worrying about drifting across the center lane of Massachusetts Avenue. I can't chance another warning from Washington cops. They let me go last summer after they caught me weaving away from an Adams Morgan bar—I bullshitted them that I'd had only one margarita. Then there was a second traffic stop when, after too many White Russians at a piano bar in Foggy Bottom, the cops had me curbside across from the Watergate, doing the whole head, shoulders, knees, and toes routine. I seem to thrive in high-pressure situations—scored a pass by the fuzz.

"Ah, Michael, there will only be two of us dining after all," Dad says, his eyes somehow still sparkling.

I look around the dining room, uncomfortable with his endless flirtations. The University Club is mostly empty, a respite from the dance club.

"My archangel, there's no need for all that. I might just get lucky tonight," Dad teases Michael as he removes the extra place setting. I suddenly wish Nic were here.

"Dad, what was the preppy boy's name you were talking with for so long?"

I succeed at halting my father's display. His aggressive eye on me is a parental reminder that he didn't raise a child without manners.

"Excuse my daughter, Michael. I was going to suggest—since our third party became ill—that you join us." Dad gives him a loose wink.

Michael grins.

"Thank you, Sir John, I'd love to, but I'm on duty," he says, holding his hands behind his back.

"I've been 'on duty' since I was an officer in the British Army, running the War Office in Palestine, but please join us anytime—after your duty." Dad's eyes are glued to our server.

"Dad, he's working!"

"Christine, I think you need a drink! Please, Michael, bring my daughter . . . what would you like, dear? Red wine, perhaps? We've been on the dance floor all afternoon, so we've worked up a thirst."

He gives Michael another wink. I bury my face in my menu, but my hands are shaking enough that I can't focus. My body feels trapped in the chair, an invisible strap holding my hips in place, stuck here alone with him and all these lies. The large chandelier becomes distorted, a massive spaceship looming above me. A full-blown panic threatens to take over. It's familiar, but it's been years since I felt this overwhelmed. The first time was in my bedroom with Simon. And then, repeatedly, for a few years in the musty laundry room, where the unfinished ceiling beams would seem to grow thick and crush the breath right out of me as I lay frozen on a frayed bath towel with my brother's face between my legs.

I grab my crystal goblet off the table and gulp down the water. My father's voice echoes as if he's talking underwater.

"Young man, please bring us a bottle of Châteauneuf-du-Pape and some warm bread."

The tuxedo-wearing archangel places his cold palm on my shoulder.

"It's pretty cool your father takes you dancing," he says sweetly.

"Not to worry, young man, I can take you, too." Dad gives Michael a mock smack with his napkin.

Michael laughs like a girl and hustles off.

Feeling Sir John's stare, I gulp my ice water and read the menu with feigned interest, grateful that the letters begin to emerge from their thick blur. I breathe slowly, reminding myself that there's no need to be afraid.

"Châteauneuf-du-Pape, Sir John." Our server shows off the label.

Dad blesses the bottle—making a grand sign of the cross like he's the pope on the balcony above St. Peter's Square. I think of the way Dad said good night when we were kids, blessing our foreheads with his thumb. Dad knows the entire mass by heart in English and in Latin; standing up, sitting down, and reciting prayers three beats ahead of the congregation. Each night after dinner, he led the family through the rosary, all of us kneeling in the living room before the cross and my parents' holy portraits. Once upon a time, he really did want to be a priest. Even though Dad had never spoken of it, my sister Kate found a letter in the attic in which he confided his disappointment over being rejected from the priesthood in England. No explanation for the rejection— just that he was heartbroken and weighing his options for the future.

Dad calls me back. "*Salute*, Christine."

We tap our crystal glasses and drink our fine wine fast, chasing down our lost high. Dad takes my hand in his. My body tenses.

He sings, " 'There's a place for us, a time and place for us, hold my hand and we're halfway there.' "

I force a smile and take a big swig of wine. I can't decide if being Dad's new best buddy is fun or frightening. Have I really gone from hating him to loving him so fast? He never seemed to like me much, constantly reprimanding me, sneering. My mind plays Ping-Pong: *Who is the real Sir John? Was having thirteen children just a cover? Did he really want all of us?* He boasts to anyone who will listen that he had hoped for twelve boys, so he could name them after the twelve apostles. One thing I know for sure, he prefers sons to daughters, waiters to waitresses, grandsons to granddaughters, and, apparently, men to women. So how does he now magically love me as if I'm a disciple? Is it just because I like girls? Or maybe because I know how to keep a secret as well as he does?

He keeps his droopy, bloodshot eyes on me while draining his glass. As if I were his subject, he examines my features, nodding with approval all the while. There's an expression on his relaxed face that is foreign, so open. His purple-stained lips are soft.

"I love you," he gushes.

"I love you, too, Dad," I say gently, and realize that I might mean it.

"Well, then it's settled, we are in love!" He laughs and kisses my lips.

He pours us more wine. Our glasses touch, and we hold them pressed together.

"To us," my father says, winking.

Suddenly I am caught in the spell. I feel warm and giddy, and I'm glad that Nic went home, that I'm here alone with my father and his loving eyes are on me. Just me.

I hesitate, then ask, "Dad, were there other men?"

Before speaking, he assesses the room and then discreetly leans closer.

"We must be careful, Mossad is watching," he whispers.

"Who?"

He takes another look at two olive-skinned gentlemen dining across the room.

"Israeli Intelligence," he slurs.

I'm not sure whether to laugh or duck under the table. But when I look over at the two men wearing boring gray suits, sipping beer, they catch my eye and raise their glasses. Just typical Washington politicians flirting with women a third their age, I figure. Dad nods, assuring me it is safe for him to proceed.

"Well . . . if you must know . . . yes. Your godfather, Harvey . . . yes, Harvey and I were lovers for many years," he reveals.

Brain awhirl, I recall my seventh birthday. Dad took Rebecca and me to Disneyland in California. Mom stayed home. It was the only trip we ever took without Mom. A plane ride, then into a helicopter. We sat in a small banquette between Harvey and Dad as I blew out my seven candles. At the Disneyland Hotel, Rebecca and I shared our own room with double beds. Dad had a suite down the hall with a king. I recall my godfather was at breakfast the next morning.

"How long? When did it . . . ?"

"For many years. Harvey was in Germany, reporting for *Stars and Stripes*. We'd rendezvous in Berlin on my way to Rome or the Holy Land, but that was many years ago, before he moved on . . . to San Francisco." His voice is low and soft. His eyes are distant.

"Does Mom . . . ?" I can't even get the sentence out.

He sits back, puts his elbows on the upholstered arms of his chair, and folds his hands, twisting his ruby ring on his index finger. He scans the large room, then moves in close. Alcohol and citrus curl around me.

"Christine, I assure you, I am not going to tell your mother about your personal affairs. I am not going to tell anyone—certainly not the family. No one. This is not information that the world needs to know. But it's important that someone knows."

I nod.

"Now, as for my life, I take it you will assure me the same courtesy. Are we clear?" His tone is cold sober.

"Yes, Dad."

"That's my girl."

For a moment, we are equals. Quid pro quo. Our long stare seals our unspoken promise as if we'd pricked our fingers and shared each other's blood. He's not the first man in my family to insist that I keep a secret. But this one feels different, a nuclear bomb, a grenade in my hand. My heart pulses in my throat. I know that, should I make one wrong move, Dad, my entire family, and I are going to be destroyed.

6
Chosen

Five East Irving Street is 251 left-handed dribbles from the playground. Some days it's more, but today, I sprint home—not wanting to be late picking up Dad at the airport. The day after we dined sans Nic at the University Club, he left on a spur-of-the-moment flight for Rome. Standing at the foot of the driveway next to our neighbor's pristine hedges, Dad tightened his already snug necktie and whispered to me, "I have an urgent meeting with the papal nuncio, Archbishop Magni—Vatican matters. But upon my return we'll hit the town . . . the Lost and Found."

As he loaded his bag into the trunk of Mom's Impala, we kissed on the lips and he began to sing, " 'So long, farewell, auf wiedersehen, good night.' "

As he slammed the sun-baked trunk closed, Mom stared at us curiously through the rearview mirror. Then he gave me another smooch and slipped a hundred-dollar bill into my palm.

Yesterday, Dad's Pietà postcard addressed to me arrived in the mail with a Pope John Paul II postage stamp, requesting that I pick him up "promptly at Dulles Airport, arriving on Alitalia. There are a few matters that I'd like to talk over with you. Alone."

I grabbed the card off the kitchen counter before my mother sorted the mail. I knew that last word would have hurt her feelings.

Instead of feeling lonely the past two weeks—Nic taking some space and Dad doing who knows what, or whom—I'm back training with laser focus. And without the hangovers.

Basketball on my hip, I run up the steep front steps two at a time, then do an agility drill across the porch to the front door. Our three-story canary yellow house is not the biggest or most impressive one in tony Chevy Chase, but it's probably seen the most action. Constant comings and goings, as well as notorious pool parties and wedding receptions, have packed Irving Street over the years with more cars than a celebrity funeral. Sunday barbecues by the pool were often a parade of my father's international cast of priests and nuns getting tanked in their trunks. The star attraction was always the frozen whiskey sours, although I could never take my eyes off the endless cavorting between the collarless brothers and the habitless sisters. After those barbecues, Father Bill would play Peter, Paul and Mary songs on his ukulele in front of the crucifix while everyone sang. After the wedding receptions there would be raucous dancing back at 5 East Irving Street in the living room, furniture pushed up against the walls, floorboards vibrating to their limit. Mom would screech with equal amounts of terror and delight while she crossed herself, praying that we all didn't fall into the basement. But her joy at being surrounded by all of her children and a gaggle of holy sisters belting "We Are Family" was worth the price of a potential Rapture.

Walking into the quiet house feels odd since Rebecca moved out. The only sounds are my heavy breath and ticks from the grandfather clock. The bare mahogany railing in the foyer—once piled high with mounds of coats and scarves in the winter, damp towels from the pool in the summer, looks naked. The single pair of shoes—Mom's dress sandals—looks lonely at the foot of the wooden steps. I miss the barrage of smells and their owners—preppy Kate cooking popcorn at all hours, Margaret and Luke's cigarettes, Gloria's lemony Jean Naté powder, Rebecca's strawberry conditioner, and Dad's Lysol spray—masking his frequent vomiting from hangovers and ulcers—in the first-floor bathroom.

"Is that my baby?" Mom calls from the dining room.

I plop down in the spot where I've eaten dinner for eighteen years—just to the left of Mom. The air-conditioning sends chills through my soaked T-shirt. I roll the basketball over my belly.

"Even in ninety-degree heat, that ball is attached to you," Mom teases, reaching into a box of Ritz crackers. Her favorite mug, with the slogan SMILE, JESUS LOVES YOU, is filled with black coffee and a film of crumbs from her late-morning dunking. If I wasn't sweaty, I'd probably sit on her lap and tell her how much I love her—something I can't seem to stop doing no matter how big I get. I'm always aware of positioning my weight just right. Causing Mom pain would be like hurting a newborn.

"Mom, I need to pick up Dad at Dulles, should I use your car or his?"

"I thought we'd both go pick him up." She brushes a few crumbs into her cupped hand, then pours them into her mouth.

"That's okay, you don't need to go."

"What if I want to take a drive with my daughter?" She pats my sweaty forearm. I cover my guilt with a laugh.

"But how about dinner? He's gonna throw a fit if it isn't ready," I warn her.

"Dinner is all ready. The roast beef is done, I'll just need to heat up the soup and carrots and throw some baked potatoes in the microwave. So there." Mom puts her hands on the table for support as she lifts herself out of the chair. Her gold wedding band is worn thin and fits tight on her plump finger.

"Who's coming over to swim today? Any of the grandkids?" I say, knowing that is a surefire way to distract her. She looks at me with deep disappointment.

"No. None of my precious grandchildren today. But little Ben got on the phone this morning and said, 'Nana, Mommy said I can come swim 'morrow. Can I?'" She lights up.

"I thought Gloria said she was coming over with the baby today," I lie.

"No, I just spoke with her this morning."

Mom looks confused as she picks up her mug and box of wafers. My mind grasps for straws.

"Somebody definitely said they were coming over today," I add with conviction.

"Hmm. Well, you better get ready, sweetie, we should head out soon," she insists.

"Mom, I mean it! You don't have to go. I can get him and you can rest." I try to steady my shaky voice.

Almost out of the dining room, she turns around slowly in front of a Turkish wooden icon of the Holy Trinity. "If I didn't know better, I'd think you didn't want to spend time with your mother."

Her hurt voice stings. Guilt covers me like sap on a sugar maple.

"Don't be silly," I say, rushing toward her and wrapping myself up in her arms, pecking her cheek repeatedly.

She squishes me tightly. "I'll squeeze you till you bleeeeed buttermilk," she teases me with one of her favorite old sayings. Sometimes I get the feeling that we both wish I was still a baby.

†

Dulles International Airport is a forty-minute drive from Chevy Chase, assuming there's no traffic on the lush green Beltway. It's a good thing Mom doesn't need gas in her Impala, because late is not an option. Neither is her driving.

"Slow down, Speedy Gonzalez," she says, as I floor it entering the on-ramp from Connecticut Avenue.

"How long should it take him to get through customs?" I ask, checking the dashboard clock again and wiping my sweaty palms on the leather seat.

"We have plenty of time, sweetie."

I wish I could believe her. Somehow, I have always known that she was too far away from me. By the time I was nine years old I knew she was too sad, too tired, too busy, for me to tell her my secret about Simon and Luke. Telling Dad was never an option. Would it be my fault? Their fault? Satan's? Would he take it out on Mom like everything else that upsets him? I've never told anyone except Miss Lange. Her first question was "Did they penetrate you?" "No, never," I said. "Thank God," she responded.

As Mom and I enter the crowded waiting lounge for overseas flights, our eyes fix upward at the arrival board. We exchange a smile when we see that Alitalia Flight 467 has just arrived, and we've escaped the lecture on lateness or common courtesy.

"I'm dying of thirst. You want something, Mom?"

"Sure, sweetie, I'll take a diet soda. Here." She hands me a twenty-dollar bill.

Inside the newsstand, unable to resist a sexy woman on the cover of *Vogue*, I pick up the magazine along with our sodas. Inside the magazine a light-skinned black model reminds me of the flirtatious drag queen at the Lost and Found. I realize there's no way Dad and I are getting to Sunday tea dance today even though Miss Darla made me promise that I'd come see her again. While waiting to pay the cashier, I fantasize about tonguing her on the dance floor.

As I wander toward the sterile lounge, I look through the glass partition that separates the international terminal from the rest of the airport. Just a month ago, Nic and I were arriving here, bronzed and buzzing with eagerness to have our film developed to relive Greece all over again. I hear her voice in my head: "I hit the jackpot with you, hot stuff." I miss being the most important person in the whole world to someone. I miss the safety of gripping her waist as she rode us out to the country for a picnic on her motorcycle, my cheek resting on her capable back. I watch the mostly sleepy-looking travelers lugging bags, entering the main waiting area. Behind a large group is Dad, wide awake and marching.

I hustle back to Mom with the ice-cold Tab. Dad speeds through the sliding glass doors—then slows, and discreetly tucks a red handkerchief into his sports coat. Odd, since he doesn't use colored handkerchiefs—only white. Spotting me, he offers a big open smile, then stops dead in his tracks. I see him see Mom. His face goes frosty, but she presses toward him, full of warmth. I hang back. He pecks her on the cheek, shakes his head blatantly at the futility of her diet soda, and marches up to me.

"I asked that you, and only you, pick me up," he whispers, with a mixture of disappointment and harshness.

I check to see that Mom didn't overhear and then make a half-hearted effort to help with his bag.

"No need, dear," he says, and races away, a horse length ahead of us. Dad is always moving fast, even to places he doesn't want to go, like home.

I let Mom drive, preferring to sit behind his foul mood

rather than next to it. The car is silent until she finally flips on the radio and hums along in her soft low voice.

The dead silence between them hangs heavily until Mom extends an olive branch. "How were things in Rome, dear?"

Dad lets out a big sigh, palm gliding over his prickly flat-top.

"Busy," he says, not looking at her.

"Were you able to attend a papal mass?" she tries with more cheer.

"Woman, yes, I told you I was planning on attending, of course I did. Stop asking such bloody stupid questions!" he fumes while Mom keeps her eyes on the road.

"Let me ask you a question: Have you gotten back on your Weight Watchers?" He dares her to respond.

My body stiffens.

"This week," she murmurs.

He grabs for the radio dial and shuts it off, nearly ripping the knob off. Silence falls over us again.

A few years ago Dad offered Mom a "chance of a lifetime."

"Dear, if you lose at least fifty pounds, I will take you on the Around the World Cruise on the *QE2*," he said.

So she put away her miniature Weight Watchers scale in a kitchen drawer, next to other rarely used things like the meat timer and the turkey baster, and committed herself to a different kind of starvation. The liquid diet.

Every day for two months, she drank the most putrid-smelling concoction you could imagine. I watched her gag it down, laugh it down, pray it down—all so that she could finally get her husband back. It worked—the liquid diet, that is. My older sisters bought her a whole new wardrobe. I saw her stand in the dining room in a wool gabardine camel-color dress, a size 14, and wondered where my mother had gone. I was fidgety and ashamed to look at her body, which had been masked under Lane Bryant tent dresses for as long as I could remember. For days she waited for Dad to book the cruise, then weeks, then months, too passive to ask for what she had earned, fair and square. He never gave her the trip, nor a compliment. And a year later, she was back in a size 20.

But what makes me just as angry is that the moment we attack him for being cruel, selfish, and a goddamn hypocrite, she will defend him. "Your father is under a lot of pressure with work. But he's very generous, sending me on trips and to Lourdes every year. Beggars can't be choosers."

"We're having roast beef, right?" I call from the backseat, my voice rising.

"Yes, sweetie. You must be hungry; you didn't eat after your morning workout."

Mom never leaves me hungry. And even though she missed so many clues about my childhood, she was keenly aware that Simon was hogging all the Oreo cookies, so she bought me my own bag and hid them from him in the turkey pan.

"Christine, I was doing some thinking whilst I was away, and I know you are busy with your basketball training, but I think a few days a week working in my office is important." He looks at me through the side-view mirror and nods.

I squirm on the hot leather seat, moving my bare legs away from the intense sun, worried about losing my focus on training and becoming his employee instead of one of his favorite things.

"I think it's vital that you start to get acquainted with the travel business. I can't run Holy Pilgrimages forever. Although I do plan to live until one hundred!" Dad's mood warms.

"It would be nice to drive in with my baby, even if it's just a day or two," Mom adds sweetly.

"Christine, let's plan on an early start in the morning, and then you and I will go to lunch at the University Club to discuss my thoughts for the future," he states, ignoring Mom. His cruelty to her is at least consistent.

"Sure, Dad, that sounds good," I lie, knowing that he'll be ordering a few bottles of pinot grigio and tomorrow's workout will be ruined.

"That's a fancy first day," Mom says, furrowing her brow.

"Dear, this is not intended as a social luncheon!" he blasts her.

She squeezes the steering wheel but says nothing, while I feel queasy at the thought of my future as a Catholic travel agent.

†

"I must be hearing things. YOU actually have a summer job? A miracle," Simon jabs as he helps himself to leftovers on the marble buffet. From my place next to Mom, I stare at a glass Virgin Mary statue resting on the thin wooden ledge that runs around the dining room.

"I train, that's my job," I snap, biting down on an ice cube, feeling cocky since I'm a better shooter than Simon.

"Good luck training now. You'll be lucky to get out of Dad's office before it gets dark every night," Simon warns, as he sits down with a full plate on the other side of Mom, next to Margaret, who blows smoke toward the ceiling. My head throbs listening to him.

"I'm not working there every day. Dad just wants me to come in a couple days a week, to start learning the business," I explain half-heartedly.

"Yeah, yeah, yeah, we've all heard it before: 'I'd like you to take over the business. I can't run Holy Pilgrimages forever,'" Simon imitates Dad's drunken loose lower lip.

"Take it from me, kid, we've all been Dad's chosen one at one time or another," Margaret adds.

"You'll go down, like everybody else." Simon laughs. He crumples his paper napkin and shoots at my lemonade glass, missing off the rim.

"Cut it out." I flick his napkin off my place mat, mumbling, "Asshole."

Simon jumps out of his chair and stands over me. "What did you say?" He shadowboxes above me.

"Hey, I thought all this ended when you moved into your own house." Mom gives Simon a soft smack on his muscular bicep. I say nothing. I wish I had bolted to my room upon our return from the airport, like Dad did, with his soup and baked potato, announcing that he must catch the six thirty news.

"Just remember, kid, whenever Dad goes to lunch and he's still gone at five o'clock, get the hell out of there, or if he passes out at his desk, don't wake him. Just leave," Margaret instructs.

"You kids are terrible. Poor man," Mom says, cleaning her eyeglasses with the hem of her dress.

"Poor man? How about poor employees? How about the time he came back from a five-hour lunch and screamed his head off, then fired the entire staff when no one would accept responsibility for misspelling Medjugorje?" Simon says.

Mom chuckles. I find nothing funny. Looking at our four reflections in the polished table, I secretly wish everyone had surprised Mom tonight with a stop-by, not just Margaret and Simon. The table would be bustling with after-dinner chaos, Mom would be merrier, and my new position with Dad would have been overshadowed.

"How about the time Dad fired me for telling a client that I would check to see if there was a McDonald's in Jerusalem?" Margaret shakes her head.

"If they care more about their bloody Big Macs than their devotion to Christ, they should just stay home," Simon mimics Dad. The three of them laugh.

"Margaret, why did he fire you the other two times?" Simon needles.

"Don't remind me." Margaret stamps out her butt. "And

I'm still sitting at home doing his damn dictations. I must be crazy."

"You said it, I didn't. But don't feel bad, everyone's been fired—not three times—but everyone's gotten the ax. Except hot dog, here. I give her a week."

I twirl my knife, finally dropping it on top of my untouched carrots.

"Well, he isn't going to fire me," I say flatly.

Everyone turns, looking at me as if I just said I was Mary Magdalene.

"You'll get fired, trust me," Simon snips.

That tone sends me back to his jealous anger over my choosing—in seventh grade—to play on Miss Lange's sister's team instead of his. He spewed attitude at me and labeled my frequent outings with my teacher as "strange." But that time with her got me away from the encounters with him in the laundry room. And as Miss Lange regularly pointed out, she taught me how to study, too. When we weren't listening to her old Anne Murray or Fleetwood Mac albums, she'd spend hours quizzing me in her music room on world capitals, presidents, and current events, and having long conversations about things she'd read to me from her "Values" teacher's manual—a new course she introduced as part of the seventh-grade curriculum.

"Are you more like a bubbling brook or a placid lake?"

Questions that Miss Lange said would help me to "know thyself."

She was a good listener, too, catching me whenever I messed up *I* versus *me* or *lie* versus *lay*. And unlike Mom, she never fell asleep when I was reading her my term papers. Most of all, she made me feel special, and except for in the classroom, I never had to share her with any other kids.

"Trust ME. He won't fire me," I say softly, rising from my seat, clearing my plate, and striding out of the room with my brother's eyes on me.

"Sweetie, grab the coffee ice cream from the basement freezer while you're up, please," Mom says.

"Yeah, why don't you?" Simon orders.

I want to say no.

"Sure, Mom," I say politely, swallowing my rage, and head down the dusty basement steps.

7
Missions

The fountain at Dupont Circle, designed by Henry Bacon, is a two-tiered white marble sculpture with three classical nudes carved into the shaft, symbolizing the sea, the stars, and the wind. With a strong and accurate arm, you could throw a baseball from Dad's Holy Pilgrimages office and land smack in the middle of the erupting spout. An errant throw could easily nail a homosexual cruising near the fountain, since Dupont Circle is a labyrinth of gay men with colorful bandannas hanging out of their back pockets—left pocket for a "top," right for a "bottom."

"Holy Pilgrimages, may I help you?" Mom answers the phone. I place her brown bag of pastries on the bare metal receptionist's desk formerly manned by Marta, a middle-aged German hypochondriac, who was fired last week when she mistakenly refused my father's collect call from Rome.

"Poor thing," my mom said on the drive in this morning. "She's been calling every day explaining, 'Dhere vus a lot of static ven Mr. Vorthington called.'"

"No, Marta, he's not back yet. But I will tell him you called. Yes, I will . . . Oh, I'm sorry to hear that . . . Well, you better have that looked at by a doctor."

My mother hangs up the phone, restraining a laugh. I hear Dad's wing tips speeding down the narrow parquet hallway.

"Was that that bloody woman again? I told Dale to tell her to stop calling! She's finished. This is a business, not a charity! If she calls again, Christine, just hang up on her."

My father hands me a file. My breath quickens. I'm nervous already, not wanting to mess up, not wanting him to yell at me for not knowing how to do whatever he's going to ask me to do. I was praying the other version of Dad—the loose guy who was doing some weird fox-trot on the dance floor of the Lost and Found a few weeks ago—was going to welcome me to the office today. No such luck.

"Let's get you started back here." He motions for me to follow him into the main room.

There are large windows with open venetian blinds, un-framed posters of holy places and shrines hanging next to crucifixes and plaques with messages about love and Jesus. On a scroll, I scan the familiar Hail Mary, resting on "Holy Mary, Mother of God, pray for us sinners now and at the hour of our death." Catholic prayers depress me.

"Dear, would you like a sticky bun?" Mom calls to Dad.

"No, dear! And I don't want that mess all over the place!" he yells.

"Tina?" she offers.

"No, thanks, Mom. Thank you, maybe later."

Dad rolls his eyes and shakes his head; I look down, try-ing to avoid colluding. My father leads me into his office and closes the door. I lay the file down in front of a gold-framed family photo from our trip to Rome in 1975.

"Now, this is the heart and soul of my organization," he says, pointing to a new gray fax machine sitting on the corner of his massive oak desk. I run my hand over it, trying to ap-

pear interested, but my mind is busy scanning through options of where to work out after I blow this joint.

"No one—besides me—uses this fax. Of course, no one has
any business being in my private office." Dad sounds annoyed,
as if I've already messed up.

I look around the room, which could be mistaken for an
office at Blessed Sacrament rectory. The wall opposite the
large window holds framed photos of Dad with priests and
cardinals and four of the most recent popes. In one, John
Paul I is wearing granny glasses as he blesses my father, who
kneels before him.

"A good man, he was." Dad stares at the picture.

"He was the shortest-reigning pope," I say, to impress him.

"No, one of the shortest, but not *the* shortest. That would
be Urban VII, who reigned for thirteen days. John Paul I's
papacy was thirty-three days. A travesty. This was taken not
long before," he says, gently touching the photo, tearful.

"Before he died?"

"Before he was murdered," he says in a low voice, glancing
at the door, holding his index finger to his lips.

"They wanted him out and they got him out," he whispers.
"Between us, the Holy Father was in good health, and those
who had access were well aware that an autopsy is never per-
formed on the pope. John Paul was preparing to make a lot of
changes inside the Vatican, particularly at the Vatican Bank."

The murder of a pope? What is my dad talking about?
Archbishop Magni? I consider my father's last urgent business
trip to meet with Magni, the papal nuncio. "Vatican matters,"
Dad had told me. But what could be so pressing about American Catholics touring the Sistine Chapel? He moves to the
window and I follow, taking a whiff behind him to see if he's
been drinking. Seems not. I take in more framed pictures of
Dad and other popes: Dad kneeling before Pope Paul VI,
gazing at John XXIII wearing his crusader medallion, talking
casually to John Paul II. Beeping sounds come from the fax

and paper starts to roll. Dad heads to his machine as I spot a man out the window in cutoff jeans and worker boots with two bandannas in his right back pocket. Light blue and black. He fingers his Tom Selleck mustache.

"Dear, I need to head over to the Vatican embassy and drop off something," Dad says, distracted by his freshly delivered fax. "Why don't you step into the mailroom and study some brochures of our upcoming tours. Get familiar, as I may want you to accompany me abroad as your time permits."

"Sure, Dad," I sing, wondering where he might take me.

Turning from the window, I catch Dad quickly slipping a hand underneath his leather blotter and removing two small keys attached to a medallion with a familiar coat of arms—the Vatican's. At the door, I glance back as he whips out his briefcase from under the desk, unlocks it, drops a file inside. His pace is rapid even by his hurried standard. What's so urgent at the Vatican embassy that requires files in a locked briefcase? I've been around the travel business my whole life and am well aware that Americans don't need a visa to travel to Italy. Nothing could be *that* urgent.

The mailroom is filled with much less intriguing things, like a silver scale to weigh packages—a much larger version of Mom's Weight Watchers scale. Metal shelving holds various-size envelopes, stamps of every denomination, the massive *Catholic Encyclopedia,* and a press release stating that Dad's business is the largest Catholic travel agency in the United States. I open the encyclopedia, checking for a mention of his company. Nothing. Flipping to the *P*'s, I search for *Papal Nuncio.* Nothing. I thumb back to the *N*'s and find *Nuncio.* It says *nuncio* is from the Latin word meaning "envoy" or "messenger." As the diplomatic representatives of the pope, nuncios are given "special credentials as well as special instructions, whether of a public or of a private nature. They also receive a secret code and enjoy the same privileges as ambassadors." So like all the diplomats living in Washington, D.C., would

Archbishop Magni, the papal nuncio to Italy, have diplomatic immunity? Nowhere in the *Catholic Encyclopedia* can I find any cross-reference about a "secret code."

On another shelf sit the brochures of the various pilgrimages that Dad wants me to study: Christmas in Bethlehem, The Shrines of Spain, Easter in Italy, The Way of the Cross in Jerusalem, Rome and Assisi, In the Footsteps of Paul, and Lourdes for the Disabled—Dad's pride and joy. Each year, my father invites some of my older siblings, "who are prepared to work," to join his Lourdes pilgrimage at no cost. He emphasizes, "This is not a free trip to shop and sightsee. You're there to serve the sick."

I have always wondered about the miracle baths. Dad brags about them like a new father: "There have been over sixty miracles in Lourdes that the Vatican has sanctioned." And Mom, a regular on the pilgrimage, shivers and jiggles every time she describes the ritual of being immersed naked into the fifty-degree water. She's hooked, returning year after year for the icy baptism and French bread. Margaret turns glassy eyed talking about the nightly candlelight procession where thousands—many on stretchers and in wheelchairs—sing "Ave Maria" and pray the rosary, inching around the Basilica of the Immaculate Conception. If it weren't for the constant prayers and processions, I might like to go to Lourdes. Maybe have a miracle of my own. Dunk away my anxious stomach, cure my remaining flat-footedness on defense, wash off the panic that seems to smother me most when it's hot and humid and I feel alone.

The four-page brochure informs the reader that since 1954, Dad has been organizing a 747 to carry terminally ill and handicapped Catholics to the small French village at the foot of the Pyrenees where the Virgin Mary appeared eighteen times to a young girl, Bernadette, in 1858: a woman in white called out to the girl, "I am the Immaculate Conception," and told Bernadette to drink from the stream and wash herself there. By doing the same, ailing people of Lourdes began to be cured, and now, a pilgrimage to Lourdes is considered the last hope for many incurable cases.

I'm not convinced of any of this. As I hold the lightweight pamphlet, I think of those who didn't get cured. Pilgrimages to Lourdes have produced sixty supposed miracles, out of how many thousands of broken hearts? Worse odds couldn't be found in Atlantic City. Even the color photos of the Virgin Mary hovering, the glow of the evening procession, and a small floral plate with a single croissant feel heavy. But Dad seems to thrive on heavy. The harder the better. No pain, no gain. I guess we both love a challenge. Every year, he's determined to charter a plane, fill it with the sick, and hire nurses and doctors to go along, whether he loses money or not—it doesn't matter to him. He insists it be a nonprofit trip, and you couldn't tear this heartfelt mission away from him any more than you could a bloody rib eye from a wolf. *Life* magazine did a profile on him and the pilgrimage in 1958.

"I'll be back shortly," Dad shouts, and then the main office door slams. My father always shuts everything as if his hands are packed with anger.

The four large wall clocks in the mailroom have small black letters above them: Washington, D.C.: 8:20 A.M. Rome: 2:20 P.M. Jerusalem: 3:20 P.M. Bangkok: 8:20 P.M.

On an out-of-reach top shelf, there are boxes marked WORTHINGTON WONDERLAND, with various dates from the fifties, sixties, and seventies. Every year, Mom writes a family Christmas letter and Dad edits it before sending it out to hundreds of their friends around the world. Most years, for a solid week in December many of us sit around the dining room table folding, licking, sealing, and stamping. I have copies of most of the printed letters from after I was born—in the sixties—but I don't remember ever seeing the Worthington Wonderland letters from the fifties. Opening up a dented folding chair, I climb up and pull down the heavy box labeled 1950s.

Inside are stacks of legal-size family letters printed on both sides in red with the Knights of the Holy Sepulchre logo above *Worthington Wonderland*—also in red ink. I read 1959, stopping on a paragraph at the bottom of the front page: "Speaking of Holy Pilgrimages, the boss man has done his share of travel this year . . . he went around the world in 19 days, made 21 stops, and the approximate number of miles covered in 1959 was about 500,000." What work can you accomplish moving that fast around the globe? Flipping through the pile, the next year down, 1958, begins as they all do: "Dear Friends in Christ." A few paragraphs in, something catches my eye: "The latter part of November, Sir John went to Russia and found Moscow a very interesting city. The early part of the year, a new country that hadn't been visited before was also included—Yugoslavia in May. Much can be written of both countries but space and time just do not permit more at this time." That's weird; those are communist countries. I know for certain from Miss Lange's drilling me about the Cold War that no American could set foot in the USSR in the fifties. *Why was Dad there? He sure wasn't selling Catholic pilgrimages to the Kremlin.* I tuck 1958 and 1959 into my back pocket, quickly searching for others. I grab '57 and decide I'd better seal up the box before Mom walks in.

In the main room of the office, four uninhabited metal desks await the accountant, our two sales agents, and Dale, the latest office manager, who Dad described as "a towhead with an eye for color." Calendars of shrines are thumbtacked over each of their neatly organized work areas. The month of June features Notre Dame Cathedral in Paris. I look at the double doors to my father's private office. I can hear Mom chuckling on the phone, and with a light foot, I head for Dad's door and enter, twisting the brass lock behind me. The overhead fluorescent lights emit a faint buzzing. With no time to waste, and no idea what I'm looking for, I move around his desk, checking on "the heart and soul of his organization": the fax machine. There is no sign of the paper that sent him out the door. I open the file he handed me earlier, just stapled pages of lists: monsignors, archbishops, and their contact information.

On the corner of his desk, I scan through neatly placed manila folders labeled HOLY LAND, LOURDES, ALITALIA AIRLINES in Dad's crisp handwriting—the slant of a lefty. A harsh ring of the phone startles me.

My heart races, realizing Mom isn't answering. *Should I?* Rushing to get out, I elbow Dad's silver pen, which clatters to the floor. I crouch down to retrieve it and pause. Under his desk, pushed far back, is his brown briefcase. The one I swear he took with him. Pulling it toward me, I notice another identical briefcase behind that one. I test the metal locks: neither of them budge.

I wipe my eyes. Feeling suddenly shaky and light-headed, I need something stable to hold on to, but Dad's rolling wooden chair is no help. I hear faint voices rise from the other room and, not able to take a breath, I quickly slide the briefcases back to what I pray is the exact position in which I found them.

8
Love

It's still dark when I jog across the dewy lawn in my baby blue tracksuit—a Christmas gift from Nic—for a run. Even before the sun rises, the August morning is warm enough that shorts and a T-shirt would have been plenty of cover, but I need to sweat out my weekend. I'm desperate to get my wind back. Sobering images of coming face-to-face with some of the best players in the country in a month cause my bloated belly to flutter. I imagine my teammates exhausting themselves on the mean streets of Newark and Philly, the cracked asphalt public courts of Oakland and Detroit, getting their already rock-solid bodies into shape for next season. I want to punch myself for being soft.

As I jog up the sidewalk, the cramp in my foot is proof that I've been spending too much time in high heels and too little in high-tops. My throat singes before I even reach the top of my street. On Brookville Road, there's no sign of life. The dense treetops hang over the two-lane road—the drive of choice when the wealthy want to avoid traffic on Connecticut Avenue.

This was my route anytime I went over to Miss Lange's house. In our three-year love affair—from sixth grade until I graduated eighth—I rarely walked to 36 Magnolia Street; instead I'd sprint to be with her any chance I got. Miss Lange's thick arms were warm and soft, and I didn't have to share them with twelve others. They were mine. Her huge breasts, too. Even though we could have chosen any of the four bedrooms on her second floor, we usually made love in what had been her parents' bedroom before they got too old to walk up the flights of steps and moved into the den. Flo, the housekeeper, kept things spotless, and the pink bathroom had matching monogrammed towels as fluffy as cotton candy— Miss Lange loved her initials on things. We would lie around for hours after sex, my lanky limbs wrapped up in her thickness, my mind on cloud nine as my head rested against her chest.

Today, my motivation is as lacking as my pace, as I crawl past Kirk Street, looking at the grand houses owned by the Washington elite—a congressman, a newscaster—and the place where Miss Lange started everything between us. I guess I was asking for something: attention. I was hungry, starving maybe, to feel special at home, because no matter how hard my mother tried to dote on all of her kids equally, she only had two arms and one heart. All my acting out at school never led to much, though once, when I rearranged the school's card catalog for kicks, Mrs. Donovan, Blessed Sacrament's librarian, took me into the hallway and whispered through gritted teeth, "I hope your brother Simon and his wife take you aside one day and beat the hell out of you." When I was in sixth grade, I went to Miss Lange's classroom one day after school and tried a different tactic. At that point, she was just my tutor. One of the nuns had asked her to help me because I was causing all kinds of trouble and getting bad grades. I told Miss Lange that I had a problem. I didn't. It was a game I made up to spend time with her. She offered to drive me home, but we drove all around Rock Creek Park as she tried to get me to say what the problem was. Finally, we parked on Kirk Street as it got dark, and she quizzed me about my fake dilemma in her idling silver Opel. I failed her test, brilliantly extending our alone time. Finally exhausted from her strikeouts and my sullen silences, she threw a pitch I wasn't expecting: "Is it that you want to kiss me?"

Out of my league, I swung anyway at her knuckleball. "Yes," I stammered.

And that was that. Soon, we were lovers, and I could barely think of anything but her every second of every day.

The giant oak trees throughout Chevy Chase provide a lot of cover, but still, I wonder how we were able to spend so much time together without anyone finding out. I guess we both must have been desperate for each other and expert liars.

Chugging along the empty road, I pass Lenox Street, where the Zapruders live—their patriarch filmed JFK's assassination. Miss Lange always avoided parking on their street. Maybe she was worried someone with a camera might capture us together. As I run faster, my body cries with sweat, soaking my clothes. The faint smell of alcohol lingers on my skin. I'm ready to collapse, but Coach Norris's criticism that I'm too slow won't let me stop. I weave my way across the double yellow line to the other side of Brookville Road, arriving at the Langes' grand corner lot. After three years spent inside the palatial home filled with priceless antiques, becoming a straight-A student and learning how to give Miss Lange pleasure, I was crushed when she decided she needed to spend time with people her own age. But I didn't let on. I don't know why I didn't kick and scream, but I don't recall begging her to stay. Actually, I don't remember saying anything; I think I just pretended to be fine in front of her and everyone else.

Her selfless-sounding breakup confused me. "Now that you're going to high school, you're going to want to see other people."

Maybe she was speaking for herself. I saw how much time she was spending with her new friend Dawn, the feminist divorcée and mother of one of her students. She was pulling away before I graduated. And so I did what my mom seemed to do: I pretended it wasn't happening, while feeling like my life raft was slowly being pulled out from under me. Inch by deflating inch, I began to sink.

There was no one to tell, so I'd hold all my tears until bedtime, when I would release everything into my pillow surrounded by all the stuff Miss Lange had given me—a collection of frogs, a découpage trash can, stuffed animals, O. Henry's short stories, and my favorite baby blue corduroys. I remember faking a cold to explain away my stuffiness. I must have still been in love with her my freshman year in high school—even though it was only a friendship after she broke off our love affair—because that year for her birthday I saved up for months to buy her a $350 bracelet with my babysitting money. I wanted to give her something special, since she was turning thirty. Once I went to high school, I would still visit her classroom, longing for her attention.

Although I haven't seen her in over a year—since we caught up over dinner at Hunan Noodle House—as I jump the hedges surrounding her gray three-story, I half hope to see her standing with her garden clippers, as her parents shuffle off the wraparound porch toward their Cadillac— off on their long Saturday outing for crab cakes along the Chesapeake Bay. Miss Lange would watch them drive off, chuckling: "Luella and Finch are straight out of a Tennessee Williams play." From what I could see, I guessed she meant the all-day bourbon. In their heavily shuttered first-floor living space, her parents spoke to me at first as one of her students, but then as one of the family. I'm sure they never suspected, when they sobered up enough to hit the road on Saturdays, that their twenty-seven-year-old daughter and her twelve-year-old student were getting high on multiple orgasms in their former bedroom.

As I wind around Miss Lange's favorite tree, a one-hundred-year-old sugar maple, I look up to the second story. I remember endless hours in her arms behind those sealed venetian blinds, the afternoons when I felt safer and more cared for than maybe I ever have.

Although she knew her parents would never come upstairs, she had a strict policy. We could never get naked until their sedan disappeared down Brookville Road. Sometimes it seemed like she was the parent, the way she took care of Finch and Luella, grocery shopping, picking up their medication, and in the summer months, acting as the unofficial grounds-keeper, despite her serious allergy to honeysuckle. When it came to yard work, she thanked me for being her "little helper," even though I was always secretly wishing we would throw down our rakes and go inside.

I pick up speed passing the crisp white porch railing and sprint down their front sidewalk, looping back onto Brookville Road. Her Opel looks small and lonely parked out front—rejected in favor of Amtrak's sleeping car. She sent me a post-card from Jacksonville, where she's vacationing with her new same-age girlfriend at the same sleepy beach town she's been visiting since we were together. Over the years, whenever we see each other for dinner, it's always at the same Chinese res-taurant where she orders the same chow mein. She is a creature of habit, that's for sure.

I still find myself staring at her breasts whenever we go out to dinner, but I no longer find her attractive. Her looks were beside the point when I was twelve, but now I know the difference. And even though Miss Lange and I have stayed friends, the older I get, the less I like her. Years ago, she often said, "People outgrow each other." I never thought that possible then, but now I know it to be true.

I get a burst of energy as I run away from her house. Fuck it, if I can fix my broken heart all by myself at thirteen, I can compete with anyone. Even if they are faster and stronger, I'm probably wiser.

†

Two weeks later, Dad's off again for another meeting with Archbishop Magni at the Vatican. I want to ask him what kind of business they're doing, but I'm afraid. It doesn't matter how close we've become, I've still been up close and personal with his temper.

"Love, the car is yours to use whilst I'm away," Dad tells me as I drop him curbside at Dulles for his flight to Rome.

I smile and kiss him on the lips. "Thanks. I'll pick you up next week."

"Alone," he commands.

I nod, understanding he means business.

"I'll be arriving early Sunday, so we should plan on heading straight to brunch at the University Club and then on to tea dance."

"Okay, sure." I nod, wondering what lie I'm going to tell Mom.

"And you'll need some money for gas . . . and for the bars, no doubt." He winks at me and hands me a white envelope with Holy Pilgrimages' return address printed in the corner. "Don't do anything I wouldn't do, love."

I like being his "love." I'm not sure how long all of this will last, but I know I am enjoying his affection. During the last eight weeks of his constant attention I fell for him, too. It happened so fast.

His sharp tongue softens its edges with me. Now, stories of his ex-lovers and extravagant trips with candlelight dinners in the Arabian Desert, and secret rumors about the Vatican, fall easily from his lips to my ears. Even his angry hands soften in my presence: removing my jacket, pulling out my chair, holding open doors, and of course, paying for everything. He wants to be with me, just me. As with any new love affair, our time is best spent alone, without distraction from others. Others who try to make sense of our new, strange relationship.

"Is this the second or third time this week you and your father have been to the University Club?" Mom asked when I told her we were having another dinner to discuss his future plans for Holy Pilgrimages.

I think my bad lie caused her to nearly choke on her hard candy, worrying me to death—as usual—that something bad would happen to her and that it would be my fault. I'm running out of believable lies, but truthfully, I don't want to give up my newfound connection.

My father gives me his shipping-off-to-sea wave, picks up one of his endless briefcases (who knows which one?), throws his carry-on over his shoulder, and heads inside the international terminal. He turns once more and blows me a kiss the way a movie star tosses one. An adoring fan, I playfully catch it on my cheek, then hop into the driver's seat, unhook the black metal latches on both sides of the convertible top, and hit "down."

The electrical motor releases a high-pitched sound, like an airplane's landing gear being tucked away after takeoff, as the canvas folds itself neatly into the back of the car. I rip open the envelope, finding three freshly printed one-hundred-dollar bills.

The humid August wind blows my loose clean hair on the drive home. I yank my sundress way up, hoping the sun will fix my seemingly permanent tan line from long hours of training in my basketball shorts. Out of nowhere, a rush of nausea comes over me, along with thoughts of tonight. Saturday night. No Nic, no Dad. *What will I do?* I try to pump myself up with the facts: I have lots of money, and a red convertible, and a storage bin of lies I can pull out to give anyone looking for the truth. But my head feels overwhelmed. All this space, but nothing to fill it up. Maybe there's such a thing as too much space? I've been in secret love affairs with women and girls since I was eleven. Miss Lange, Nic, a handful of high school classmates, plus a few boyfriends along the way. Before all that it was Simon and Luke. The picture of being with no one is trying to hang itself inside my head. I start to panic. Heat rises from my body. The humidity, now stifling, makes it worse. I turn my face toward the open sky and gulp in a big breath.

The dark green exit sign for Connecticut Avenue looms over my head, and I watch it expand and land on me. The massive metal is smothering my chest. An old station wagon next to me seems to grow larger, too—invading my space. Driving down the exit ramp, my hands, feet, and face feel fat, like I've ballooned from 125 to 225 pounds.

I grab for distractions—the radio, the air-conditioning, the vents—anything to get my mind off the panic. Waiting at the traffic light, heart racing, I look around for a friendly face that might help me. But what would I say? "Hello, stranger, will you talk to me for a few minutes, until this panicky, distorted feeling goes away?"

A massive middle-aged man sits in the driver's seat of a station wagon, talking to three hysterical kids in the backseat. The youngest one happily shows me her Cabbage Patch doll out the window. I force a smile at her. It helps. I wave good-bye as I turn onto Connecticut Avenue. I take deep breaths, and eventually I slip out of the panic.

As I turn the convertible into our driveway, Mom's Impala sits alone. Tears stream down my face as I look at the four brown doors. If only she could escape. I can't tell her. About him. About me. I can't tell her how the love I have for her is so big, it hurts. And even if I could, would she be rested enough, happy enough, full enough, to love me back that much?

Once a year, on my birthday, I do get a delicious taste of her big love. And no matter how many years she writes "You're my lucky 13" in my birthday card, I can't help excusing myself from the table and bawling my eyes out in the first-floor bathroom while my cake is being sliced. Mom, like the chocolaty dessert, has always been divvied up among too many people to ever allow me to feel full.

9
Condemnation

I'm barely into the first week of my sophomore year of college when the shit hits the fan.

"It's fucking bullshit," I yell, speeding away from the public high school where Nic teaches. My aggression toward the accelerator is nothing compared to the anger I feel after the crushing meeting with my basketball coach.

Now a safe distance away from her school, Nic rolls a joint, shaking her head in solidarity from the passenger seat. I run a stop sign for no good reason other than I feel like it.

"Ya know, I bet she was just trying to motivate you," Nic says.

I turn the van's large steering wheel hand over hand like a bus driver, merging onto Veirs Mill Road, and hit bumper-to-bumper rush-hour traffic. Nic rolls up her window, then bends down, hiding below the dashboard to light the joint. Knowing the drill, I roll up my window, too, keeping the smell of pot away from nearby cars.

My mind spins. Every which way I turn Coach Norris's words, I can't make them mean anything else. Nic rises with a mouthful of smoke. She offers me the joint as we inch along, and I take it. I need it.

"How can she already know I'll never be a starter? I'm only a sophomore!"

"I'm telling you, coaches say that shit to light a fire under you."

"Have you ever told one of your players that she'll never start?" I ask.

Nic takes the joint back, considers the question, then shakes her head.

"I'll just ask her about it when she comes over this weekend," Nic says.

"No, then she'll know I told you," I explain.

"She knows you're going to tell me everything, you're my girlfriend."

"No! I don't want you asking her," I insist.

Nic looks at me and, playfully, blows smoke in my direction, giggling.

"Go the back way," Nic suggests, pointing east.

I barely avoid the oncoming traffic as I floor it onto a side street of brick ramblers just like Nic's. Their occupants probably have crushed dreams, too, and have settled for what someone told them they could accomplish in life. Fuck that. I look at the simple, small homes and know I don't belong here. I would never tell Nic, but I don't like driving this big brown masculine box, either. If one were to rip off the passenger door and stencil on a logo, it could pass for a UPS truck.

As I pull up in front of Nic's rental, I feel nearly as underwater as I did when I walked out of Norris's office with a fake smile plastered on my face, having just had my dream deflated. I turn off the ignition even though I want to drive away and hide somewhere so no one can see my hurt. I have barely enough energy to grab the door handle. My pulse seems to be missing. Nic gathers her things from the floor.

"I'm quitting the team," I declare.

Nic opens her door and gets out of the van. I hear her chuckle.

"Very funny, hot stuff."

†

I did quit the team a few weeks after my preseason meeting in Coach Norris's office, but Mom and Dad didn't get a bill for my sophomore year, even though I didn't play at all—it was really decent of Norris to not yank my scholarship away. When I told her I was leaving the team, she didn't try very hard to convince me otherwise. I lied, telling her my decision was because I wanted to focus on my studies. Another year of riding the bench seemed much worse than being seen as a quitter. Dad's initial response was tinged with disappointment: "When you make a commitment, you keep a commitment." Maybe that's why he's still married to Mom . . .

†

If I were Larry Bird, I could just raise my arm and rest my palm on the ceiling from the top bunk in my dorm at my new school. But I fall short by a forearm. I got stuck with the top bunk because by the time Mom dropped me off at Mount St. Mary's College, a Division II school an hour and a half from home that recruited me to play basketball junior year, my two roommates had grabbed the prime real estate in our suite. Nothing has been sweet so far. In fact, I have felt awkward ever since I climbed into Mom's Impala with my suitcases piled high in the back and we began the drive on 270 North. I feel like such a fraud.

After a month here, I am still completely uncomfortable

sharing a room with two freshmen I have nothing in common with. My roomies are both from New Jersey and became instant best friends before I even had time to set up my hot-air popcorn popper. We are pleasant to one another, but mostly I keep a wall between us, not telling them much about me and staying to myself. I play pickup games in the gym every day after school with my teammates, eat in the cafeteria with a couple of them, or alone, and then study in the library. Other than my fellow players, I've only really talked with Todd, a New Yorker with an asymmetrical haircut who's always dressed in black. My first week here, I was heading to philosophy class, and he told me my ankle boots were "flawless." He gave me his number, a first. I haven't called, but I'm pretty sure from the way he walked—all hips—that he's gay. Most days, and nights, I stay away from my dorm room until I'm ready to crash or until Nic is supposed to call on the hallway pay phone—conveniently located outside our door.

Tonight, with the room dark except for the glow of three bedside clocks and a desk lamp, I'm about to nod off when I hear the hall phone ring. My bunkmate slides back from her desk—wood scraping sharply on the vinyl floor—and walks out of the room. A few moments later, she returns.

"Tina, are you awake? The phone is for you," she whispers from below.

"Yeah, okay," I say, climbing down the small ladder attached to the bottom of the bunk.

I tighten the drawstring on my pajama bottoms—Nic's baggy red sweatpants from the high school where she teaches. The black receiver dangles from the metal cord inside the glass phone booth. Slipping inside, I close the folding door for privacy. I feel safe in here. For one hour most nights, I get to fully be myself, no hiding, talking on the phone with Nic.

"Hello?" I say playfully, knowing it's her.

"Hey, hot stuff. Did I wake you up?" Nic's voice is unsteady.

"Hi, babe. No, I'm up."

"How was practice?"

The question surprises me, since she knows official practice doesn't start until mid-October.

"You mean pickup?" I ask, trying to gauge if she's stoned.

"Yeah . . . pickup games . . . game."

"Great. Mr. Sheehan was watching us today, and he said I grabbed at least eight rebounds over all the forwards and centers."

She goes silent.

"Are you okay?"

The only response is her uneven breathing.

"What?" I say impatiently.

After a deep breath, she says, "It's not the same . . . here."

"I know. I hate it, too. But we'll see each other next weekend."

"You didn't have to transfer."

Her tone is clipped, and dead serious. I don't feel like hearing for the hundredth time that the bed feels empty. It's not like sleeping in a top bunk is some fantasy come true, but turning down the chance to play basketball again, along with a full scholarship for the last two years of college and my M.B.A., didn't really feel like an option.

"I'm just not sure," her words stumble out.

"Of what?"

She takes another big breath.

"Us . . ."

"Not sure?!" My breath shortens, my heart speeds ahead.

She falls silent. I stare through the glass box, my eyes following the row of door handles all the way down the hallway, dead-ending at the open bathroom door. I prop my foot against the glass.

"Not sure what?"

She hesitates, dragging out her words.

"How I feel . . ."

"About what? Like you aren't sure if you love me?"

"Yeah . . . I'm not sure . . . I think I need some time," she apologizes.

I clutch the metal phone cord, which refuses to bend. The word EDISON—her school—is spelled out in chunky white letters down the right side of my sweatpants. My brain seizes and sentences refuse to form. My chest feels like it's pulling in every direction. Finally, she tries to explain. "I'm sorry, but you left, and now I don't know . . ."

Like waves cresting, emotion rises from my belly, curling through my chest and throat, and crashing out of my eyes and down my face. I use my T-shirt as a tissue. Then the heaving starts. I try to wrangle for control. Out of nowhere, a chubby girl with a towel wrapped around her head stares at me from outside the pay phone, jolting me. I quickly wipe my eyes and reach for a smile to prove I'm fine, but it's futile.

"Are you going to be much longer?" the girl mouths from the other side.

I shake my head, cover the receiver, and mouth back with a lifeless shrug, "My boyfriend." She nods with mild sympathy at my guy trouble and shuffles away in her flip-flops. At least I feel safe knowing if she's going to gossip about my weeping, late-night call, she'll be sure to say that I was on the phone with my "boyfriend."

"How about I call you this weekend?" Nic offers, like she's bargaining with a child.

"Sure," I mutter softly.

"Okay," she says.

"Bye."

I hang up, dropping my head into my hands. A whirlwind of thoughts, mostly regrets, blows through my mind—my stupid cheating, my blatant flirting, my overconfidence that she would never leave. But then, like a crazy person, I have the opposite feeling. Hope strikes. Maybe Nic's just having a bad day. I am convinced she's not breaking up with me. But then, just as fast, a lump swells in my throat, recalling her tone—different from anything I've ever heard from her. Different from the emotion-filled threats of the past.

In a daze, I enter my dark room, the desk lamp now off. The freshmen are tucked in, and only the hum of the mini fridge sounds alive. I slowly climb the ladder to my top bunk and pull the covers over my head. Rolling facedown, I mute my cries into my pillow, soaking the floral pillowcase Mom picked up on sale. Eventually, needing air, I let a sob slip out.

"Tina, are you okay?" my bunkmate calls from below.

"Yeah, I'm fine," I pipe up, doing a bad impersonation of being fine.

I swallow hard, cough, roll over noisily in my bed to mask the crying. For sure, my bunkmate knew that was a woman who asked to speak with me, the same woman who calls regularly. I can tell both roommates suspect things, the way they look at each other when one of them answers the pay phone and it's Nic. If I fall apart, they will figure it out for sure. I bite my lip and bury my face back into my pillow. *Fuck! I have no idea how I'm going to get through this night.*

One of the only people I am able to confide in about my breakup is Dad. While I am away at school, he writes to me often, always telling me how much he misses me and trying to pin me down for our next dinner. His last letter, written on British Airways Concorde stationery, ended with a guilt-inducing "Well, love, just want you to know I'm thinking of you and love you very much even though I don't see much of you. Strange—life will be over and we'll be asking why? Keep me in your love and prayers. Miss you. Love and Blessings always, Dad."

During one of our reunion meals, I tell him that Nic and I aren't together anymore. He doesn't seem to care much about the breakup, maybe because I lied and told him it was mutual. Maybe because when something isn't about him, he mostly seems uninterested.

At the end of my first semester at the Mount, I am summoned to the dean of students' office. He closes the door to his office before speaking.

"Your roommates have filed a complaint," he says, going on to explain that they claimed I hit on them and made them feel uncomfortable.

In a state of shock, I feel ashamed and embarrassed, even though as sure as I am of being a great jump shooter, I am sure I never, ever looked at those girls with a shred of interest, never mind doing anything but trying to hide my sexuality from them. Still, their intolerance and flat-out lies, probably due to their suspicions about my lifestyle, result in the dean transferring me to a "single"—a two-hundred-square-foot box with cinder-block walls, and a very hard get for someone still new on campus. I would have been glad for the chance to be roommate-free, only now, my housing situation makes me feel as if I have leprosy. Also, I'm not sure if it's a coincidence or not, but there's a gay gal on my floor—a funny party animal named Max—who fortunately does have roommates who seem to love her.

Trying to salve the pain of being moved into a single because my roommates told lies to the dean, I'm determined to do an even better job of passing for straight during my second semester at my new school. My plan is to stay focused and firmly committed to my business degree, particularly after learning from my advisor that by taking just two extra classes in economics, I can earn a minor in the subject. I like the sound of it: "I'm majoring in business with a minor in economics." Lots of my decisions get made because I like the sound or look of something. Truth is, I'm not even sure how I feel about economics. Or a lot of stuff I do.

In March, during the playoffs, I have a lot to prove, both on the court and off. As captain of the team, I lead the Lady Mountaineers to one win shy of making the Final Four and am voted Most Valuable Player. I don't even attend the annual sports banquet to pick up my trophy.

10
Mysteries

Finding myself single at the end of my junior year and back at home for the summer, I'm in need of something to fill my time and a way to make money. So when Dad offers me a full-time job for a few months, answering the phones, filing, typing envelopes, and doing brochure mailings, I grab it. Since we are partners in crime, I figure it will be a breeze.

These first few weeks of vacation, Dad and I have been making up for lost time, since we couldn't spend as much time together while I was away at school. No matter how late we stay out or how much we drink, Dad never misses 6:30 A.M. mass, or even seems hungover. Even when I nod off at my office desk, he lets it slide, never getting mean. Anyone else, he'd fire on the spot. All I get is another invitation to lunch. I haven't had the chance to snoop around the office much because he hasn't been away in nearly a month—an eternity for him. But I look forward to another peek around. I know he's got more secrets for me to uncover.

Staring into the ladies' room mirror at the University Club,

I fluff up my curled hair, making a sexy face, and kiss the mirror, leaving a bright red lipstick print behind. A toilet flushes, and I rush out before anyone steps out of the bathroom stall. Breaking rules, even something as minor as my lipstick graffiti, makes my heart race with the exhilaration of a game-winning shot, as I hustle back to the table where Dad and his Middle Eastern business associate, Hassan, are still deep in serious conversation. Dad invited me to join them after their business meeting for an early dinner—code for "Dad wants to start drinking as soon as possible."

Swaying through the crowded dining room in my new summer dress—a fitted mini—my confidence soars in response to stares from the mostly male crowd. A new bottle of Châteauneuf-du-Pape—our third, on top of the gin and tonics we began the evening with—rests next to the gorgeous arrangement of white roses in the center of our round table. I'm flying high on the right balance of excellent appetizers, expensive booze, and the beauty of the dining room.

I love everything and everyone right now.

". . . Archbishop Gagnon was concerned for his safety," Dad tells his guest as I arrive at the table.

Hassan stands, pulling out my chair, his smooth brown face filled with courtesy and respect, as I sweep my dress against the back of my legs and settle into my seat. No matter my attraction to women, I, much like my father, appreciate a real gentleman. Dad's drunken nod continues far too long as he eyes Hassan up and down approvingly. The Arab looks sharp in his slim black suit, loafers, no socks, and expensive watch. His patchouli scent reminds me of Nic's masculine cologne. I'm confused, unsure of what's going on between them, if anything.

Who is he? What does he do? What does he want with Dad?

I've learned very little about Hassan tonight, although it's obvious he and my father have many mutual contacts in the Middle East. They toss around unfamiliar names and anecdotes as I smile politely, enjoying my clams casino and the grand dining room. So far, I've learned that Hassan seems to spend quite a bit of time in Rome, speaks Arabic and Italian, and, like Dad, understands Latin. Maybe it's his limited English, but Hassan is very reserved, unlike Dad, who as usual does most of the talking.

"Sorry, I didn't mean to interrupt," I jump in, trying to hijack Dad's cruising of Hassan and get the conversation rolling again, curious about an archbishop "concerned for his safety."

"My dear, you could never be an interruption," Dad insists.

"I think is very truthful." Hassan smiles.

He clearly understands English better than he speaks it. I take a sip of my red wine, the bold flavor swishing in my mouth as I muster the nerve to interject.

"Who is Archbishop Gagnon?"

Dad looks at me, then straightens his silverware, brushes the tablecloth as if there might be crumbs, despite the fact that we haven't eaten our main course or touched the bread-basket, and besides that, no waiter in this joint is ever going to let a single crumb sit on the impeccably set table.

"A good man, Canadian bishop, he's been in Rome now for . . ."

"Since *Humanae vitae*," Hassan adds with a scholar's certainty.

"Yes, starting with Pope Paul VI—he's been running the Pontifical Council for the Family—many years now in Rome."

"Why would he be unsafe?" I press.

"I told you Christine would be taking over for me at Holy Pilgrimages one day." Dad gives Hassan a wink, as if to say she's one of us, it's safe to tell her. "Toward the end of his papacy, Paul VI had Gagnon look into some concerns the Holy Father had inside the curia, wanting to weed out some problem cardinals and others involved in things the Vatican prohibits . . ."

"What kind of things?"

Dad hates when I interrupt, but doesn't scold me for a change. Maybe Hassan is a calming influence.

"Freemasons," Dad explains. "When the archbishop completed the report, the dossier was put in a safe until the Holy Father could look at it . . . but it was stolen."

I wait. Nodding, wanting more.

"So the pope never saw it?"

"He died," Hassan says.

"And the next one was murdered . . . John Paul I never had a chance," Dad adds.

Dad and Hassan shake their heads.

"Deus lo vult!" Dad proclaims, as if that explains everything.

I feel clueless in their world of Vatican hierarchy, Latin, and stolen dossiers.

"Someday I must write the book," Dad muses.

Hassan clears his throat, eyes Dad, then looks across the room as a few middle-aged men, olive-skinned and stone-faced, walk toward our table. They pass by—giving Hassan a long stare—and then zero in on Dad. Nobody flinches.

One of the men bumps into my chair, hard, prompting Hassan to reach toward me, to ensure I'm okay. His strong warm hand on my bare shoulder feels good.

I am okay. It wasn't intentional. Or was it?

Hassan calls toward the men, saying something in Arabic, I have no idea what, but it sounds harsh. Then again, all Arabic sounds a bit aggressive to my untrained ear.

"Bloody Jews," Dad spews quietly.

The three men are gone, and Dad signals to our waiter.

"Are you ready to order, Sir John?"

"Not quite, *s'il vous plaît,* but my glass seems to have a hole in the bottom," Dad teases.

"Mine too." I play along and reach for Hassan's wineglass, holding up his glass, pretending to examine the bottom.

"Yours looks fine, Hassan," I say sarcastically.

We all laugh as the waiter pours the wine. I look to the door, still curious about those men. After the waiter leaves, I have to ask, "Dad, were they Mossad?"

Dad smirks. Is that pride across his face?

"Christine, your father tells me you have much intelligence of the world, and I can see he is true," Hassan notes.

Dad nods vigorously.

"Too bloody smart for her own good!"

Dad leans in and kisses my lips. Alcohol reeking from him, his moist skin wets mine. I'm embarrassed at his drunken attention. It's one thing when we are alone, but Dad's sloppy, exaggerated love gets weird in front of strangers. Hassan takes my hand and squeezes it, less fatherly. Looking at his brown eyes, thick dark eyebrows, I smile. He smiles back—only a few crow's-feet. His curls of black hair have no gray. I'd say, if Dad's sixty, and I'm twenty, Hassan's probably in his early forties. I like being the baby bear of this group, a familiar role I find intoxicating, as long as I'm getting the right kind of attention. For as long as I can remember, I've gotten a rush running with the grown-ups.

Over espresso Dad suggests we head to the Lost and Found, getting assurance from his guest that he's up for dancing. I conclude Hassan is definitely gay, otherwise Dad wouldn't suggest a men's bar. After all the alcohol we've consumed, I have no idea how the hell we are going to bump or grind—we'll have to hold each other up or pray the caffeine kicks in. Dad and I wait for the valet while Hassan heads upstairs to his room to drop off his sport coat. Often Dad has overseas guests stay at the University Club, which has about sixty private hotel-like rooms, although you have to be a man to stay here, still no women allowed except in the dining room.

Somehow, I drive us in Dad's convertible—Hassan in the passenger seat—out of the circular driveway, down Sixteenth Street, through downtown D.C., and into the rough-and-tumble projects of Southeast. Between Dad's lazy eye and the fact that he's a horrible driver—drunk or not—there's no choice but for me to drive. Dad's been known to back into poles and cars in the parking garage beneath his office building. Although he'll argue with Mom or most anyone who insists on driving when he's blotto, he actually seems to like that I drive, happily getting into the backseat.

Inside the club, Dad, Hassan, and I stand at the bar. Still in need of energy, I tell Dad I'll have a Coke.

"A Coke? You mean a Coca-Cola?!" Dad finds it absolutely deplorable when people have the opportunity to drink alcohol and they don't.

Fortunately, he's too drunk to yell at me for not drinking.

Dad hands Hassan a vodka cocktail, plops a hundred-dollar bill on the bar for the boyish bartender, and stumbles—nearly sideways—to the men's room. Watching him, I get the familiar knot in my stomach but home in on the pounding beat instead. For a Wednesday night, there's a decent crowd. Mostly men, as usual. Hassan moves closer to me, leaning in, so he doesn't have to shout.

"All of your family is beautiful?" He stares at me.

I think I know what he means, so I laugh—never really knowing how to handle a compliment. Mom usually makes up a reason why the praise anyone gives her isn't true, so maybe that's where I learned to throw away flattery. In fact, most of us Worthington girls handle a flattering remark like a hot potato.

"You want to dance?" I shout, diffusing thoughts of Dad, hoping he's not facedown in the toilet or face-to-face with a stranger.

Hassan and I head to the dance floor. Shutting my eyes, I settle into the bass, hands in the air, spinning in circles, the lightweight hem of my dress swirling freely, the air-conditioning refreshing on my dull head. I feel hands around my waist and am pulled by Hassan, my cork sandals support-ing my weight evenly, against him. For as long as Donna

Summer belts, I let the handsome Arab do as he wants with me, knowing we are hidden from my father's eyes, packed into the middle of the flashing dance floor. Reds, blues, yellows blink beneath our planted feet. We dance easily and playfully together.

In the car, as Dad sings show tunes in the backseat, I focus on the potholed roads in front of me, always eager at closing time to get out of this dangerous neighborhood. My buzz is still alive, but I'm glad to be a little more clearheaded—the adrenaline from the dancing helped—for the drive home. Dad insists on being dropped off at the office, drunk enough to believe he's capable of getting an early start without going to bed. You don't have to be a rocket scientist to know he's going to be facedown in faxes and paper clips in less time than it takes to say the rosary. We drop Dad at the office, making sure he gets inside the building safely, and I speed off for the short, familiar drive to the University Club.

"Sir John never stops," Hassan says, laughing.

"Yeah, he makes me tired and I'm only twenty," I joke.

"You are not twenty? No, much older."

He seems genuinely surprised.

"Have you known my father a long time?"

Hassan nods.

"But you aren't a travel agent, right?"

Hassan shakes his head, smiling.

As I pull up to the valet, I fumble to shut off the music and turn to Hassan, laughing at myself. All at once, he leans in and kisses me on the lips, his hand on my thigh. I pull away, aware of the valet opening my door.

"Come inside, I show you my room."

"Oh, okay," I say, wondering if that's even allowed.

Unstable, I get out of the car, attempting to feign sobriety for the valet and hiding my guilt for actually wanting to go up to Hassan's room. I drop the keys into a white-gloved hand, but somehow they land on the cement.

"I'll be right back, I just need to pick up something," I lie, slurring a little.

We walk into the lobby, and an attendant by the door smiles. I fake like we are heading for the dining room, and at the last minute, pivot toward the elevators.

As we wait, I lean against Hassan for support, staying hidden, out of sight of the front desk. I'm not sure if he knows women can't be in his room, but he doesn't seem to care.

Hassan opens his door, turning on a table lamp. Holding the wall, I enter the dimly lit guest room, feeling a little queasy. The wallpaper design looks blurry; the light fixture refuses to stop swaying. The small room holds a single bed and little other furniture, not nearly as impressive as the common areas of the building. More University than Club. Hassan walks toward the bathroom, dropping his wallet and emptying his pockets on the dresser. "Maybe they bring some drinks for us," he suggests.

I move over to the chest of drawers, wobbly, grabbing the corner of the dresser, hoping the room will stop spinning if I just hold still. My eyes rest on a pile of papers, folders, a mess of coins, a leather case—unzipped—and a key chain with what looks like a coat of arms—something familiar. The Vatican coat of arms? Like Dad's. Curious, I flip open a folder; again there is a coat of arms at the top of the pages. I lean in for a closer look, but Hassan opens the bathroom door, startling me. I stumble back, arching against the dresser.

"Do you need . . ." He points to the bathroom, picking up the phone.

"Yes," I say, inching my way to the door.

A loud knock stops us both. Hassan, holding the phone, hollers, "Yes?"

"Mr. Hassan, it's the manager," a man calls from the hallway.

I know we're in trouble, so I slip into the bathroom.

Sitting on the toilet, I hear the manager explain their policy—no women allowed in the rooms. And Hassan's apology. He's either a good actor, or he really didn't understand the no-chicks thing.

"No women allowed anywhere but the dining room," the manager says loudly.

I leave the bathroom, spotting the manager at the door prepared to escort me out. Thankfully, the room has stopped spinning—maybe the fear of authority has sobered me up—but either way, Hassan insists on walking me to the car, despite my assurances that I'm fine. He offers me his arm down the hallway and in the elevator, where the three of us ride silently to the lobby. The tall jerk sees us to the front door.

"You're welcome anytime in our dining room, accompanied by a member," he chides.

Fuck you and your clams casino.

Hassan leads me to the car, which the valet has left parked off to the side of the entrance, letting me know the keys are inside. Opening the door, Hassan eyes my bare legs as I steady myself into the driver's seat, then comes around and slides into the passenger seat. Before I can start the engine, he pulls me toward him, raising my dress, and gets on top of me. We make out, his breath fresh from a mint he must have snuck while I've been blurry. I wish I had one. His smooth skin feels soft and warm against mine. Almost girl-like. Reaching down and unzipping, he pulls out his penis. I touch it—not as big as I've experienced, but he's hard, and I'm turned on by the danger of it all. Neither of us seems to care that we are in the driveway of the University Club, we're so completely distracted by getting into a comfortable position so he can fuck me.

It's fast and mechanical, and after one long last kiss, he's out the door.

"I don't believe you are twenty."

Pulling up my underwear, I feel my wetness, even though he's the only one who had an orgasm. I make sure the passenger seat is clean, aware that I'll be turning over Dad's car when I drive myself to work. The thought of sitting at my desk at Holy Pilgrimages in less than five hours brings dread. Working there has its pros and cons. Right now, I just can't think of any pros.

Rolling down all the windows to keep myself alert for the drive home, I notice the valet attendant smiling at me. He probably watched the whole thing. I feel ashamed, but too tired from the long night, and alcohol, to dwell. Pulling out of the driveway, I turn on the radio to the soul station and listen to Marvin Gaye singing into the night.

†

A month later, Dad takes me to Tandoori Gardens, an expensive Indian restaurant off K Street, filled with mostly well-dressed businessmen and a few women. I've never eaten Indian food and had no idea they start their lunches with vodka. I reach for the puffy bread as Dad pours us both another shot and returns the icy bottle to the gold bucket on our table. Dad pulls the white handkerchief out from his breast pocket and taps his moist forehead, as I consider my second shot of vodka on top of last night's lineup of White Russians at the piano bar where we spent the evening.

"Have you given any thought to where you'd like to travel this summer, young lady?" Dad says casually.

The lure of another trip gives me goose bumps. Like my dad, I feel drawn to adventure, but also to the finer things. I lean over and kiss his clammy cheek, neither one of us quite cooled off from our muggy walk across town.

"Um, well, I didn't know . . . I was going somewhere."

"It's important that you see the world, particularly if you're going to be taking over the office someday."

I play along with his vision of my future. There's no reason to tell him I find Catholic tourism as boring as watching professional bowling. There's no reason to share my real feelings about mass, confession, visiting churches with Mom, saying the rosary every night after dinner, celebrating the bland Passover meal on Holy Thursday, or any of the trappings of Catholicism, frankly. It doesn't feel like the moment.

I want to live and work somewhere exciting. Exotic, sexy places, not just Catholic ones. I adjust my snug sundress and down the shot of vodka. Once I get over the burn in my throat, a looseness flows through me, a smile blooming on my face.

"You've not been to the Holy Land, am I right?"

"No," I say, not liking his suggestion.

"Well, you must get to Jerusalem."

Dad looks around for our waiter while I gather my nerve.

"How about that cruise—the one that's part of your Egypt tour?"

Dad laughs, shaking his head.

"So you'd like to cruise the Nile, Queen Nefertiti?"

I nod, hoping he doesn't give me a lecture on selfishness.

"You are your father's daughter," he says, beaming.

11
Desert

Royal Jordanian Airlines is a client of Dad's, so the luxurious first-class service and unlimited cocktails make for a comfy twelve-hour flight from New York to Amman.

Dad decided we would fly to Jordan for a few days, since he has some work there, before I head off alone to Cairo and he travels to Rome for an audience with the pope and meetings with Archbishop Magni.

"Dad, what's your favorite thing about the Middle East?" I ask, adjusting my tray table.

He stretches his arms behind his head, something he never really does—as if he were lying on grass stargazing. I sip my vodka tonic through a tiny black straw. The weight of the cut crystal feels at home in my hand.

"The desert. There is nothing quite like the desert."

I consider what could be so special about miles and miles of sand that isn't the beach.

"I'd be afraid of getting lost there."

"Getting lost is the best part," he says dreamily.

His eyes practically roll up into his head, as if reaching for memories.

" 'The greatest thing you'll ever learn is just to love and be loved in return.' "

Eyes wet, he takes my hand and kisses it.

"You'll love the desert, too."

Dad's in charge of everything when we travel—even holding my passport and itinerary. Eventually, he'll have to hand them over when we part ways, but for now, I'm very happy to let him be my tour guide. After landing at Queen Alia Airport, Dad marches us through customs as if he's on speed. I'm half asleep, dragging my bags behind me. One of Dad's many travel edicts is never pack your jewelry in your suitcase and always have a change of clothes with you in case they lose your luggage. Dad presents our passports, and I search my bag for my sunglasses. Out of the corner of my eye, I catch a glimpse of Dad removing a red handkerchief, like the one I saw him put away at Dulles Airport. As if he wants the customs officer to notice, he dangles it and then places it back inside his sport coat. And as if it were a magic trick, without opening any of our bags, the customs officers whisk us through, giving Dad a familiar nod. In return, Dad offers a playful salute as he marches away, carrying his bag and briefcase. *Was that some kind of code?* I've never given Dad's frequent trips to Jordan much thought until now. *Why Amman?* From the contents of Dad's annual brochure, Jordan isn't a popular destination like Rome or Jerusalem.

We find our driver smoking a cigarette in the main terminal, holding a sign with our names on it.

"Good morning!" Dad puts his bag down and extends a hand, introducing himself. "Sir John."

"Welcome to Jordan, Sir John. My name is Sahib."

His shirt is mostly unbuttoned, revealing a thick gold chain hanging against his chest, black hair sprouting like pea shoots on his mocha skin. His tight flared pants and leather

sandals seem to be a popular look with the guys in the airport. Sahib takes my luggage—Dad never traveling with more
than a carry-on—and we begin our twenty-minute ride into
Amman.

I take off my beige linen jacket—wrinkled as a lizard—
and catch the driver's brown eyes glancing at me through
the rearview mirror. I'm too jet-lagged to flirt or give him
attitude. Instead, I stick my face out the back window as Dad
snoozes next to me. Strange lands are probably old hat to
him, but my senses are in overdrive. Odd music cries out
from the car radio; a voice whining over a steady jangling, as
if someone's banging pots and pans. The air, dry as a sauna,
smells new, more complicated than Europe. Even through
my Ray-Bans, the sun is blinding white. There's not a tree
in sight, just endless waves of sand. It's swimming weather,
but I purposely didn't ask Dad if our hotel has a pool. Those
kinds of questions make him snap, usually labeling the asker
"selfish" or "entitled."

Arriving at our hotel, I step out of the backseat and immediately hear a girl's voice: "Tina!"

Precious, my secret high school girlfriend before Nic, and
her Jordanian girlfriend, Noor, rush the car. Precious, a statu-
esque beauty, hugs me, squeezing the way one does when they
are still in love with you. A few extra seconds in an embrace
can tell a whole story. Noor gives me a tomboy's backslap.

"How was your trip?" Noor asks, her highly educated Jordanian accent so proper, she could almost pass for British.

"Long, but I just watched movies and listened to my Walk-
man."

"Don't let her fool you. She slept and then slept some more
after quite a few vodka tonics," Dad teases. "Now, who do we
have here?"

He eyes Noor the way he eyes busboys. Maybe he thinks
she's a young man. I wonder if her masculine Arab features
remind him of his long-lost Omar.

"Dad, this is Noor and Precious—you remember, Precious and I went to Immaculata together."

"Of course," he says, distracted, turning back to Noor. "Now, are you Jordanian, my dear?"

"Yes, sir, my family name is Kawar. I attend Georgetown University with Precious."

"Kawar. That's familiar."

"My grandfather opened the first hospital in Jordan."

Braggart.

"Wonderful. If I catch a fever, I'll know who to call! Shall we find the bar, ladies?"

He grabs all the bags, still holding his briefcase, and strides toward the entrance in search of a porter. Dad's energy has rebounded after his catnap. As we follow our leader inside, I do my best to dismiss my nerves and embarrassment over my father's wanting to socialize with my friends.

"We'll just have one drink with him, okay?"

†

Hours later, we sit under the black sky, stars flickering along with my buzz after three rounds of drinks. Dad and Noor have exhausted the topic of Israeli-Palestinian relations. Thankfully, they are on the same side of the conflict. The Arabs' side.

I've seen Dad's political conversations turn ugly and mean if someone supports the "bloody Jews" or "their bloody occupation."

"We should get going," I announce.

Dad slowly licks his lips, eyes rolling toward me in slow motion. He's bombed, as usual.

"Slowly . . . slowly, Christine. There's no rush," he slurs.

"Noor and Precious told some friends we were going to meet them for dinner, so we should go and let you relax."

"Relax?"

I stuff my swollen feet back into my heels, ignoring his edgy tone. His sad droopy face stares at mine. I play light in front of my friends—not wanting things to become any more uncomfortable. Like a highly trained surgeon removing a bullet, it takes great skill to excuse oneself once Dad crosses into the land of incoherence. I've been handling him since I was a small child, taking his mood temperature. When he would pass out in the driveway late at night—engine running, convertible top down, a Gregorian chant blasting—Mom would say, "Someone needs to go wake him. We don't want to disturb the neighbors." And like a fierce brave warrior, I would attach armor over my fear and go gently shake the crusader, without setting off a war. Mom must feel she's part of a threesome: Dad, her, and booze.

"Do you guys want to go get the car while I run up to my room quickly?" I suggest to Precious and Noor.

"'You guys'? I only see one 'guy' at this table."

Precious and Noor gather their things.

"Thank you so much. It was a pleasure meeting you, Mr. Worthington."

Noor extends her hand.

Dad leans in, kissing her on both cheeks, nearly falling over. My stomach twists with shame and anger at him for getting so drunk. For behaving in an oddly seductive way toward Noor. He would sometimes do that with Nic, too. Of course we ignored it. But maybe there's something to it—Noor and Nic both with their dark features, short hair. Who the hell knows, maybe Dad does find them attractive? It's just another thing I don't want to think about.

"Good night, Mr. Worthington," Precious says as they walk away.

In silence, I gather my jacket and feel Dad's drunken stare.

"Dad, you should get some rest, go to your room."

"Go on. Your friends are waiting," he says with deep hurt in his voice. "I didn't realize you had friends in Jordan."

"I told you on the plane. I didn't know they were going to meet me here. But I can't be rude . . ." Defensiveness and guilt pour out of me.

"Not to worry, I know you prefer not to have your old man around. That's fine."

He looks at me like I'm breaking up with him. A frustrated sigh slips out of me, as if the kid I'm babysitting won't eat his applesauce.

"There's someone they want me to meet," I lie, knowing full well I don't want Dad coming with us and making a bigger fool of himself.

" 'You are sixteen, going on seventeen, fellows will fall in line . . .' " he sings, voice cracking, losing notes in his throat.

I soften, too. He reaches for his blazer on the back of the chair, clumsily. After a few tries, he finally gets his hand inside his breast pocket and pulls out his wallet and my blue passport. A second passport slips out along with his mouth spray. I reach under the table to retrieve it. It's different from mine. Darker, maybe black.

"Leave it!" he insists.

He puts his foot on the passport, masking what I'm pretty sure reads JORDAN.

"No need to get dinars, everyone takes the dollar," he explains as he hands me the usual hundred-dollar bill from the thick wad in his wallet. I lean over, and we kiss on the mouth.

"I love you, Dad."

He puts his thumb on my forehead and makes the sign of the cross, blessing me. "*In nomine patris, et filii, et spiritus sancti,* amen."

Dad would have made a great priest. His passion for ritual and prayer—so ingrained in him—is heightened when he's drunk. But so is his gut-wrenching sadness.

"I'm the loneliest man in the world," he stammers, reaching for his wineglass like a blind man. "Someday I must write the book."

†

After a night of dancing at an Amman disco—where the cool Jordanians hang out, supposedly—I roll into the empty hotel lobby at nearly 5 A.M. I stumble toward the front desk, in desperate need of aspirin and food—too wired to sleep. The employee, a twenty-something Arab, smiles, discreetly glancing over my creased sundress.

"May I help you?"

"Can you tell me what room Mr. John Worthington is in . . . please?"

The night's festivities put my head in a fog. I can't remember the rooms my father and I checked into yesterday. Only that mine is across from his and I have no idea where my key went missing. I'm too embarrassed to admit it.

He smiles in recognition.

"Sir John? He is staying with us. Would you like me to call him?"

"I'm his daughter. I just need his room number."

"Very good. I will be happy to call him."

"Can you just tell me the room number?" I snap, more harshly than I'd intended.

The man flinches at my tone, but politely dials. I don't like it when people don't realize I'm important, too. I turn my back to him, leaning up against the front desk, looking around the barren lobby. A few travelers sit on an upholstered bench with their luggage piled in front of them. The cool marble feels good against my back. My stomach gurgles with hunger pains.

"I'm sorry, Sir John's not answering."

I walk off, irritated with him, and head over to the restaurant, hoping for some breakfast. As I settle into a table too big for one, I see Dad rushing out the front door of the hotel, carrying a briefcase, dressed in his usual suit and tie. A blue glow illuminates the parking lot, the sun threatening to rise. I start to go after him, but seeing two Middle Eastern men greet him, I decide to watch instead. They exchange professional handshakes and nods. I can't tell if they've met before, and their faces are mostly blocked by a large pillar. After a few minutes, Dad passes the briefcase to one of the men, who walks away briskly, now out of my sight. Is that Hassan from the University Club parking lot? Dad and the other man continue their conversation. After a few moments, they walk toward a waiting dark car, light rising in the distance. A driver gets out and opens the shiny back door for Dad, who slips into the backseat, while the Middle Eastern man gets into the front passenger seat. The back window opens and Dad's arm appears, resting on the door, as the expensive car rolls away.

My stomach begs for some food to absorb my all-nighter. I can't help but wonder how on earth Dad is able to appear so pulled together, after I left him hours ago slurring his words, still drinking. How does he function? As a family, we've done our best to cover for him in public, Mom making excuses, my older siblings having concerned and loving one-on-one conversations with him about his drinking—only for him to blow up, storm out, and give them the silent treatment for weeks. But what about the Vatican? What about Archbishop Magni? Does Dad control his drinking around him? As far as I can tell he's never had a stopping point, drinking until he's nearly passed out, eyes rolling back as if he's possessed. I'm worried that one day he might wake up from a drunken slumber facedown in St. Peter's Square.

†

Out my twenty-first-floor hotel windows, the Nile is as lightless as onyx. After a few days in Cairo, if I had to describe the mood in two words, I'd say sexy and black—the eyes of my private driver and the luxury sedan he picks me up in, the lobby of my hotel, the bellman's uniform, and this placid river below me. Very sexy. Very black.

The rush in my throat has been charging nearly non-stop since the Middle Eastern pilot advised us to fasten our seat belts for landing in Cairo. The adventure of being in such an exotic place—having my own room in this five-star American-style hotel all alone—feels tantalizing and mysterious. I love it. I want more. Dad warned me that the summer temperatures in Cairo are a good fifteen degrees hotter than home, but desert air doesn't drain me the way Chevy Chase humidity does.

Slipping on my best black dress and open-toe high heels, I ride the glass elevator to the top floor of the hotel, which opens onto a glitzy circular bar buzzing with mostly men with dark-caramel skin, sipping cocktails, engaged in passionate conversation, hands active in the air. I slide onto a tall leather chair at the bar. If not for the harsh clip of Arabic and the piped-in music—a mix of clanging and humming—I could be among the University Club set. A man of about sixty, sitting one seat over, smiles, lifting his drink to me. I smile back and order a vodka tonic. The view behind the bar is breathtaking, overlooking all of Cairo—the Nile River stretching as far as the eye can see.

"Put on mine, please," the older man tells the bartender, pointing to my glass.

"Thank you, sir," I say.

"I'm Ahmed," he announces.

"Tina. Nice to meet you." I offer my hand.

His kind eyes and soft speech put me at ease. The bartender, Rashid, joins our conversation. I'm eager for everything they can tell me about Egypt and the Middle East. I learn Ahmed is from Oman, here frequently on business, and the playful Rashid is studying law, bartending to pay for school. Rashid's dreams are all about going to America, while

I'm hungry to know what I should expect on my Nile cruise. I'm thrilled for tomorrow, when I'll fly to Aswan to board the small ship that will sail me down the river to Luxor.

I tell them about my day of sightseeing with the driver and my own tour guide—a smart Egyptian woman, Fatima. While I scaled the steep ladder inside the Great Pyramid of Giza; rode a camel; happily exchanged my dollars for Egyptian pounds near the Sphinx, where Dad told me I would get the best rate—"They are hungry for dollars in Egypt"—Fatima waited patiently, beautiful silk scarf covering her head.

Ahmed announces he must retire for the night, but I stay until closing with Rashid, who offers to take me to a nightclub nearby. We dance for a while to mostly old disco music, then lose each other in the crowd, stumbling back together later in the night. Drunk and sweaty from nonstop dancing, I am happy he takes me back to the hotel with no expectations, no detours. It's nearly 4 A.M., and the only thing I feel like lying on is my Egyptian cotton sheets.

As I pass by the front desk, doing my best to keep to the semblance of a straight line, the hotel worker calls from behind the front desk, "Miss Worthington?"

I immediately feel guilty—the muscle memory of bad behavior and secrets. *What did I do now?*

"Yes?" I ask, avoiding his eyes.

"There was a man here to see you, a friend of your father's," he announces.

I immediately run through Dad's list of who I was scheduled to meet and when. I know I'm going to be seeing one of the brothers who runs Happy Tours here in Cairo—Dad's Middle East agent. But that's after I return from the Nile cruise. Another brother from Happy's runs the ship, and I'll be meeting him tomorrow when I arrive in Aswan. But who could have come here to the hotel?

"A friend of my father's?"

"Yes, he waited for a while in the lobby."

"I think it was a mistake," I assure him.

"No, he came to take you to the airport," he explains.

The clock behind the desk reads 4:10 A.M., and I know there's been a mistake.

"My driver said they'd be picking me up this afternoon, but thank you," I mumble sleepily, and drag myself up to my room.

Too tired for makeup removal, I strip off my dress and climb under the clean-smelling sheets. Lying in bed, I consider the odd airport pickup. Baffled, I recall my driver's exact words when he dropped me off after our sightseeing today.

"I'll be picking you up at three thirty tomorrow for your flight to Aswan. Get some sleep," he said.

No way he could have meant A.M. I lie in bed, praying to go to sleep and forget how strange all of this seems. I cling to the impossibility of a middle-of-the-night pickup with all my might, till finally the looming slim chance that I'm wrong, and Dad's wrath if I miss the Nile cruise, scares me into picking up the phone.

"Front desk."

"Hi, this is Tina Worthington in 2120."

"Yes, Miss Worthington."

"The man who came to pick me up—could it be possible he would get me that early for a flight to Aswan today?" I ask incredulously.

"Certainly, ma'am. Our airport is very busy and one must arrive many hours before the flight in order to get a seat," he explains.

"So, that's normal? Three thirty in the morning? You think that guy was definitely for me?"

"I'm quite sure, ma'am." He sounds confident.

I hang up. Bone tired, I stay in bed, cataloging possible

lame-ass excuses I can give Dad for missing the cruise—the whole reason I wanted to come to Egypt. I'm fucking dead in the water. Then, all at once, I'm called to action, kicking off the covers and bouncing out of bed, grabbing the phone.

"Front desk."

"Hi, it's me again. Do you think I can still make the flight if I leave soon?"

"The flight to Aswan leaves at eight, so I'm not sure."

Like all those times with women, and men, and basketball, when I refused to take no for an answer, I keep pushing.

"Can you send someone up to my room right now to help me pack, and get me a car to the airport?" I beg.

"Yes, yes, I will send someone right up," he assures me.

At the Cairo airport, I run through bland, chaotic terminals, cluttered with a pileup of luggage carts, toward what I'm told is the flight to Aswan. As I push through a large group of people, I hear my name, "Tina!" in the now familiar Middle Eastern accent.

I turn to see a tall, handsome Arab man—maybe thirty or so—smiling and walking toward me. He's completely unfamiliar.

"Yes?"

"You were at Allah's disco last night, right?" His grin has me suddenly worried. *Did I black out?*

"Oh, hi . . . sorry, I need to catch a flight to Aswan," I cover.

"You're the American who's going to Aswan?"

"How do you know?"

He laughs.

"I work with Happy Tours. I came to your hotel this morning, early, but you weren't there. Now I know why!" He laughs again.

"I thought when my driver said three thirty pickup, he meant this afternoon."

"We were able to get you on the flight to Abu Simbel—impossible this time of year. You will go there first, and then you will go to our boat afterward. That's why so early," he explains, handing me a ticket.

This is like a creepy scene from a movie where I'll be thrown on a private plane and stabbed with a syringe, an American kidnapped and held hostage while suffering from amnesia. I take a deep breath, trying to clear my head. Dad's arm is long, organizing everything for me—the fancy hotel, the personal service, and now some side trip to a place I can barely pronounce.

"What's Abu Simbel?"

The disco agent's raised eyebrows remind me of Dad when I ask what he deems a stupid question. "Bloody Americans know nothing about the world outside of their own backyards!" Dad regularly complains.

"Something you will never forget," he assures me.

Even on the other side of the world, Dad provides the unforgettable. I hope someday, like my father, I will be capable of making anything happen.

†

The hefty driver stares at my naked legs as I board the bus with mostly middle-aged, English-speaking tourists in floppy sun hats. I barely slept on the small plane—which had maybe twenty seats—and I'm deeply hungover. Although it seems everyone from D.C. to Cairo went the extra mile to get me this exclusive once-in-a-lifetime sightseeing opportunity, all I want is a bed, a pillow, and some blackout curtains.

The bus parks among a long line of other vehicles, and the group files into the blistering heat. Wobbly legged, I follow the crowd, curious, but also eager to lie down. Summoning the power of mind over matter, I make the long walk silently through the desert surrounded by chatty, excited tourists with cameras poised. All of a sudden, we turn a corner and it appears. Shockingly magnificent, at nearly 100 feet tall and

115 feet wide, the Great Temple was carved out of a massive rock during Ramses II's reign. It stands alone in the middle of the desert, and it takes my breath away.

After taking the tour of the main temple and meandering through parts of the smaller temple—dedicated to Ramses's favorite wife, Nefertari—I bow out, losing steam despite the gorgeous scenery. Dying to sit down away from the scorching sun, I am greeted on the bus by our driver, who sits wide legged with the windows down. I smile politely and head to the back.

"Did you like?" he calls.

I nod.

After a few minutes he asks, "Coca-Cola?" gesturing as if he's drinking a bottle.

"No, that's okay," I deflect, and go back to resting my head on the hot window while he speaks to some men out his window in Arabic.

A moment later, he appears in the back of the bus holding a bottle of icy Coke.

"For you." He smiles, sitting across from me.

I slide over to the aisle seat and take it, grateful—it's probably exactly what I need. Gulping it down, I feel his eyes on my bare legs again. He probably doesn't get a lot of blondes in short shorts in the middle of the Nubian Desert. Then, with the entitlement of a man with diplomatic immunity, he reaches his hand between my legs. I let him touch me for a second, then move his hand away. The driver gets my message and walks back to his seat. I feel surprisingly strong, allowing and disallowing. My decision. Not his. I close my eyes, desperate for a long rest, hungry for my cabin on the river, where I will be my own beautiful companion.

†

I step into the suite of the ship's executive director, Phanes—a pint-size Egyptian whose family owns this Nile cruiser. The lights are dim; the leopard couches are shaped like half moons; beads hang in doorways; church candles burn. If they weren't Dad's friends, who had invited me to their private quarters for dinner, I might worry from the look of things that Phanes and Tat were hosting a Middle Eastern séance. Dad explained that Phanes, the black sheep of the family that owns Happy Tours, and Tat, the ship's hairdresser—whose hair actually looks like a black sheep's—are lovers. Despite my exhaustion and need for an immediate nap upon boarding—skipping the first excursion, to the Aswan Dam—the guys insisted I join them tonight for dinner.

I settle into my vodka tonic as Phanes and Tat sit across from me, legs crossed, with the ease of people who are used to having whatever they want, whenever they want it. There's no rush for anything. No pushing, no hunger. Their servant sits outside the door, awaiting their needs. Life is elegantly simple: an olive offering here; the private servant silently refreshing cocktails; spotless cream shag carpet; an exact crease in their expensive linen trousers; Tat's shiny tasseled loafers, perfectly coiffed hair, and smooth, well-cared-for skin.

Their neatness, beauty, and entitlement are seductive, turning me on like nothing else I can think of. The other-worldliness of it all sparks my hunger to see every corner of the world. *Is this how Dad feels when he travels? No wonder he doesn't want to be home.*

"How did you meet my dad?" I ask, leaning back into the luxurious fabric, matching their relaxed pose.

"My family. You know, Happy's works with Sir John. And we have had many evenings together in Cairo," Phanes explains, lighting up a black cigarette.

"Never on the ship?" I pry.

"We have invited him many, many times, but always Sir John must keep traveling," Phanes explains.

"He only works." Tat laughs.

"Well, he doesn't ALWAYS work, right?" I smile, testing them.

They smirk like teenage boys with a secret.

"Did you ever go out dancing with him?" I dare boldly.

They look at each other knowingly, for the first time at a slight loss as to who wants to speak. Then Tat confesses, "Sir John likes to dance."

"I know, we go out to clubs together," I share, playfully imitating Dad's drunken moves.

Phanes and Tat crack up as I sip my vodka, enjoying the safety of being around people who understand, who accept the way things are, and who are like me.

"Your father told us." Tat winks.

Their familiarity and acceptance of Dad is comforting. I like that they appreciate him. And me.

"Does your family know about you two?" I ask Phanes.

Tat rolls his eyes and looks to Phanes, his hands passing the question to his lover like a silver platter.

"Egypt is a traditional country, my family, too, and we don't speak of it."

Tat can't resist adding, "It's for the reason, they give him the job on the ship."

Phanes picks up his drink silently, the hurt rising in his eyes, his family's shame about his being gay impossible to mask. Tat rests his hand on his lover's knee, giving it a gentle shake, a reminder that he is loved, no matter that his family put him out to sea.

12
Defrocked

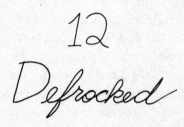

Driving alone to Shescape, I'm smart enough to know putting the convertible top down is not an option. My white ass would be asking for trouble. Washington, the Murder Capital, is notorious for having one of the highest per capita murder rates in the country. So, with windows up and doors locked, I blast Chaka Khan and make my way to the lesbian dance club on the wrong side of the tracks—two short blocks from the Lost and Found. I create my own parking spot along the side of the warehouselike building—a shorter walk for me and my Candies.

"How do you walk in those, Tina?" my mom asked as I stood in the dining room an hour earlier, wanting to rush out but feeling guilty. Another Saturday night alone with her crossword puzzle and a box of Ritz crackers, while her husband is off doing God's work with a bishop and a bottle of Sambuca.

"Tina, help me. The clue is 'Not allowed by the Party.' Seven letters. Begins with D and ends in E." She sounded desperate for an answer.

It was so obvious.

"Divorce, Mom," I told her.

Before stepping out of the car, I slip off my skirt. The matching lightweight houndstooth blazer is long enough to cover my ass. Barely. I had, unsuccessfully, begged the salesgirl at Commander Salamander to sell me just the jacket, because I knew immediately that I'd be wearing this padded-shouldered jacket not as part of a suit but as a dress. Or as Precious calls it, "a very wide belt." She's the one who got me into clothes.

Before she became my sophomore-year girlfriend in high school, my fashion sense was a set of colored watchbands that I changed to match the ribbon in my hair. But stylish Precious handed me a pair of designer jeans and platform shoes with a cork heel, and I've never looked at anything monogrammed again. I did wear the matching skirt to get out of the house respectfully, in front of Mom. But my intentionally ripped black hose brought on the Inquisition:

"Do people really dress like that?"

"My baby's going out looking like Raggedy Ann?"

"What happened to all the sweater sets I bought you?"

As I lock up Dad's Buick, I promise myself: out of here by 1 A.M. and no tequila shots because I have to work out tomorrow. Two women step out of a shiny red Mazda RX and join hands. They could be brother and sister. Dark, tall, lean. One beautiful femme, one handsome butch. I reach the entrance first and wait for them, holding the door.

They smile at me.

"That's sweet," the femme says. Her fingerless gloves, strapless cutup dress, short black boots, and deep cleavage could have been ripped from the pages of *Vogue*. I smirk and follow her flawless bare back into the club. Waiting in line behind them to pay the cover charge, I smell the cologne coming off the butch—Grey Flannel. As the couple steps toward the small window, I step in front of them.

"I've got it," I say, sliding a one-hundred-dollar bill to the little redhead working the door.

"That's all right," the butch says.

"No, no, I insist."

I can feel the femme staring at me. Receiving a bunch of drink tickets with my change, I hand them over while looking into her brown eyes. *Gotcha.* I feel a tingle up my back, adrenaline shooting through me, like I'm ready to take the court.

Shescape is actually big enough to play a full-court game of hoops. At its center is a large round dance floor with a four-foot wall around it—a roller rink waiting for the derby to begin. Gals lean against the wall smoking and drinking, waiting for someone to make their head spin. I love watching the locals who drop in from the neighborhood. No one would fuck with these tough chicks—some with linebacker-size thighs, shaved heads, and round asses raised up toward the disco lights. They move with the ease of maple syrup, pouring themselves into each other. One grinds on the dance floor, one hand on her drink, the other on her woman's ass. Her girlfriend has her hands up in the air like she's waiting to get frisked or praise Jesus. Shescape may be 80 percent white girls, but it's the girls from Southeast who get the party started.

Nic and I came down here last New Year's Eve. As soon as we hit the dance floor, she became aggressive, in a way I'd never seen her. She shoved her hand down my pants, reenacting a scene from my graduation night.

I had let two Latin men sandwich me on the dance floor at the bi club in Georgetown, and my hands found their way around. She must have seen the whole thing while sipping her White Russian.

I head to the bar for a drink, catching an older platinum blonde in a sexy vintage dress checking me out. She leans arched against the wall, sipping out of a thin glass. I stare back, stone faced, trying to act cool.

At the large three-sided bar, an androgynous woman wearing a FREE NELSON MANDELA tank top and a red bandanna on her head is zipping around like a machine.

"Absolut sea breeze with lime, please."

Rosie the Riveter is off and running. I survey the club—mostly couples.

"Here ya go, baby." The bartender sets a tall glass in front of me with a straw. I hand her a twenty and lose the straw.

"Keep it," I say, then down half my drink.

I check on Platinum, who's posed up against the wall now, talking with two women, a six-foot big-boned gal with cropped brown hair and a pretty sun-kissed chick with dirty blond hair in a ponytail. Platinum catches me looking at them and smiles; her friends turn around and look. Polishing off the rest of my sea breeze, I take the dance floor. Madonna's "Borderline" bounces out of the speakers, and the brother and sister beat me to the dance floor. The butch catches me out of the corner of her eye and glides her girl away across the wood floor. Smooth move. I dance alone, getting lost in my own universe; happy the sea breeze has kicked me into gear. Happy to be moving my muscles. I close my eyes, dropping into the free zone. Anything goes.

"Ya mind if we dance with yew?" Platinum says in a heavy southern accent. She sways next to me, moving her asymmetrical bangs out of her eyes; her two friends dance together. If I had to guess, I'd say she's thirty-two, straight, mad about Bowie, cool enough to have gay friends, and drunk enough to check out a lesbian club while she's in town from who the fuck knows where down south.

"I'm Violet," she slurs.

I lean into her, not feeling like shouting. "Tina."

She dances close.

"Well, Miss Tina, I've been wantin' to tell you since you walked in how much I love your dress." She looks me up and down. "You're flawless."

"Let's get a drink," I say, gently resting my fingers close enough to her cleavage to invoke a shriek. I walk off the dance floor. She follows me to the bar.

"What would you like?" I ask.

"A Bloody Mary. You want to go do a line?" She's wobbly on her feet.

"Maybe," I say, flagging the bartender.

"A Bloody Mary and an Absolut sea breeze . . . and two shots of tequila."

I turn back to her.

"So, Miss Thing, what do you do . . . besides wearin' a blazer as a dress?" Her tone is charming and seductive.

"I work. I go to school on a basketball scholarship. And I am trying out for the Olympics," I tell her, crossing one ripped leg over the other, leaning against the bar.

Her laugh is a scream, like she finds me outrageous.

"The Olympics! . . . Okaaaaay." She says it like she thinks it's about as likely as me asking the DJ to play the hokey pokey.

"What, you don't believe me?"

I stare at her boldly, looking at her chest. She smiles and shakes her head, sucking on her Bloody Mary.

"Well, I don't believe that's not a padded bra." My eyes stay affixed.

She laughs again, then clears her throat and falls into me. "Well, Miss Thing, maybe we should find a basketball court and you can shoot for me."

"Maybe we should go to the bathroom, and you can shoot for me."

I hand her a shot, taking the other, and we clink our glasses. We down the tequila, quickly stuffing lime slices in our mouths. She settles, quiet for a moment, looking at me.

"Let's go," I whisper.

She grins and sips on her drink.

"Bring it with you," I say, walking away.

Not looking back, I move through a small room behind the

bar with a sleek pool table and head toward the neon sign, RESTROOM, passing by a few tough-looking girls. In the small dark hallway is a shiny pay phone and two black doors to the bathrooms.

"Here ya go, Miss Thang, no padding, just Kentucky originals." Her voice is low, just behind me. Alone in the hallway, I turn to her. She stands with her pink nails pulling back her deep-V-neck Doris Day dress and revealing most of her breasts.

She moves toward me, not releasing her dress. Totally exposed. I throw one arm behind her back, press the other hand on her breast, and begin to tongue her deeply. She's noisy with pleasure as I slowly dance her past the pay phone and into the darkest corner. Comments spring from women leaving the bathrooms.

"There's a Holiday Inn down the street."

"Fuck the hotel, I'll watch."

Our hands are everywhere. I catch her in a flash of light— fuchsia lipstick covers her face and chest—everywhere my mouth has been.

"Violet? Violet?" a soft southern voice calls.

Violet pulls her dress over her exposed breasts and wipes her mouth with her thumb and index finger.

"Nice, Violet." Her dirty-blond friend stands looking at us, tosses her hands in the air, shakes her head with disgust, and walks away.

"Who's that?"

"Sandy . . . my girlfriend," she says quietly. "But we really aren't together."

I walk over to the pay phone, cleaning lipstick off my face, and rip out a sheet from the yellow pages hanging by a chain. A broken pencil lies on the silver base. I pull out my black eyeliner pencil from my pocket and write my phone number while Violet puts her image back together.

"Call me when you're single," I say, handing her my number.

13
Lust

There was a time I slept on a cot, they tell me, in the bedroom that is now all mine. Three of us sisters shared the back room on the third floor—the girls' floor—where, according to my parents, no boys were allowed. But in the quiet of the night, rules and hearts got broken. Since mine has always been the hottest bedroom—the farthest away from the air-conditioning unit in the third-floor stairway—I now heat up my curling iron in Kate's old bedroom, with her peeling découpage door; roll out my makeup on the worn Formica bathroom counter; and try on outfits in Helen's former room, with a full-length mirror on the back of the door. With seven sisters now gone, I can spread out my beauty rituals over three bedrooms. Thankfully, the bathroom—once busier than a girls' dormitory—is finally all mine.

Tonight, I settle on an off-the-shoulder black minidress, white fingerless gloves, and ankle boots, and I'm definitely wearing ripped hose again. I wrap three bangles on my left arm and finish with a big swipe of soft pink lipstick and extra black mascara. My heart starts racing as I head downstairs, wondering what lie to offer my mother this time. I certainly can't say, "Mom, I'm having dinner at the Foundry with an older woman I tongued last week at a lesbian bar."

As I head for the kitchen, I hear Simon's voice, and the usual tightening of my stomach begins.

"Hi," I say, bracing myself for a critique.

"Whoa, looks like Kate got into your closet, cut up your gloves and your stockings." Simon offers his typical sarcasm.

"For your information, smart-ass, I did cut the buttons off Frances's coat, but only after she tore the zipper off my prom dress," Kate barks at Simon.

"Tina, aren't you glad it's just you and me now?" My mother pats my shoulder, sensing my irritation.

"So where are *you* going?" Kate drills.

"To find a needle and thread, I hope." Simon laughs.

"Out."

"Oh, 'out.' Out where, chump?" he challenges me.

It gives me great pleasure to ignore him, since I can't do what I really want to do to him.

"Mom, I'll be home later. I'm going to a party at Nic's house."

"I haven't heard that name in a while," Mom fishes.

"She's been away with her boyfriend . . . and Dad said I could use his car."

"Of course he did, kiss-ass," Simon says.

"Night, Mom." I peck her cheek, ignoring the others.

"You shouldn't be going out, you should be in the gym working out." Simon shakes his head at me.

"Maybe you should be at your own house with your wife on Saturday night," I throw back.

Simon furrows his brow. He's not used to me throwing a jab. He stumbles, grasping for a comeback, while Kate laughs. I hightail it out of the kitchen, slapping the door jamb on my way out, imagining it's his stubbly face.

"And you better not drink and drive!" Simon shouts at me.

Fuck him.

Parking anywhere in Georgetown is a pain in the ass. After four loops around the cobblestone streets near the restaurant, I settle on a parking lot across from the Foundry.

When Violet called me on Sunday, I knew our Shescape encounter wasn't just a drunken one-night feel-up fest for her. I'm still not sure what it was for me. But I told her, "I'd love to have dinner with you," in my most mature voice. Walking from the car, I take a few deep breaths to calm my nerves. God, I need a drink.

The Foundry gives you the feeling that someone might still be making muskets in the next room, in order to drive out the Royal Navy. My father would hate this place. He gets agitated when discussing the fall of the redcoats to the colonists. "You bloody Americans don't know how to win graciously," he'd say.

"Hey, Miss Thing, look at you." Violet greets me by the hostess station with a gentle kiss on my cheek. Her low-buttoned lightweight blazer is all that's between me and her purposefully exposed bra. Her floral perfume smells so much better than Nic's. Violet takes my hand. "Come on, I reserved one of the booths with the curtain."

I smile at a few men in suits at the bar checking us out, proud to have this beautiful woman leading my way and happy to be ogled, too. As I watch her full hips sway in front of me, her pencil skirt snug as a well-made bed, I'm certain no one here would ever suspect she likes women. We step down into a small room with about ten booths, each covered by a floor-to-ceiling burgundy curtain, offering a completely private dining experience.

"Isn't this fine?" Violet coos, as a waitress steps forward to pull back the curtain for us. The tabletop—a thick wooden slab—is set with heavy silverware, white cloth napkins, and a small glass vase with red roses and baby's breath.

"May I get you ladies a drink?" our perky waitress asks. She's probably a student from Georgetown, with her good skin and tortoiseshell headband.

"Do you have Pouilly-Fuissé?" Violet asks.

"No, bring us a bottle of Dom Pérignon, please."

Violet lets out her high-pitched scream. The waitress laughs, says, "Okay," then closes the curtain.

"Well, excuse me, Miss Thing!"

"I got this tonight." I nod at the menu with confidence, knowing we can order anything on the menu and I'll still have money left over for the club.

We look at each other, smiling. Violet is so alive, no longer dulled by Bloody Marys. Her hazel eyes dance, and her face is far more beautiful—freshly made up like a doll's, with red narrow lips—than I remember. I wipe my sweaty palms on the banquette.

The waitress calls from the other side of the curtain, "Knock, knock."

"Who's there?" I joke, and everyone laughs.

Our champagne is presented and poured into red crystal champagne flutes. "Thank you." I nod.

"*Merci beaucoup,*" Violet adds.

"Ladies, we have some awesome specials tonight . . ."

"What's your name?" I interrupt.

"Sarah."

"Sarah, we are going to take things slowly."

"Oh, sure, take your time. There's a bell right here." She points to the corner of the booth next to Violet where a knotted rope hangs. "When you are ready, just pull and I'll be right over."

Sarah moves the silver champagne stand closer to our table and yanks the drape closed.

"Let's not save any libations for the gods tonight," I announce, holding my glass in the air.

"Where did you come from?"

"Well, I was born down the street at George Washington Hospital. I was supposed to be born at Georgetown, a Catholic hospital. But my mother's OB/GYN was vacationing in Bermuda," I say with a straight face.

"Where did you come from?" I ask, downing my champagne.

"I was born and raised in Louisville, Kentucky, and came to D.C. to work for my congressman."

"Wow, you work on Capitol Hill?"

"Yes, ma'am."

"I was there on a field trip once in seventh grade—with my lover, Miss Lange."

Violet nearly chokes on her champagne, then finally coughs out, "WHAT? You had a 'lover' named Miss Lange in seventh grade?"

I nod. "Yeah, well, Jane—Miss Lange—she was my homeroom teacher. We were together for three years . . . secretly."

"Oh my God, that's child abuse."

"No, no, it wasn't, you don't understand. I was really mature for my age," I brag.

"What am I gonna do with you?" she says, pressing her body forward, her breasts resting on the tabletop.

Nervous, I take control, feigning the confidence of a quarterback. I call for her hand, kissing it, and then put her index finger in my mouth, the way I would a grape Popsicle. She makes a tiny groan and wraps her bare foot around my calf. The foreplay calms me.

"What do you want to do with me?" I say playfully. I grab as much as my hand will hold inside her bra. And we are on. Our starving faces come together, creating a hot centerpiece; tongues pushing, hands squeezing. Utensils clink together noisily beneath us. In the midst of our making out, we move our flutes out of the way.

"You ladies okay?" Sarah calls.

"Fine," I say, jerking myself back against the banquette.

"All right, just let me know." She sounds mistrustful of us behind the curtain, or maybe it's my Catholic guilt. I reach for the bottle and give Violet's glass a long slow pour, then move it to her red-stained lips. As her lips part, I gently pour the bubbly in her mouth; then I finish off the rest.

"Come here," Violet whispers, moving her face toward mine over the table.

"No, lean back." I reach my hand under the table, open her crossed legs, and gently slide my body down the booth, under the table. The space is barely big enough for me to fit sitting back on my knees. Two Ferragamo heels welcome me, like ladies in waiting.

"Oh, darling!" Violet releases a little scream, equal parts desire and fear, as I push up her skirt. My wide hands slide down her hips, taking her panties past her thighs and finally removing the twisted fabric from around her feet. As I throw my face between her legs, smothering myself in her wetness, she wraps her legs over my shoulders. Her warm hands dig through my soft curls and finally settle down, holding my head exactly where she wants it. Her short breaths quicken as my tongue moves religiously over her. My heartbeat pumps against my chest; my face is on fire, listening to her getting closer. Purposely, I slow down, pull back, teasing her desperate body. She thrusts her hips forward, pushing her swollen flesh into my face. But it's not enough; I want her chest, too. Reaching up under her jacket, I find her nipple pushing out from her bra. She moans loudly, and I quickly cover her slack mouth—a gentle reminder that we are behind the red curtain.

Violet reaches back, unhooking her bra. I slide my face away from between her legs and push the base of the table back a few inches, making space for me to squeeze up against her, like a boa constrictor slithering from underneath the table, mouth landing all over her freed breasts. I'm reborn here, wide mouthed and ravenous for all of it to fit in my mouth. As I suck her nipple, my hand slides down, feeling the wet leather seat. The smell of floral perfume is everywhere as I enter her easily with my fingers. Violet groans. Her nails dig into my back inside my dress. I pump my forearm—pushing deeper into her.

"Ladies, how's the bubbly?" Sarah shouts from outside the curtain.

Stopping my body on a dime, my heart refuses, speeding ahead with adrenaline.

"Darlin', we are just fine. Not ready for you . . . THANK YOU!"

Violet's cover is smooth.

"Okay, just pull the rope." Our waitress sounds disappointed in us.

Slowly, I begin to move again, licking my way off her breast, down her silky torso, landing my breathy kisses just below her belly button. My hands reach between her legs, opening her lips but not touching. Her body shudders.

"Oh my God." She takes my head, forcing it between her legs. Happily buried again, I hear her breath speed up; her throat sounds like a motor revving; her hips rock rhythmically. Knowing she's ready, I mask her mouth with my palm. Violet's moan explodes into my hand, her wetness into my mouth as she climaxes—her warm body electrocuting against me; her glowing doll face making a final surrender backward against the soft leather banquette.

14

Coronation

"FUCK!" I shout, discovering that the digital bedside clock reads 10 A.M.

My alcohol-soaked brain struggles to solve a normally easy calculation. If it's 10 A.M., what speed do I have to drive in order to get to Dulles Airport for a 10:30 A.M. arrival from Rome?

I'm missing an important part of the equation: *Where am I?*

My father's voice reverberates in my head: "I'll be arriving early Sunday, so let's plan on heading straight to brunch, and then onto tea dance at the Lost and Found."

I dry-heave at the thought of a drink. My temples throb. Lying on my numb shoulder, Violet doesn't budge. Her nakedness is spread out on the queen-size bed like a *Playboy* photo shoot, a cream satin sheet covering just below her knees. I assume this is her four-poster bed, but how did we get here? I'm too embarrassed to wake her up and ask. I roll away from her dead weight—135 pounds, I'd guess, of voluptuousness.

Standing brings on another rush of nausea and chills, so I sit naked on the edge of the bed, trying to find a clue amid the expensive antique furniture. The hardwood floor looks like a natural disaster, with tossed lingerie, high heels, a tequila bottle, and one fingerless glove. The rest of our clothes form a trail from the doorway. This is no time to be hungover, or horny, or late.

Sir John is waiting.

The silk curtains aren't doing much to keep out the bright morning sun as I scan the residential street below for my father's red convertible. A Cadillac, Mercedes, and other expensive cars are parked outside the crisp Washingtonian townhomes on this unrecognizable street. *Where did she tell me that she lived?* I vaguely recall leaning up against the wall at a bar, watching a drag queen sing. The rest is a blur. One story below, there's no sign of my father's car. I slip on my underpants, feeling tight and sore between my legs, as if the sex went on all night.

I check the clock again, feeling lost and massively confused, the way I did in Sister Mary Claire's chemistry class. Too many mysterious elements; a missing nucleus. *Fuck, what am I going to do? What would Jesus do? Or Ted Kennedy?* I finish dressing and rush into an upstairs hallway. A flight of wooden steps with an antique runner down the middle looks vaguely familiar. Down the floral-wallpapered hall is a narrow table with a red lacquer Princess phone. I walk quietly toward it. On the hallway table, calla lilies fill a cylindrical glass vase. I pray no one else lives here. Across the way is a powder blue bathroom with a claw-foot tub and a large sink with spotless silver hardware. I grab the phone and dial.

"May I have the number for Alitalia airlines?" My voice—huskier than normal—startles me. A vision of sharing a pack of cigarettes with Violet on a couch must be real, and would account for my Lauren Bacall register today. I jot down the number and dial. The warm Italian accent on the other end is soothing to my battered everything. I pray for a miracle with a silent improvisational medley of the Lord's Prayer, a Hail Mary, and an appeal to Saint Christopher, the patron saint of travelers, probably surprising him by begging him to delay a flight rather than ensure its timely arrival. As the agent looks up the flight information, I scope the hallway, wondering if Sandy, the sort of ex-girlfriend, lives here. A lot of lesbians think breaking up means moving into the other bedroom. Women, more than men, it seems, can't say good-bye.

After a few minutes, I learn that Sir John's Roman flight is going to be twenty minutes late. Rushing back into the bedroom, I find that Violet is still comatose. I have no choice but to wake her.

"Violet? Violet? Where am I?"

She releases a soft groan.

"My bed," her voice cracks.

"Where's my car?"

Her eyes open wide.

"It's not in the alleyway?"

"What alleyway?"

A small, sleepy chuckle falls out of her soft lips.

"Out the kitchen door, in the back." She smiles at my relief.

I lean in and kiss her with a closed mouth, realizing I haven't brushed my teeth.

"I gotta go."

"Noooooooooo, you can't."

She playfully pulls me into her.

"I'll be dead if I don't get to Dulles right now . . . what's the best way from here?" I say, not telling her I still don't know where "here" is.

"The end of the street, turn onto GW Parkway, to 495, then follow the signs."

I walk coolly out of her room in last night's clothes, then dash like mad into the bathroom and quietly open the medicine cabinet. I squeeze some toothpaste onto my index finger and scrub my drunken, sex-filled night out of my mouth. Hustling down the stairs, I spot my purse lying on a beautiful navy blue couch in the living room. A full marble ashtray and an empty pack of Dunhills sit on the coffee table. There's one sure way to never get playing time: smoke.

All these distractions make me want to cry and scream. I grab my purse and rush out the kitchen door. The sauna-like air drains what little energy I have. Unlocking the car door, I make a swear-to-God promise to work out twice as hard tomorrow and every day this week, no matter what. And definitely no more drinking. I turn the ignition, hear a hiccup, and then nothing. Pumping the accelerator, I turn it over a few more times.

"COME ON! COME ON!"

Scanning the dash, my eyes land on the gas gauge: empty.

"FUCK, NO WAY!"

I pump again, keeping my eyes on the needle. It won't rise.

"Fuck you, Saint Christopher."

I wish I could just punt. Give the ball over to the other team. But the head honcho is waiting. I jump out of the car and run back inside, sprinting the stairs two at a time.

"I knew yew'd be back, Miss Thing." She smiles from the bed.

"My car's out of gas."

"Oh, darlin', take mine. The keys are probably in the kitchen."

"Okay, thanks."

I dash out of the bedroom.

"You can drive a stick shift, right?" she shouts.

My heart sinks. I head back into the room, feeling like a total loser. Nic tried to teach me to drive a standard a few times, but I hate not being good at stuff in front of other people, so I gave up.

"No," I sigh.

"Come on, I'll drive you." She jumps out of bed and finds her bra.

"No, I have to pick him up alone!"

Her face drops into a sad clown expression. "Well, how ya gonna do that, Miss Thing?"

She stares at me as she slips on her bra and panties. There's no time for me to be distracted by her body, but I am.

"All right, yeah, sure, that would be great, if you drive. I'm just going to make a quick call, all right?"

She nods, and I hustle into the hallway to call the person I need most right now. I dial. Her hello is pleasant but holds that familiar shadow of sadness.

"Hi, Mom!"

"Tina, I was worried sick! Where are you?" she asks, a hint of anger coating her words.

"I am so sorry, I . . . fell asleep at Nic's house . . . I stayed to help her clean up after the party . . . and then just fell asleep. Sorry . . . anyhow, I have to pick up Dad. I might be a few minutes late."

"Where are you now?" Mom says, sounding upset.

"I'm . . . in Wheaton, but I ran out of gas . . ."

"How are you going to pick up your father?" Her voice is filled with mistrust.

"Well, one of Nic's friends . . . my friend, too . . . Violet . . . she offered to drive me to get him. So . . ."

My mother is silent. Worse than any other thing she can be. Mom doesn't raise her voice, but her disappointment is deafening. Inside her withdrawal lives the intolerable pain of having her child lie to her. I can feel it the same way I did when she caught me smoking in fifth grade, sitting on the hill at Chevy Chase Playground with Boo Hayes, fellow troublemaker. Mom saw us puffing away, but when I got into the backseat of her car, she still asked, "Were you smoking?" And I lied, "No." It's a pattern now, a constant game of hide and seek with the truth. I feel guilty, but it doesn't stop me.

"And I think Dad might want to have brunch or something.

I'm not sure, but he said something before he left . . . but I'm not sure . . ."

Her silence continues. Violet enters the hallway, dressed in a slinky pink halter sundress, trying to fasten her necklace as she rushes into the bathroom.

"But . . . hopefully, he won't want to," I mutter.

"I'm sure it won't kill you to go to the University Club for brunch, dear."

Her dig lands in my gut. I'm desperate to make it better for her, wishing I could reach through the phone, put my arms around her snowman middle, kiss her cheek, and tell her I'm sorry for lying, and sorry that he doesn't invite her to brunch, and sorry that he's so mean to her. I want to drown her with my love. To gush that she's the most special person to me in the whole world. But I don't have the time for that now. Violet comes out of the bathroom, smelling like an expensive perfume my father might bring back from Rome.

"Mom, if he calls, can you please tell him that I'm on my way?"

"I'll tell him. You'd better go."

"Okay, I'll call you—" The phone clicks midsentence.

On the ride to the airport, my eyes are glued to the car clock while I flip through my Rolodex of possible lies. Violet drives her BMW at a steady eighty, watching for highway cops. With still another twenty miles before us, his jumbo jet has already touched down. I'm screwed, and my stomach knows it. There is no way that picking him up late, with a stranger, without his car, still in last night's smoke-filled clothes, isn't going to bring on a tongue lashing. The longer he stands at curbside pickup, the worse his ulcers will get. Oddly, or not, his first ulcer was removed—along with half of his stomach— the year I was born. The family Christmas letter from that year reads, "In February, under doctor's orders, John spent two weeks resting in Hawaii, and was fortunate enough to have his close friend, Harvey, vacationing in Hawaii at the same time." Now that I know what I know about my father and my godfather, it is just too obvious. How is it possible that Mom didn't know Dad and Harvey were enjoying more than balmy weather and pig roasts? In the years that followed, Dad had two more operations, and his doctors have told him, "Eat small portions, very slowly." But like everything else, Dad does things his way, pushing and punishing, never stopping to take care of himself. Like a guy in a hot-dog-eating contest, he crams food down, barely chewing. Then, minutes later, he excuses himself from the table and heads for the first-floor bathroom. The vomiting always sounds violent, like he's at war. His stomach firing back from being torpedoed with heavy artillery. When the dining room table was full with all of us at home, my siblings would lob quiet sarcasm back and forth as my father's dinner echoed into the toilet down the hall.

"Anyone for seconds?"

"Mom, I don't think Dad likes your cooking."

"Was that shepherd's pie I just heard?"

"Poor man. He really should eat more slowly" was always Mom's response to his nightly visit to the bowl.

My mother eats like a tortoise; my father a hare. And when it comes to keeping food down, she wins by a mile.

"I hope he likes me," Violet says, as if we've been seeing each other for months, instead of a day, breaking me out of my daydream. "Tell me about him?"

Explaining my father—or what I know of him—in twenty minutes is as impossible as explaining the Immaculate Conception. *Jesus, I pray he likes her, too.*

"He likes to be called Sir John."

"Sir John?!" she screams.

"Yeah, he's a knight," I say, knowing it will impress her.

"You messing with me?"

"No, he's a Knight of the Holy Sepulchre . . . was knighted by the pope."

"How do you get knighted by the pope?"

"You help the church in the Holy Land and give money and . . . I don't know . . . he supports an orphanage in Jerusalem."

Her wide-eyed expression is the same as that of everyone else I ever told.

"How does your father afford to support an orphanage with thirteen kids of his own? Who are you, honey, the Kennedys?"

I laugh off her words, knowing this is the part where I run out of answers. We're different from the Kennedys—less tragedy—but we are two large Catholic families with plenty of secrets. They had Mafia connections; we seem to have Vatican connections. John F. Kennedy was concerned about the CIA; Sir John seems concerned about the Mossad. And although they preferred different genders, both Johns have engaged in countless affairs, resulting in untold damage to their marriages.

Arriving at Dulles, we slow down as we circle past the various airline terminals and the passenger cars loading and unloading at the curb. As Violet speeds toward the Alitalia sign, I spot my father, glaring as he looks back and forth between his double-faced watch and the approaching cars, tapping at his forehead with a white handkerchief.

"Let me get out first, so I can explain . . ." I hop out before Violet comes to a full stop, then lean back in the passenger window. "Don't worry, he knows I've been with women."

"Dad!" I call, rushing to him, oversmiling. "Sorry."

Even though I'm twenty, I'm sure his tense face and hard eyes are a sign that he's about to ground me for the rest of my life. Ever since I can remember, I have been afraid of him and been pretending I wasn't. Even now that I'm suddenly his favorite, I know better than to expect a reprieve from his fury.

"What the bloody hell?! I've been standing here for a half hour in this heat."

"Dad, I'm so sorry, I . . ." The words turn to sobs as I drop my head, hiding behind my uncombed hair.

"What the . . . ? What's wrong? Dear, dear . . ." His tone softens.

He puts his bags down next to me, and I look up, afraid but ready to confess all my sins.

"Hiiiiii, I'm Violet. So nice to meet you, Sir John."

Violet gives an awkward curtsy, like she's meeting the queen. My father's face brightens as he assesses Violet's snug sundress and heels; her sports car with the driver's door jutting out.

Dad turns to me with his familiar smirk. "My dear, why didn't you just say so?" He gives me a wink and turns to Violet, extending his hand.

"Pleasure, Violet. I trust you will be joining us for brunch?"

Violet smiles. "I'd love that, Sir John." She gently puts her arm on his shoulder.

"And after that, who knows where we'll all end up?!" he jokes.

"Or if we'll even be standin' up," Violet teases.

"Touché, my lady."

I can tell Dad appreciates Violet's femininity, her lovely, well-made dress, and that unmistakable wild, I'm-up-for-anything sway in her walk. He never called Nic "my lady." Dad slowly escorts my belle to the driver's side and closes her door, then ducks into the backseat with his bag, letting the Lady and her Tramp lead the way.

Dad digs into his carry-on as Violet leaves the airport. Suddenly his arm stretches into the front seat, his large hand holding a velvet box in front of my face.

"I thought it was time for this," he announces.

"Should I open it now, while we're driving?"

"I believe presents should be given when least expected. Any day. Every day," he explains. Inside the black case is a beautiful ring. Violet squeals with delight.

"Oh my goodness," she says admiringly.

"Emeralds and diamonds and white gold," Dad boasts.

"Thank you, Dad. It's really beautiful. I love it, thank you," I gush, slipping it on my ring finger.

15

Hallelujah

My hangover has mellowed by the time we arrive at the University Club and settle in to my father's regular corner table. No more queasiness or headache. What's left is the good part: the loose, horny, relaxed me, ready to test the drinking waters again. We all agree on a pinot grigio, a good way to ease into our brunch. My father is thrilled that Michael is covering a sick waiter's shift, Sunday being his usual day off. Violet lathers on the southern charm. Her "Sir John" this and "Sir John" that are a balm on his perpetually malnourished ego. She shrieks with delight over his world-class stories, making us the liveliest table among the well-mannered crowd. Although he always plays his Vatican cards close to his chest, Dad shares his beloved tales about his private audiences with various popes and boasts of his close relationship with cardinals and bishops from around the world.

"You met Pope John Paul?" Violet's tone sounds full of awe. She's good with Dad, an avid listener. It likely serves her well with the congressman.

"I have met every one of them since Pope Pius XII."

"When did he rule?" Violet asks.

"Reign, my dear. Reign. 1939 to 1958."

"Violet's not Catholic, Dad," I explain.

"Well, then we must correct that and get you baptized!" Dad teases.

Violet squeezes Dad's arm, laughing loudly, bringing some stares from nearby tables. I look to Dad to see if her boisterous personality offends him. But all I see is two people who seem to appreciate each other as much as they appreciate gracious living and fine wines. By the looks of them both, you'd think they were bona fide heterosexuals.

Dad shocks us with a story about his eating the eyeball of a bull with some archbishop in Africa and boasts to Violet about taking his thirteen children on transatlantic cruises on the Cunard fleets.

"First class," he brags.

"Christine had the privilege of meeting Alfred Hitchcock!"

"What?!" Violet shrieks.

My father nods for me to tell the story.

"I was nine . . . and got his autograph one night at dinner," I begin. "And he signed his name, and drew that profile face that he does of himself. And then when I got back home from the trip, I decided I'd take it to school to show my class. But when I was looking at his autograph more closely, it was really hard to read his name because, you know, it was like chicken scratch the way he signed it, and I figured the other kids wouldn't believe it was really him . . . so, I took a pen and fixed it."

Violet breaks out into hysterics as my father lets out a deep howl, as if it's the first time he's heard this story, instead of the one hundredth time. Violet leans over and kisses my cheek.

"That is the most adorable thing I have ever heard. Ever!"

She turns to my father. "Sir John, I've really fallen for your daughter."

"Well, my dear, that makes two of us." He picks up my hand and kisses it, looking deeply into my eyes, and sings, "'The greatest thing you'll ever learn is just to love and be loved in return.'"

I smile at him, wishing he could share this part of himself with my mother.

"Are you all ready to order some appetizers?" Michael asks, pouring a new bottle of wine.

"Yes, Michael, I think we could all use some nibbles." Dad eyes Michael, as he always does, and Michael smiles at him openly. Violet taps me under the table, obviously wondering the same thing I am.

"Perhaps you'd like to join us later, as we continue our afternoon on the dance floor?" Dad smirks.

"I might just take you up on that, Sir John," Michael replies, as he picks up my father's fallen linen napkin.

"Well, I hope you will . . . my archangel."

He eyes Michael's crotch, and a wide-eyed Violet hits me again under the table. There just wasn't time on the way to the airport to share Dad's deep affection for effeminate young waiters, and men in general. I squeeze Violet's hand under the table, trying to calm her need to squeal like a wasted sorority girl. Michael observes his other tables.

"I'm off at four," he whispers.

"Marvelous, we are in no hurry. And we won't save any libations for the gods." Dad lifts his glass, continuing, "*Salute* . . . to the four of us . . . at four."

Tea dance is in full swing as we stagger into the Lost and Found with Michael, who is the only one walking a straight line. He graciously holds the club door open for Violet and me. The air-conditioning does little to temper my out-of-control blood alcohol level. Sir John stumbles ahead to the man in leather chaps taking the cover charge.

"Keep the change," my father garbles, passing a crisp one-hundred-dollar bill into the doorman's heavily ringed fingers.

"Thank you, Sir John," he says.

My eyes try to shake off the seasick feeling that lots of sex, little sleep, and three bottles of pinot grigio are having on me. Michael sways his tight ass up to my father, putting his thirty-something hand on my father's seersucker suit jacket, leading the obviously intoxicated sixty-one-year-old into the main room of the dark club, like one would lead their aging grandmother across an icy sidewalk.

Old disco blasts out of the speakers as hairy-chested, glistening men pump their fists and grind their groins on the dance floor. Their passionate baritone voices create a thunder.

Violet interlaces her fingers in mine and helps me cross the swirling, packed house. I need a bounce in my step, but first I need the room to stop spinning. My pickled limbs know they need to swing and sweat out some of this booze, or God help me.

"How ya doin', Miss Thing?" Violet puts her arm around me as we reach the bar.

"I'm fucked up," I admit, laughing.

"Me too. We drank waaaaay too much." She doesn't seem as drunk as I am. Her eyes are awake and intense on me.

"What . . . to . . . drink . . . my fair ladies?" Dad speaks slowly, almost losing his balance and falling on us.

"Nothing right now, Dad," I say, steadying his skinny body against the bar.

He looks surprised and turns to Violet.

"I'd love a Bloody Mary, Sir John. Thank you." Violet gives him a kiss on the cheek. "The ladies' room, first!" She takes my hand and leads me away—crossing the floor, impossible without her help. I'm an out-of-control bumper car, smashing into mustached men in tank tops, bears in leather pants, and young androgynous hustlers on the lookout for wealthy-seeming men or fallen drink tickets. We make it through the rough seas and land in the dark restroom. Violet leads me past the urinals, toward the four stalls. The last one has an open door that she pulls me through, locking it behind us. Her tongue immediately lands in my mouth as I rest my limp body against the door.

"You're flawless," her tongue fishing in my mouth for a bigger response.

My motor has stalled. Stepping back, she reaches into her bra, pulling out a folded dollar bill in the shape of a triangle—a paper football ready to be kicked with the flick of a finger.

"Oh my God, your dad is a hoot." She laughs, unfolding the bill.

White powder fills the center. Digging in with her pinky finger, my bombshell scoops some into her long nail.

"Here, darlin', this'll help." She holds her fingernail under my nostril. I snort it, recalling the few times Nic's friends brought coke over to her house. It made for really tense games of horseshoes and sleepless nights.

The powder stings my nose, bringing a quick rush to my forehead. The alertness feels better than the heaviness I walked in with. Violet scoops herself a hit, then offers me another one. She puts the powder on the tip of her index finger and rubs it on my gums. A charge rushes through me, and I'm now ready to burst out of the gate and run the Kentucky Derby. My thighs want to kick, feeling their power again. The dance floor is calling. I pull Violet's waist against mine, holding her round hips, and kiss her.

"Let's go dance," I say, unlocking the door.

As we pass the urinals, Violet and I look at a guy's hard bare ass with some interest, then laugh our way onto the dance floor. Dad and Michael are dancing like robots together. I try to get a little rhythm going by dancing between them, while Violet flies into her arm-swinging groove. With fingers snapping, bob flopping, ivory heels twisting, she grabs the attention of the gay boys around her. A burly shirtless guy gyrates his way over to me, and Dad nods. Michael decides to sit this one out and squeezes his way off the jammed dance floor.

"Good afternoon," my father shouts. "I'm Sir John . . . my daughter Christine." He extends his hand to the shirtless guy, showing me off.

"Bruce," the bear says, smiling.

Pulling out something from a pocket of his leather pants, Bruce unscrews the top, puts the glass vial to his nostril, and inhales. He hands it to my father, who looks lost, the way he might if handed a pair of cleats and a metal protection cup.

"Thank you, Bruce. What is it?"

"Amyl nitrate," Bruce shouts.

"Anal what?"

"Poppers," he explains.

"What do I do with it?"

"Just sniff it!"

I continue dancing as Dad takes massive hits up his nose and then passes the vial to me.

"CHRISTINE! JUST SNIFF IT, DEAR!"

I inhale—knowing the drill—in both nostrils and pass it over to Violet. We all take flight into the heavy bass on a re-mix of Michael Jackson's "Billie Jean," our blown-out heads cracking wide smiles.

Violet grabs my hips, laughing. "Feel better?"

I jump up and down with my arms swinging wildly in the air, feeling madly and passionately in love with the music.

I hear my father over my back.

"Bruce, is that genuine leather?"

I glance over, catching my father's right hand on Bruce's boner. His favorite ruby ring prominent, catching the rainbow of disco lights spinning around us. Another horny dog in a leather collar runs to the scene and gets behind Dad. They all hump each other, using the music as an excuse. Dad catches me looking.

"Christine, I'm feeling free!" he shouts.

My head rush has passed, and in its place, a pain surfaces in my heart at witnessing my father in the middle of these men. I force a smile at their threesome, then turn away. Violet passes a vial of poppers my way, and I aggressively sniff, searching for my own freedom.

16
Inquisition

Our swimming pool was built when I was five years old because Dad realized that, as the older kids were becoming teenagers, summer jobs, boyfriends, and girlfriends were making it more and more difficult to keep all of us in our Dewey Beach rental for the summer. Nearby Rehoboth wasn't a big gay resort back then; otherwise he might have found a way to continue leasing that massive oceanfront house. They tell me that Dad would drive down to be with us on weekends—unless he was overseas. But most beach days, it was just Mom and thirteen kids covered in Coppertone. She would easily be inducted into the Patience Hall of Fame, if there were such a thing.

I roll out to our backyard in my bikini—beach towel wrapped around my neck, black sunglasses covering the evidence of my two-day binge. The tall, faded fence is a warm backdrop to the row of azaleas and the dark mulch tossed between them. My mother gave up on grass a long time ago: too much trampling. Our backyard is what Miss Lange described as "lived in" when she came over to swim one rare day that the house was empty, the coast clear. It was the only way I ever got her to set foot in 5 East Irving Street.

Today, the humidity adds an extra dose of lethargy to my morning. I needed three aspirin just to get out of bed. I'm eager for a chaise lounge and too sluggish to care about my noisy nephew Tate, in the shallow end, screaming about his monumental feat.

"Awnt Tina Tuna, I'm swibbing!"

His mop of brown hair is like a wet bird's nest.

"Yay, look at you go so fast," I mumble.

My mother stands, dripping perspiration, at the edge of the shallow end. Adoringly watching her grandson, she talks quietly with Margaret, who's wading—purposely keeping her head above water, so as not to turn her newly highlighted hair chlorine green. The steaming pavement has me walking like I'm on midday August sand.

"Awnt Tuna, you funny." Tate laughs as I dash on the balls of my feet to the group of beach chairs near the deep end. I feel the two women's eyes on me, the way classmates dissect the new girl at school.

"Hey, sis, hi, Mom," I offer, laying a towel on the chair.

"Well, good afternoon." Mom's tone holds layers of questions and judgments.

"Come talk to us." Margaret's attempt at an innocent attitude fails.

I'm desperate to collapse and sleep, but there's no time to rest when the weary is engaged in an epic cover-up, bigger than John Paul I's murder. The crystal blue water sparkles in the fierce sunlight, looking more inviting than another walk across the cement. I hop over to the diving board and climb up on the low white platform.

"Here I come, little man!"

Despite my light-headedness, hitting the end of the board and springing into the air is effortless—a move I've made a thousand times. Bending into the cool water silences so many aches and pains, and seduces me to hang loose as jelly underneath the surface, wrapped in the water's easy embrace. I swim the length of the pool underwater, seeing Tate's flapping turtle legs in the shallow end.

Being immersed in the quiet, safe deep brings back thoughts of all-day swimming in the Aegean Sea with Nic. Bliss. Only darkness or a sexy topless Euro-gal got me out of the clear Mediterranean water.

"AH, I GOT YOU!" I grab my nephew's pruned feet.

He yelps with joy.

I give him a big kiss on his forehead and fall back underwater like a crazy drunk playing Tea Party until my lungs shout, "Give me liberty or give me death." And I burst out of the water, gasping for liberty.

"I'm the Cookie Monster!"

Tate delights in my immaturity.

"What happened? You decided not to work out this morning?"

Mom never asks about the details of my training.

"I'm going to do a long workout tonight," I lie, knowing that a short shoot-around is about all my hangover can handle, unless miraculously, I could do basketball drills underwater.

"What time did you and Dad get in last night?" Mom asks.

"Gosh . . . I don't even know, sometime after midnight."

"It had to be well after midnight, because I was up until one o'clock!"

Ouch. She has never taken this tone with me. I didn't even know she possessed this angry voice. I dunk my head back into the water, creating a waterfall through my long hair. I reach out for the splashing toddler and pray that Mom and her strange new attitude will paddle away, too.

"Where did you all go?" she presses.

All? Fuck, did Dad tell her Violet came, too? Shit, I hate this.

"The University Club."

"Till one in the morning?" Margaret chimes in.

I dunk all the way under.

Surfacing, I try to find my confidence. "Yeah . . . I mean . . . we were there till . . . I don't even know . . . forever. Then he needed to stop by the office for something, so we drove him there . . ."

"Who's 'we'?" Margaret asks.

"Ohhhh . . . my friend . . . Violet."

"So you went to the office?" Mom is relentless.

"Yeah, we waited for so long . . . in the car, um, I don't know what he was doing . . . I mean for an hour or more—I thought maybe he passed out . . . you know, um, how he is . . . but . . . then he came out and said he needed to drop something at one of the embassies, so—"

"On Sunday?" Mom interrupts.

"Yeah . . . and so, then . . . he was wanting to—of course—get something to eat, and 'cause . . . it was getting late . . . we just grabbed a bite in Georgetown."

"Where did you eat?" Margaret asks, adjusting her sunglasses.

This cross-examination is going to give me an ulcer. I hear the phone ringing faintly through the open kitchen windows and hustle through the water toward the steps.

"I'll get it! It might be my friend about working out tonight."

My arms and legs push harder through the resistant water, the way you do in a bad dream when you have to escape evildoers with machine guns through quicksand.

"Well?" Margaret calls, as I rush up the pool steps.

I pretend not to hear her and disappear inside the screen door.

†

I have always loved the back stairway at 5 East Irving Street—a narrow and more private option than our grand mahogany staircase that climbs from the entry foyer to the third floor. The hidden stairs, like the *scavi* beneath St. Peter's Basilica, have a mysterious, sneaky quality. They were built for the help—an unobtrusive way to get to the kitchen. As I tiptoe down, cool as KGB, I'm hoping to avoid detection. After a lifetime of sneaking up and down the bare hardwood, I know to place my foot on the back of each stair—any contact with the creaky front hardwood will blow my cover.

After my afternoon siesta in the cool of Kate's old room, my mission is simple: get to the kitchen, raid the fridge of as many carbohydrates as possible, find ginger ale at any cost, and get the hell out before any more interrogation from Mom.

The early-evening light in the kitchen brings on a moodiness. Miss Lange used to call it "the blue mood." She would get depressed at that time of day. I would go visit and stay until the sun made shadows through the venetian blinds. I hated leaving her sad face for home. I'd sit in the plaid armchair at her bedside. The Tiffany lamp and overhead light never went on during her blue moods, no matter how many jokes I told her or how many chapters of *Lady Chatterley's Lover* I read aloud.

The fridge is jam packed and could feed the three of us through the blizzard of the century. After raising a family the size of an orphanage, buying in bulk is in Mom's nature.

"Tina, is that you?" Mom calls out as the basement door swings shut.

"Yup," I say, grabbing a package of cold cuts and the Swiss cheese.

Mom pats my shoulder as she enters the kitchen, carrying a large frozen Tupperware container. She pops open the microwave, plops the hard block of dinner inside, and hits defrost.

"Your father is on his way. Why don't you set the table for me, please?" Her voice is chilled and clipped.

"Sure, Mom," I say, kissing her on the cheek. "Is it just the three of us?"

"Yes, just the three of us . . . still seems strange to say that," she muses.

When it's the three of us, I set Dad's end of the table; but if it's just the two of us, I set Mom's end. I don't know what they do when I'm not home. I grab silverware and head off to set the table, avoiding her. The dining room has inlays of dark wood between the cream plastered walls. Large carved mahogany pocket doors can close off the living room from the dining room, although they rarely do. The religious statues decorating the thin wooden ledge that runs around the entire room create a solemn mood. The memory of Erie's ironing dotting the whole room fills me with nostalgia for a fuller house.

As I set the table, I absentmindedly fold a paper napkin and place it under my father's fork. Catching this mortal sin, I yank it out and blow my nose—still stuffed from plowing through Violet's coke last night. Inside the eight-foot marble-top buffet are white linen napkins reserved for Papa Bear's place. The rest of us, including Mom, have always used paper napkins. I pull out three of his cloth napkins, deciding we all deserve the royal treatment.

Smells of stew fill up the house, and I'm optimistic the meat and potatoes will soak up any leftover alcohol from my sinful Sunday. The front door slams with Dad's heavy hand, and I automatically tense.

A beige linen suit flies past the dining room—his sweaty blotched face beelining to his mostly empty kitchen—not noticing me filling our water goblets. From the wrinkle of his suit, my hunch is he's coming from a short nap slumped over his desk after a long liquid lunch at the University Club with a clergyman. A foul mood always follows these lunches, especially when he's coming to a place he'd rather not be. I put my ear on the wall and listen.

"Hi, dear."

"Would you mind telling me where you were today?" he snaps.

"What? . . . I told you, I needed to help Margaret with Tate while she saw her lawyer—"

"All day?!"

"Most of the day, and then—"

"AND THEN WHAT? THERE ARE INVOICES SITTING ON YOUR DESK THAT NEED PAYING. THESE NEED ATTENTION, AND YOU SAID YOU'D BE IN LATER."

"Dear—"

He interrupts.

"NO, DEAR, I HAVE A BLOODY OFFICE TO RUN AND YOU ARE ON SALARY, SO THERE'S NO EXCUSE FOR BILLS NOT BEING PAID, BECAUSE YOU'RE LAYING AROUND, SHOPPING, OR LUNCHING, OR WHATEVER YOU AND THE GIRLS DO . . ."

"We were not shop—" Mom's voice weakens as the tsunami hits.

"I AM WORKING EIGHTEEN-HOUR DAYS, SEVEN DAYS A WEEK, AND YOU ARE SITTING AROUND, STILL NOT DOING ANYTHING ABOUT THIS WEIGHT! PLEASE, DO SOMETHING ABOUT THIS EXCESS!"

Pressed against the paneling, my body trembles with anger; the light switch digs into my shoulder. Finally, I burst into the kitchen, distracting Dad from his evil routine.

"Hi, Dad, you look nice!" I give him a kiss on his lips, receiving his perspiration, but no love.

He stares at Mom, still revved up.

"How about some iced tea, Dad? Mom, what would you like to drink with dinner? Jeez, that smells good. Hmm, I'm starving. Can I put out anything else, Mom?"

In the middle of them, I'm a skilled, if hyper, matador, quickly pulling the animal this way and that way. Tricking him into ramming his bull head into thin air, instead of into someone's rib cage.

"Yes, Tina, put the bread and butter out."

I force a smile at Dad, hoping it will dull his blade. My

sweaty palms anxiously squeeze the breadbasket and butter dish, heading out of the kitchen. His wing tips are on my heels, following me through the tiled hallway and into the dining room.

"Did your mother ask you about last night?" he whispers.

"Yes. I told her that after we had brunch at the University Club, we took you to the office, and waited for you, and then went to dinner in Georgetown."

"Where?"

Mom enters the room, catching our sotto voce exchange, and I let out a cough alerting Dad that she's at his back.

"Mom, let me get that."

I rush over to her, taking the white ceramic bowl, placing it on the buffet. Removing the glass lid, I welcome the steam up into my face—a soothing distraction. Dad takes his place at the head of the table, while Mom and I pile large helpings on the china plates at the buffet. The wide gaps of silence, and the shared knowledge of the hidden truths among us, bring on an uneasy rumbling in my belly. I give Dad his plate, and he gives me a wink, reminding me that we are the masterminds of these lies together.

"Did you get some rest today, Christine?" He smirks.

"Yes, I did, Dad."

I sit to the left of Dad, and Mom takes the other side. The sea of empty chairs around us adds to the awkwardness. Things will never be the same again. Even if "the same" was screaming, incest, chaos, and siblings cutting up each other's prom dresses once in a while, it was a great big family in constant motion. And now, we sit at Dad's end of the table, dying a slow death, our secrets tugging at the seams.

"Tina, why don't you say grace," Mom's tone suggesting that I need it.

"In the name of the Father and of the Son and of the Holy Spirit, bless us, O Lord, and these thy gifts which we are about to receive from thy bounty through Christ our Lord, Amen."

"Amen," my parents chime in, as we all make the sign of the cross.

Like well-mannered folks, we all place our napkins on our laps. Dad looks at all of our cloth napkins as if he's not special anymore.

"I thought we should dine graciously tonight." I wink, indicating my napkin. He lightens up.

"Yes, we should. Whatever happened to gracious dining?"

His lazy eye seems to be searching for the good ol' days.

"Where did you all eat last night?" Mom asks with a perfect balance of passive and aggressive. I glance at Dad, who quickly stuffs a large bite of food into his mouth and points his fork toward me to answer.

"I told you . . . didn't I? We ate at Mrs. Simpson's." My heart pounds against my number thirteen practice shirt, catching my mistake as soon as it leaves my mouth.

"I thought you said you ate in Georgetown. Mrs. Simpson's isn't in Georgetown." Her brow creases.

"What does it matter?! We ate at Mrs. Simpson's, and we had a lot to discuss about the future of the office. I've been doing a lot of thinking. Christine is the right one to carry on Holy Pilgrimages." Dad turns to me. "Your business degree can be put to good use."

Mom reaches into the breadbasket, taking a sourdough roll. A loud bang startles me as Dad drops his fork onto his dinner plate; his eyes case her as she spreads the I Can't Believe It's Not Butter.

"Dear, is that part of your Weight Watchers program?" he barks.

"Dad!"

He spins his head toward me, reacting to my aggressive tone. His raised eyebrows and tight face force me into submission, and I feel afraid to fight for her and risk losing him. I throw a Hail Mary. "Dad, what made you decide to start the business?"

He settles. "Now, that's a long conversation that we should have over dinner this week. Which day are you coming into the office?"

"Uh, I'm not sure yet," I hedge.

"I'll be in all week," Mom interjects.

His rolling eyes scold her again for playing hooky today. Blowing on his stew, he turns back to me. I take a piece of sourdough, hoping to soften my mother's ache with solidarity, and send a silent "fuck you" to my father for abusing her calorie count, and her.

"Why don't you plan to come in tomorrow? Monsignor Galliani will be arriving and I'd like you to meet him before we head out to lunch."

"Sure, Dad, I can do that."

Back to our meat and potatoes, the silence is long and uncomfortable—a big empty space as a result of their dysfunctional marriage. Her Irish eyes rarely smile around him. Maybe they should have had more than a few dates before they decided to get married. Their long-distance courting, and his marriage proposal via first-class mail, were all the rage during World War II. Mom couldn't see his body language or his glances at fellow soldiers. But would she have noticed even with a long face-to-face courtship? Or swept it under a rug like she does so many things?

"Tina, did you order the crab cake?"

My father slams his hand onto the table and aggressively wipes his mouth, shaking his head in her direction.

"The brunch menu at the University Club does not include crab cakes!" he yells.

Silence returns to the room. I want to jump out of my skin. My stomach pain sharpens with each second of angry silence between them. His outrage has subsided, but it lurks just below the surface, like a killer shark. I pray my crab-obsessed mother doesn't dare go back in the water. I pretend that I'm enjoying soaking up the gravy juice with my crust.

"Mom, this is excellent."

"Looks like there'll be over one hundred and fifty of us at the reunion . . . it's going to be fun having all the Allens and the Marshalls and all of us together . . . you're going to drive up to the Cape with me, right, sweetie?"

"What's the date again?"

"July 20th, but I'll go up a few days early, if that's okay with your father." She looks to him for approval.

"Do what you wish, just make sure the invoices are up to date before you leave."

"Do you think you'll take the train up?" she asks him.

Dad's mouthful prevents him from giving her another tongue lashing, but he's chomping at the bit. We wait politely for him to finish chewing.

"I've got an office to run. There's no way I have time to get to a bloody family reunion, for God's sake!"

"Not even for a day or two?" she persists.

"NO, DEAR, NOT FOR A SINGLE DAY!" he yells. "I SAID GO TO YOUR REUNION FOR AS LONG AS YOU DAMN WELL PLEASE, BUT SOMEONE HAS TO WORK AROUND THIS PLACE!"

"Well, I just thought it would be nice if the whole family were together."

Dad belches loudly, his stomach calling for a reunion with the first-floor bathroom. My leg shakes against my chair, wanting this ungracious dining experience to end.

"WHAT THE HELL IS WRONG WITH YOU, WOMAN, ARE YOU DEAF?!"

He stands up and throws his linen napkin onto the table.

We follow his fast-paced tear out of the dining room, shaking our heads in unison, as the bathroom door slams. Mom wipes her watery eyes and bites her lower lip, trying to keep it together. There's no room for me to allow the lump in my throat to escape. She needs fluffing up after being beaten down.

"Is it too much to think your husband would come to the family reunion?" she asks wearily.

I smile, knowing this is not the time to tell her: "Yes, in your case, it is too much to think that your husband would come to the family reunion, and it's also too much to think that I'm going." The noisy dumping out of my father's stomach overtakes our quiet. I take a deep breath, not sure who I feel the most sorry for in this moment. His violent vomiting grows louder. It's a toss-up who's the bigger victim here: Dad's stomach or Mom's heart.

"How about seconds?" I joke for her sake.

She can't help but laugh, which gives me permission to join her. It's a troubled laugh, as if I'm being squeezed too tightly in the middle of this threesome.

17
Visitation

If you drive south on Connecticut Avenue from Chevy Chase Circle, in thirty minutes you will land at Dupont Circle if there is no traffic. After a short but detoxifying run this morning, I'm in a confident mood as I ride shotgun with Mom to Holy Pilgrimages. She hums along to the easy-listening station, packed into the driver's seat of her Impala—her safety belt stretched to its limit.

"Mom, I'm not going to be able to go to the reunion."

"What! Why not?" She adjusts her weight with a strained face.

I can't tell her that I have eyes for a congressional aide, or that I have a master plan to be the only Worthington swimming south of the Mason-Dixon line that weekend—other than Dad. I've been scheming to have the greatest pool party since Margaret's senior-year luau, when Dad blended stiff whiskey sours for her underage friends while the pig on a spit got roasted. I'm envisioning something more lavish: champagne on ice and canapés. And lots of gay people. A first in our backyard, assuming you don't count some of my father's clergy pals who have dipped their toes in our pool after Sunday mass. The thought of having my people in our backyard with no racing heartbeat, no fear of my brothers shouting, "You fag!" and no hiding my attraction to girls, is a relief.

"I have to train," I say confidently, knowing it's partly true.

"I'm sure they have basketball courts on Cape Cod."

"It's not the same. I have the guys at the playground."

"Honey, this is the first, and who knows, maybe the last reunion. You need to come," she asserts, as if she forgot I turned twenty this year.

"Plus, Dad wants me to be at the office at least once a week, and you're going for a whole week, right?"

She turns away from the red stop light, her gaze landing on me. Her brow is pinched, eyes squinting.

"I'm sure your father wants you to be with your family, Tina," she digs.

"He's not going!" I insist.

"That has nothing to do with you. Now, I'd like you to drive up with me."

"No!"

She hits the accelerator with the green light, like I do when I'm mad. Her tight angry face is a shock—the way you never expect the sweet neighbor to be the ax murderer. We've had our opening argument on the subject. I can't defend myself or cross-examine her. That's breaking our family code among my siblings and me: we treat Mom like the saint that she is.

"Tina, I rarely ask anything of you." She pauses, letting the guilt smother me. "I am asking that you be part of the family and come to the reunion."

Part of the family? Her disapproval stings, makes me defensive and frustrated because I don't know how to fix this. Upsetting her kills me. But I don't know how to be with Mom and be all of me. As long as I can remember, I've had the sense that I'm too much and should cut myself down to a size she can handle. Mom's right, more and more I avoid being home and at family functions, because I'm suffocating under the mask I must wear in our family. I need air.

"I really have to train here, Mom. Sorry."

The saint retreats, and we drive the rest of the way feigning interest in everything but each other. As we drive around the bustling, hustling Dupont Circle, I innocently glance at the action. A few young guys sip coffee out of paper cups and eat donuts, all the while shifting their bodies, eyes roaming like a searchlight over the small park.

†

Inside Holy Pilgrimages, my father's overseas voice can be heard all the way from his private office. Shouting through the phone, across oceans and deserts, he reads the itinerary of his upcoming pilgrimage to Fátima at his overseas agent. Mom takes her place in the receptionist's swivel chair, since Dad hasn't approved any of the "bloody fools" that Dale has interviewed.

"Mom, would you like me to get you a coffee?"

She keeps her head buried in her file of invoices. "No, thank you."

The wall between us seems to have been built in a day. *What happened? I'm her lucky thirteen, and she is my first love.*

"Well, good morning, Christine. Morning, dear." Dad has a bounce in his step, the way he does when I shout to him at the Lost and Found, "Dad, do you want to dance!?"

He offers both of us kisses. Maybe he's warming up his "love thy wife" muscles before Monsignor arrives. Why can't he warm to the fact that this "bloody woman" delivered thirteen of his children, spending 117 months pregnant? Nearly two weeks of labor.

"Christine, I'd like to show you a few things before Monsignor arrives." Dad motions for me to follow. Mom looks up as we walk away. I feel her eyes on our lying backs as we disappear down the hallway and into his office. Dad closes the door behind us. It smells innocent enough, like vitamins and cologne. But no matter how many overhead lights and desk lamps may be on, it feels dark and mysterious, now that I know Dad is hiding secrets in here, even if I don't know what they are.

"Did you get some breakfast this morning?"

"Yes, I grabbed some after my run."

"Taking after your father." He smiles.

He walks over to a large, brown wooden file cabinet, while I contemplate what he means. I'm guessing the last time my father ran was when he was a choirboy, late for mass.

"I was a scrawny kid with thick glasses, but I could run forever." He holds up a three-inch navy blue ribbon that says FIRST PLACE. His face looks fifty years younger.

"How old were you, Dad?"

"Nine." He goes distant. "And Mother was going to get to this race. Promises, promises. The race started, but no Mother. I didn't care, it made me run faster. No tears for that woman . . ."

I take the ribbon from him, admiring it.

"Did she ever see you run?"

"No, she was too busy with all her gents. Bloody woman," he says with grief straining in his throat. His story makes me want to cry. Not because my long-gone grandmother seemed more interested in her men at the expense of her children, but because he's telling me something about himself without being three sheets to the wind.

He takes the ribbon back, handling it like the treasure it is.

"So what are your plans for the reunion?" he asks, sliding the file drawer closed.

"I'm not going," I say quickly, and he beams with pride. "Mom's not happy, but . . ." I add.

"Too bloody bad. There's no reason for you to go if you don't want to go. I don't blame you!"

He walks over to the window and looks out. Something catches his eye, but he speaks through his lust. "The three of us should plan dinner and the bar that weekend."

I can tell he's a fan of Miss Kentucky, the way he smiles at me. "I'll call Violet."

"Yes, you should. Let's plan on Saturday. Maybe I'll have some of your good luck and meet someone."

A knock on the door startles both of us back into our straight postures.

"Yes? Come in," he says formally.

Dale stands at the door, his green scarf adding a wild pop to his pale yellow suit.

"Mr. Worthington, Monsignor is here," Dale announces with an exaggerated arm sweep. A surprising wave of nerves floods my chest at the sight of the man Dad said "holds much sway at the Vatican." He's nothing like the imposing presence I'd imagined. With a slim build, and of average height, he's able to look my father squarely in the eye. His brown eyes dance, like someone who gets to eat the best pasta dishes anytime he wants. The perfectly clear, olive-skinned face lights up at the sight of Dad.

He wears the black garb with a bright white collar around his tan neck.

"John, *buongiorno*!" He carries a briefcase similar to Dad's.

"Monsignor!" Dad gushes.

Monsignor blesses the back of Dad's bowed head. In the other hand is an oblong gold band with a crucifix.

"Monsignor, my youngest daughter, Christine."

I step up to shake his hand, but he holds my shoulders upright, pecking each cheek with his warm skin.

"Is dis de basketball star?" His accent is a well-tuned musical instrument.

I'm shocked to hear that Dad has been bragging about me. The priest moves into the center of the office, the briefcase remaining close against his thigh. He catches me staring at the case as he sits opposite Dad's desk, placing the briefcase out of my sight.

"Christine tried out for the Olympics at one point. When she's done with her athletics, we're going to see about her taking over Holy Pilgrimages!"

He chuckles easily. "But John, you will never retire."

"No, I won't! This you know, Father, but I will need some help . . . especially with the Holy Year in 2000."

"John, how old will you be in 2000?"

"Eighty, and still traveling five hundred thousand miles a year, God willing!"

No matter that they seem to have a genuine friendship, Dad never loses the obvious admiration on his face. He puts men with a collar up on a pedestal. Dad gives me a nod, indicating it's time for me to leave—a gentle reminder that I don't belong in the middle of these briefcases and their secrets.

"It was so nice to meet you, Monsignor."

"*Arrivederci*, Christine." He gives me a quick wave, and I leave the office, dying to know what treasures lie within that leather case.

The sound of typewriters and business calls fills up the main room of the office, where Dale and his staff are actively pursuing Catholics with a yen to travel. Everyone seems wrapped up in their holy sales, unaware of my presence, so I fly back toward Dad's office to eavesdrop. Their low conversation sounds serious, but it's impossible to make out. After a few moments, their voices rise to the door, and I fall back, hiding in the mailroom, watching them from out of sight.

"Dale, we are heading out," Dad announces, exiting his office with Monsignor following behind empty-handed.

"Okey-dokey, Sir John," Dale says.

The men walk down the hallway and exchange small talk with Mom. Then they are gone. I sneak out of the mailroom toward Dad's closed office door. The overhead fluorescent lights have been shut off for some reason. He's not one to conserve energy. Ever. Maybe this is a message to potential intruders to keep out. I hustle around the desk and check underneath, then move the front briefcase out of the way and count two more behind it. Ignoring my shaking hands and thumping heart, I lay the front one gently on the neat desktop and reach for the two metal releases, expecting them to be locked. Careful not to make a peep, I slowly open the case.

The briefcase is jammed with money. It almost looks fake, like the paper bills stacked five feet high on the Bureau of Engraving and Printing tour.

I pause long enough to take in what I'm seeing. Then I hear Dale laughing and quickly close the briefcase, placing it back where it belongs underneath the desk, and silently hustle out of the room.

18
Sin

At 8 P.M. sharp, the weekend of the family reunion, Dad is manning the punch bowl in his white suit and, shockingly, a pink tie that Violet bought him and brazenly insisted he wear. We'd won him over to our plan for a Pink Party at the house while Mom was away by telling him we'd invited equal numbers of men and women.

Upon opening the Saks Fifth Avenue box, he playfully informed Violet, "My dear, real men don't wear pink."

She teased, "It will look scarlet in the candlelight, Sir John, and besides, you can take it off later in the night—it might come in handy."

Her Mae West banter earned a belly laugh from him—a modern-day miracle. Between sips of his pink punch, Dad obsessively eyes every arrival through the side gate, as if awaiting his pink Prince Charming. His Sergeant Pepper has been laid out the way a sommelier lays out a fine bottle, easily viewed beneath his thin linen trousers. European cultural norm or not, it still feels weird to see your Dad so exposed.

Watching him watching the gate is turning my stomach upside down, knowing I lied straight to his blotchy face when I first suggested throwing this soiree weeks ago. I said, "Dad, it will be a really small party—like twenty . . . guys and girls." I emphasized "guys" and he seemed to spring to life. His smirk built into a joyful laugh, and I knew I had succeeded.

"Well, my dears, how old are these 'guys'?" Dad asked, giving Violet a wink.

I piled it on. "Some my age, some Violet's age, and probably some guys from the Lost and Found."

Fuck. Now that the night has arrived, I'm worried that Dad will be upset at the man-woman ratio. I invited fifty gay women and two gay men. When I flipped through my address book, it was weird to see so many names from the bars, but nobody I'd call a friend. Sometimes I wonder if exes are the only people I really trust enough to keep around. This morning, panic set in, so I begged Violet to call any gay guy she knew.

"Honey, I've only lived in D.C. for a few months, but if this was Kentucky, pretty boys would be riding each other in every corner of this Victorian tonight!" she hooted.

I get busy flirting around the pool, complimenting outfits, offering drinks, making introductions. The only queer I don't entertain is Sandy, Violet's beautiful blond ex, who's been avoiding me the way you do the kid shouting "Marco Polo."

Her cold shoulder makes her intriguing to me. I eye her tan bare legs, hanging out of her pink miniskirt, and then trace up her thin body to her soft straight hair that she has released from her usual tight ponytail. She's pretty, in a beachy, blond way.

The gate swings open as Heather, a.k.a. Garbo, makes an entrance—all five foot ten of her—and something stirs between my legs. Despite having a massive crush on her for years, I've never had the guts to ask for her number. As far as I'm concerned, anyone that sexy is excused for being snobby. I coolly observe her gliding in with her entourage and fantasize that she secretly wants me as much as I want her. Taking a long look around the backyard, I'm giddy that I have gathered this hot group of women.

"What the hell?" Dad says, loud enough to be heard across the pool while observing another pack of lesbians filing through the gate. I don't recognize any of them until about the tenth one walks through. My heart shoots into my throat, seeing Nic holding the hand of a plain-looking girl my age, with long dark hair like Morticia from *The Addams Family*. My face grows flushed with jealousy. Nic's friends Patsy and Patsy bounce in last, clumsily slamming the tall gate behind them. I have run into them a few times out at the clubs, but they barely speak to me.

I watch Nic with my highly trained peripheral vision as she scopes the crowd and her gaze lands on me. I pretend she's not here, keeping my focus on a bunch of jocks that I'm entertaining by the candlelit diving board. "What's the number-one come-on line in a men's bar?" I pause. "Can I push your stool in?"

The women erupt into laughter as I gulp down my second glass of vodka punch.

"Hi, hot stuff," Nic says, checking me out from a few feet away.

"Hey!" I fake a smile, noticing the new gal clinging to her tan arm, even as she gives me a rough kiss on the cheek. After a month spent with a girly girl like Violet, Nic's boyishness reminds me of a different version of myself.

"This is Maggie." Nic nods toward her date.

"Hey."

"Hi," Maggie says shyly.

"Hi, there, I'm Violet Powers, Tina's girlfriend." Violet appears out of nowhere, throwing out her hand like she's greeting constituents on Capitol Hill.

"Nic," Nic says, all business, offering Violet a firm handshake.

Violet puts her arm around me, clutching my bare shoulder.

"Darlin', you need another drink." Violet takes my pink cup. "Would you ladies like some punch?" She directs her question to Nic, flashing a big fat southern smile.

"Don't worry, we'll grab it," Nic sends back.

"Oh, honey, I wasn't the least bit worried," Violet says, and heads off, touching my curls as a parting gift.

"Mag, want to grab us a drink?" my ex babies her new girl.

The reality of being replaced nearly takes my breath away; a nothingness fills my insides. Insignificance is more painful than stepping on a nail.

Maggie nods and heads off toward Dad, who's ranting to Violet about a group of hefty lesbians who have just squeezed through the gate. There are still no guys. I'm screwed.

"So, how've you been?" Nic's tone is warm and familiar, like we might still be lovers.

"Good . . . good." A wave of emotion floats around my heart. I push it down.

Her long stare has me scrunching my hair.

"You sure look good," she says, glancing at the bar area.

Then she strokes my cheek with the back of her hand, whispering, "I miss you."

I'm choked up, unable to speak.

"I messed up, and I have a feeling I'm gonna regret it forever," she confesses.

I look into her eyes, unsure of everything, just as Violet slides back between us with Maggie in tow.

"Darlin', your daddy is asking for you." Violet takes my hand and pulls me away.

"Here." She hands me a full glass, and I empty half of it in one gulp.

"I'm gonna have a chat with that PE teacher if she lays another hand on you."

Violet glares like a wildcat back toward Nic. I head over to the bar, where Dad is filling the punch bowl with another fifth of Absolut. A few lesbians linger nearby.

"How ya doin', Dad?" My buzz is kicking into high gear.

"What the hell is this?!" he demands with his voice raised.

I see some dykes turn toward us, alarmed.

"What?" I whisper, stepping closer to shield the guests from his rage.

"You said twenty-five guests. There's at least one hundred here!" he yells, waving the ladle above the punch bowl.

"I'm sorry, Dad, I didn't invite all these people," I plead quietly.

"Well, I don't see people, I see women!" He slams the spoon on the tablecloth, breaking it in half. The partygoers go mute.

"Dad, please calm down, I'm sure the guys are coming later."

He glares at me, looking straight through my manipulation.

"We cannot disturb the Dorans or any other neighbors, so be sure this bloody music is turned down by 10 P.M. sharp!" he shouts as he storms toward the back door. A loud slam punctuates all the questions across the faces of my concerned guests as Prince begins to go crazy:

"Dearly beloved . . ."

"Ladies, how about some punch!" I throw a left jab toward the back door, as if I'm punching Dad. The backyard erupts into laughter, and we're back in business. I slip out from behind the bar and grab Violet, pulling her toward the dance area.

Women converge on the concrete dance floor. Sisters bump, grind, bounce, and sway with each other. In the center of them all, I grab Violet's round ass as she tongues me deeply right next to Nic and Maggie, who are moving in a slower, conservative step. I feel Nic's eyes on us while Violet makes her point, refusing to take her mouth off mine. I salute my new girlfriend's aggressiveness, while another part of me wants to punish my old one for dumping me. I feel someone's arms around my waist, pulling me off Violet, and get spun around into Sandy's drunken dance. Her aloofness has been taken hostage by the vodka.

Violet watches us dance extremely close before finally pulling me away from Sandy and back into her needy embrace. Nic hovers. I catch her critical eye on my girlfriend. We both know Violet's attempt at aggression is weak compared to my ex's dominance. Violet's obvious clinginess embarrasses me, a turnoff. Unsure who to turn to for attention, I'm suddenly second-guessing everything. *If I were single tonight, would Nic come back? Tell her safe bet, Maggie, not to let the gate hit her on the way out?* But I've changed. I'm not interested in those boyish things: camping and smoking pot and drinking beer. I'm not sure I ever was, but I did feel loved and protected by Nic.

Dancing in the middle of all this static, loose from alcohol, I want to get away, go play. I search for Sandy, curious about her bold move, her sudden change of heart. I see her heading into the house alone, carrying a fresh drink and a cigarette.

"I'm gonna turn down the music a little before my dad goes off again!" I shout to Violet over Michael Jackson's "Thriller" while Violet sways over to the punch bowl for a refill. I slip into the house, craving a thrill. Something taboo seems more exciting than what I can easily have. Moving through the empty kitchen toward the dining room, I hear Dad's baritone voice singing "Edelweiss" in the living room. I peek around the paneled corner and find him sitting, legs crossed, on the couch, serenading a tall glass of wine. He's over the angry interlude and seems fully grounded in his sloppy drunk phase. I knock on the bathroom door, hoping Sandy will let me in.

"Yeah, okay, be right out," the Patsys shout in nervous unison.

I slip into the hallway and slide up the back steps quietly so Dad won't hear the steps creak. I take a quick glimpse around the second floor, wondering where Sandy went, hoping she didn't leave. Energy races through me as I listen for any sign of her upstairs. I have no idea what I'm going to say if I do find her, but I keep hunting anyway.

All's quiet on the boys' floor, so I climb the wooden steps to the third floor, where a soft light falls out of my bedroom. Inside, I catch Sandy in a private moment, holding Violet's purse in one hand and applying lipstick with the other.

"What's up?" I say, feeling a smirk take over, loose in my buzz, my hand resting on the doorjamb.

"Hey there," she says, and stumbles toward the door, placing Violet's lipstick cap back on.

She holds it out. "Want some?"

I examine her mood. Her normally defensive attitude is gone. There's a playfulness on the surface. Faking interest in her Revlon, I step closer to her, taking hold of her small waist. Sandy doesn't resist. Even though she's older by a few years, she's not strong like me, not as confident or daring. I love the surge I get from taking control, like my veins are filled with power fluid. I wonder if this is how Luke and Simon felt all those years ago.

"What're ya doin'?" Her southern accent is evident for the first time.

"I was thinking of kissing you," I say, asking permission.

Standing inches from her downturned face, I lift her chin and kiss her gently. No tongue. She keeps her mouth tight, not ready to surrender. My heart races, a mix of turn-on and the thrilling anxiety of hoping Violet doesn't find us.

"You're pretty," I say, stepping her back effortlessly, like a ballroom dancer.

Allowing me to lead, she gives me confidence. I glide her back to the edge of the bed. She sits. I fall easily to my knees and push open her cooperative legs. Sex makes me forget what time it is, where I am, who I am. It zaps the right or wrong out of everything. I put my hand on top of her heated underwear. She releases a sigh of pleasure, and I kiss her hard, climbing on top of her. We seem to want each other—oblivious to an outside world, to Violet. We breathe hard, alcohol curling together, the taste of cigarette on her tongue. I reach between her legs, sliding my hand inside the elastic band. Finding her hard and wet, I begin rhythmically rubbing. I get uncomfortably aware that in Sandy's sightline is the first poster I ever bought—Kareem Abdul-Jabbar—taped on the wall. And right below that, on the radiator, she must see my childish gifts from Miss Lange: an oversized stuffed bunny, a polka-dotted family of beanbag frogs. Even though I'm proud of countless trophies, plaques, and my gold medal from the U.S. Youth Games, my room feels stupid and babyish, especially compared to Violet's grown-up town house where Sandy still lives in the guest bedroom.

I make no attempt to quiet Sandy's orgasm, knowing we are three stories and a promise away from anyone ever finding out.

"You're not going to say anything, are you?" I ask, moving flyaway hairs from her smeared mouth.

"Nah, it's nothing Violet wouldn't do." She sounds resentful.

I climb off her and straighten my outfit in the full-length mirror, spotting Violet's lipstick on the floor. Despite my flushed face, I need a makeover. I fluff my disheveled hair and dab some lipstick on my cheeks. Sandy stares at my reflection in the mirror.

"You do this a lot, don't you?" she snips.

Her question knocks the wind out of me.

"Nah," I lie.

As I leave the room, sadness and embarrassment battle for space.

I make it down the back stairs to the first floor, overhearing Violet and Dad laughing in the living room. With my senses distorted by my heightened anxiety, they sound underwater. I tiptoe around the corner, holding on to the paneled wall, its surface warping against my palm, as I grab a peek of them. Seeing Violet and Dad sitting close together, relaxed on the blue floral couch, relieves me. As usual, Sir John holds court; she is his captive audience. Dad adores being adored.

My panic attack fades and my sensations normalize. Thankfully, the back door handle feels right-size as I walk outside. The party is still hopping and gorgeous Heather is still parading around in her backless ivory dress. I'm ready for more.

As I strut around the pool toward the diving board, Heather saunters by and says, "Great party, Tina."

I stop at the punch bowl for a quickie, then head up onto the diving board, feeling eyes upon me. Kicking off my pink heels, I slowly unzip my snug halter jumpsuit and peel it off. A light summer breeze sends a chill through my naked body.

"Hot!" a dyke calls out from a dark corner.

Whistles follow as I gracefully walk to the edge of the board and spring off in a forward dive. The hollers are muffled under the water. I remain below the surface, swimming the length of the pool, the alcohol buzz heightening the potent charge of being the star of this show. From the shallow-end wall, I hear the crashing of water. As I surface, rowdy women—all shapes and sizes—undress and jump into the pool. Nic watches me from the dance floor, no longer wrapped up with Maggie. She smiles at me, her lonely eyes saying what my heart feels, what I wish I could say: *I'm sorry. I messed up. I miss you.*

"Come in, Nic!" I shout.

Maggie desperately starts to undress, as if taking it personally and needing to prove a point.

Wearing sunglasses, Heather wades nude into the pool and lies outstretched on the steps at the shallow end, smoking a joint. She's as intriguing and alone as Garbo.

"Hey, hostess, you want some?" Her low, sultry voice is a perfect match for her glamorous updo, which she's keeping out of the water.

"Yes, I would," I call playfully, and swim toward her. Up close, her eyes are painfully bloodshot. Pink party eyes. She puts the lit end of the joint into her mouth and pulls me toward her with her long legs. She blows the smoke into my mouth, and I seal it in—allowing the marijuana to work its magic. She takes the joint out, careful not to burn her full lips. I slide my body onto hers, water disappearing between us, and we kiss deeply and playfully—like two people just having fun, no love. She laughs when we part, tossing her head back and looking around like she just won a bet. Proving something to someone. I'm not sure who.

"Thanks for the hit." I place my hand on her cheek, insecure and fighting for the last power play. I swim away, submerging myself again. The silence amplifies my racing mind, my fears of being caught for every sin. Countless white legs kick in the glowing water, and I swim faster toward them, wanting to escape the baggage of tonight and the weight of too many secrets anchored inside me.

19
Confession

"It looks so erect," Violet screeches from the passenger seat.

"You know those Mormons," I joke.

As I speed Violet's brand-new Mercedes around the Beltway near Kensington, a few days after the Pink Party, the phallic-looking Mormon temple lights up the night sky—a cross between Dorothy's Oz and the Disneyland castle. The windshield wipers flap hard as I cross lanes flooded from a summer storm. As I barely catch the Latter-Day exit, Violet stomps her heels with excitement. "Darlin', where are you taking me?"

After a three-hour workout at the playground this afternoon, I dropped into Chevy Chase Market for two ice-cold bottles of Pouilly-Fuissé and some gourmet snacks. Nothing but the best, made possible by my father's deep pockets and forgetful nature. His amnesia regarding his poolside rant is one-sided—I'm still secretly licking my open wound from being yelled at during the party. His leaving me two one-hundred-dollar bills the morning after—on the still-gooey dining room table—did little to dull the pain.

"Your dad wants us to go to the Lost and Found when he gets back from Rome," Violet announces as I barrel us toward the temple.

"When did he say that?"

"At the party."

She lights her Dunhill with a nearly empty Bic.

"While you two watched the sunrise?" I tease, masking my jealousy at their closeness.

"Darlin', you can't believe the things he was telling me."

"What?" I say, pulling into the parking lot of the Mormon temple.

"That he works for the Vatican and that's why he's always in Rome." Her eyes are electric.

"WHAT?! He was toasted, don't believe him. He exaggerates. What else did he say?"

"That's it, and then he nodded out for a couple minutes—bless his heart—and then he was talking about your mom and what a saint she is."

I squeeze the steering wheel, a possessiveness taking over. *He's my dad, not yours.*

Violet takes in the majestic temple through the rain-splattered windshield.

I throw the car into park and kill the ignition. We sit among rows of empty parking spaces. The fog adds an eeriness to the illuminated structure and the conversation. I look up at the imposing building, wondering if the Church of Jesus Christ of Latter-Day Saints has followers secretly working for its leader, or is it just the Catholic Church that does that?

It's impossible to wrap my head around this story. Why would he tell her and not me? Why would he call my mother a saint and treat her like a sinner? What would the Vatican hire my father for? I feel a strange need to protect him, my family, myself. "Stay out of our secrets," I want to tell her. I consider the briefcases, his special relationship with Archbishop Magni, the wads of cash, and the talk of Mossad watching him. Is he a spy for the Vatican? A courier of some kind? I don't know what to believe.

"What do you think he does for the Vatican?" she muses.

I reach into the backseat for the wine and the bottle opener I took from the kitchen drawer before Mom got home from the office. I'll bet she'd be shocked to know Dad speaks kindly about her. But probably not as shocked as she'd be to learn that horny naked women were squirming around in her pool on Saturday night, or that her baby, the ringleader, was the horniest of them all.

In the two days since she returned from the reunion, I've been avoiding Mom by working out during the day and going out at night. I can't bear to look into her disappointed eyes right now. I'm afraid she'll see guilt in mine, or notice the pink stains under my fingernails from dyeing all the hors d'oeuvres with food coloring. I am already nervous about having to drive with her to the office, hoping there won't be a stream of increasingly suspicious questions about what I did while she and my siblings were at the family reunion. Dad and I agreed it's best not to say a word about the pool party. "It doesn't concern your mother," he said. I love that he is trying to protect me, cover for me after all the covering I've done for him. It still blows my mind to think that just a few years ago, I mostly just felt anger, fear, sometimes even hatred toward him. Now, I'm his best friend, and here he is shielding me from Mom.

I twist open the cork and pour the chilled chardonnay into crystal goblets that I took out of the china cabinet.

"*Salute,*" I say, wanting to drop the whole Vatican mystery.

Violet stares into my eyes, moving a strand of hair out of my face. "I love you," she whispers, kissing my nose.

Not expecting the L-word, I glance away. Violet stays on me, as if awaiting a response. I take a long sip of wine.

"Me too," I mumble, not meaning it, but when it comes to the truth, I'm in the habit of being tongue-tied, just going along with things. I'm angry that I have to keep track of a million lies, never really being me—whoever the fuck that is.

Maybe I will feel "in love" tomorrow, or next month, but today, I'm sure I'm not.

I love her body, but I'm overwhelmed—sometimes even turned off—by how much Violet seems to love me and how needy she can be. When I see neediness, it's as if I'm seeing a brown bear. I want to run like hell.

The chardonnay goes down easily as we sit quietly, listening to the rhythm of the rain, looking at the magnificent spires desperately reaching into the sky for a God connection.

Giggly from polishing off two bottles of *vino* while we waited for the rain to stop, I lead Violet into the foyer of 5 East Irving Street. Too much alcohol and too many cigarettes have me light-headed and ravenous. Thank God the house is quiet. Mom always goes to bed early when Dad's away.

"Let's raid the refrigerator," I joke, pretending I'm a stoner.

Violet laughs, wrapping her arm around me. We walk like pals toward the kitchen, giving each other a drunken peck on the lips.

"Tina? Is that you?" Mom says from just around the corner. We drop arms and straighten up like cadets. I shove Violet behind me. Entering the kitchen with a casual bounce, I can feel my smile is way too exaggerated. Mom sits at the breakfast bar with a box of Ritz crackers in front of her. The half-eaten package is ripped open.

"Yup, it's me, Mom," I overenunciate.

"Is someone with you?"

I wave a frozen Violet out of the hallway and into the kitchen.

"My friend . . ."

"Hi, Mrs. Worthington," Violet says shrilly.

"Mom, this is Violet," I pronounce, slowly kissing Mom's warm cheek.

"Whew, you stink! Were you smoking?" Mom snaps.

"No," I lie.

"Well, you must have been around it . . . and you reek of alcohol, Tina."

"No, we . . ." I stammer, feeling guilty for lying about this and so much more.

I look to Violet. She's better at the spin, since she spends her days bullshitting constituents on behalf of the congressman. Violet does her power walk—the charm oozing from her extended, polished hand. She always drinks more but seems to handle it better.

"Mrs. Worthington, it's sooooo nice to meet you!"

"You too, Violet," Mom says flatly.

"Ma'am, it's all my fault. I was smoking like a runaway train, and the windows were up. Can you believe this rain?" she screeches.

Mom is low-key, raised by Nana to be kind and loving and polite but not overly demonstrative, and certainly not loud. Mom's solemn face scrunches up at Violet's high-pitched outburst.

"Where were you girls?" Mom asks.

"We went to Georgetown, but then . . . we couldn't find parking, so we went over to Hamburger Hamlet . . ."

My lie is way too complicated.

"I thought they were renovating Hamburger Hamlet."

"We ate at the Hamburger Hamlet in Old Town, near my place," Violet jumps in.

If Mom were a detective in the interrogation room, she'd be pacing right now, rubbing her hands together, ready to tear our lies apart.

"You drove all the way to Old Town for a hamburger?"

Mom eyes Violet's fuchsia heels, dangling from her two fingers.

"Yeah, Violet needed to get something for work tomorrow."

"Why would you need something for work tomorrow?" Mom plows on.

I feel where she's going, and I need to put a stop to this.

"Mom! Why are you asking a million questions?" I snap.

Mom's face reddens as she turns on me.

"Tina, you are telling me all kinds of stories that make no sense, you have had too much to drink, and I'd like to know what's going on."

Her tone breaks me. My shoulders begin to shake, my head falling in shame. Violet rubs my shoulder and takes me in her arms, hugging me. Sobs overtake me, and I'm unable to pull away from Violet's affection.

"Darlin', it's okay, don't cry." Violet rubs my back.

Halting our intimacy, Mom's voice is stone cold.

"Violet, I'd like to be alone with my daughter, please."

"Oh, yesss, of course, I'll just wait . . ."

She leaves the room. I walk over to Mom, desperate for her fat arms to squeeze me till I bleed buttermilk, desperate for her warm neck, desperate to bury my nose into her freshly cut and colored hair. Wobbly and hysterical, I lean like a blow-up doll into her. She wraps an arm around my waist. Heaving into her chest, I drench the neckline of her nightgown with my tears. The familiar safety of her hug is comforting. I'm exhausted from juggling lies like knives, hoping none come down on me. I want to show Mom all of me, once and for all, proving to myself that she loves me—no matter what. Something surges inside me—like a sewer unable to contain the runoff after a bad storm, I begin to overflow, debris bubbling up to the surface, everything I've hidden in plain sight.

"Mom . . . I don't really date guys much because I like . . . girls better," I say, weeping.

Falling apart, I sink into the straight-back chair—the cool black wrought iron against my back offering no real support. Mom's tense body doesn't seem interested in wrapping me up snug as a bug, like she used to, like I want her to.

"Tina, I'm worried about you. You are drinking too

much . . . you're going out every night with strange people too old for you to be hanging around. It's not normal."

She didn't hear what I just told her—maybe unable to take hold of such a sinful subject. Her response is typically indirect. But I need something more from her now, as all the pain of hiding my whole life is banging on my chest. What is "normal," anyway?

I've never felt normal. And I suspect Mom has known I was never exactly normal. The family Christmas letters that Mom always wrote called me "bossy" at three; "never happier than when she's playing football with her brothers" at six; "a real tomboy" at eight. And when the family gathered to watch Simon's home movies of his wedding, my thirteen-year-old strut to the pulpit in my pink gown to read from the book of Corinthians brought teasing from Simon's wife: "Tina, you walk like a boy!"

And chuckles from Mom.

"I don't date guys 'cause I don't want to," I blurt, wiping tears on the back of my hand, knowing that now I'm the one being indirect. But I can't say it any better. More clearly.

She pulls out a cracker from the plastic wrapper and cups it tightly in her hand.

"Sweetie, I think you're tired and need to get some sleep." She sweeps my interest in girls under the carpet. Does she prefer I simply go back in the closet? I slump out of the kitchen and find Violet sitting on the floral couch in the living room. She gives me a sad look; she heard it all. Embarrassed and ashamed—maybe for not being more lovable to my mom—I wave Violet toward the front door and keep walking. We limp onto the front porch, still drunk despite the sobering conversation.

"I'm so sorry, darlin'." She goes to hug me.

I move away, not feeling worthy of hugs and kisses right now.

"Let's talk tomorrow," I say. "I don't want her coming out here looking for me."

Violet takes the hint, kisses me on the cheek. "She's just in shock. If I ever told my mother, she'd have a heart attack or try to have me committed—you're braver than I am, Miss Thing."

"Bye," I say, heading for the front door, not wanting her to see me cry.

†

When I roll downstairs the next morning, still in my short summer nightgown, the house is church quiet. I plop myself down on the bottom step, not caring about my unladylike position despite not wearing panties. The fog from last night hasn't lifted. *Was it all a dream?* Maybe I was drunk enough, and vague enough, that Mom didn't understand what I was saying. God, I hope so.

I'm suffering my penance for my confession—a gut filled with knots and nausea to go along with another hangover, another morning workout lost. Despite multiple tooth-brushings and a long Listerine gargle, my throat feels raw, and my sinuses are filled with nicotine from smoking Violet's fucking Dunhills. The headache thumping across my forehead is the only constant companion I've had all summer. *What did I do? What should I say when I see Mom? What about Dad?* He's not going to like that I told Mom about me; he likes being the only one in the family to know my secret. Thank God he's not due back from Rome until next week. Maybe Mom will keep pretending I never said anything last night. Maybe Mom won't tell Dad anyway. *Fuck.* Right now, I wish I could snort last night's confession right back up my nose and down my throat. I wonder how many memories you can kill with a hit of poppers? Or a line of cocaine? Or a half dozen sea breezes? Or a case of Pouilly-Fuissé?

Resting my chin on my shaky hand, I count the number of runs in the sea foam wall-to-wall carpet—a gift from our dearly departed black Lab, Sambo. An image of our dog lingers in my memory: lying at my parents' feet as they sat lover close in this exact spot, dressed in their Christmas Eve best. The snapshot caught Dad in a nanosecond of love for Mom, a result of the perfect mixture of whiskey sours and Johnny Mathis's Christmas album. Lady Anne ate up his hand-holding and serenade: "A beautiful sight, we're happy tonight. Walking in a winter wonderland." No matter if he gives her a crumb or the whole cake, she's grateful. "Something's better than nothing" has always been a favorite expression of hers. And, still, always, she gives him everything. No matter what Dad does or says, I think Mom treats him the way she wishes he'd treat her. Maybe someday.

I pull myself up, using the railing as a crutch. My stomach is crying out for something to soak up last night's alcohol. What I eat in the morning depends on how much I drink the night before. If my first meal of the day is burgers and fries, I got hammered the night before. Scrambled eggs and toast: I was in bed by eleven.

Dragging myself into the kitchen, I see the ticking sunflower wall clock and am reminded of how alone I am in this cavernous house. A wave of dread lands me in one of the wrought-iron kitchen chairs. Unable to hold my head up, I lay my cheek on the cool countertop. Tears crash out of me. Fluid pours over my bloated face and into my messy hair as I heave uncontrollably on the Formica. I don't know what to do. Maybe I should stop drinking so much.

Flipping my cheek to the other side, a sharp pain in my neck rises from too long in an uncomfortable position. I watch the clock, wishing I could go back in time and erase last night. The black second hand moves—tick, tick, tick—like a bomb threatening to go off.

The last time I watched the kitchen clock this long I was in seventh grade, on the night of Rebecca's graduation party at a classmate's house. Miss Lange was there, and I was jealous because she was hanging out with other kids; I couldn't wait to grab any tidbit about my lover when Rebecca walked through the door at 11 P.M. I'd been waiting in the living room all night, unable to concentrate on the television.

"All the adults got really drunk and Miss Lange was doing the bump with Bucky Smith," she detailed as I hid my possessiveness. That information sent me spinning into insomnia, while I replayed Rebecca's words obsessively, sitting in this exact position, watching the second hand inch along, until the sun rose. Waiting and waiting and waiting until I could call her. Twelve years old, and too mature to count sheep. But not too mature to bypass the phone and instead pound on her front door at 9 A.M., waking her and her parents, rushing upstairs to cross-examine her.

"Why were you being such a flirt?" I demanded, clearing off her bedside table with one furious hand.

My question deserved an answer, but all I got was a question. "Why are you being so immature?" Her hangover was obvious in her gravelly voice.

"ANSWER ME!" I screamed, ripping the wet cloth off her forehead.

She rolled up urgently to a sitting position and reprimanded me: "If you raise your voice again, you are leaving."

And with that I flew off the king-size bed, bumping into her card table—where she had been laboring over her beloved thousand-piece puzzle for months. And with two angry hands I destroyed her nearly completed Mount Rushmore.

Remembering her words, "Why are you being so immature?" a surge of anger overtakes my tears. *Fuck her, she's the one that wanted to be with a twelve-year-old!* Mom would never understand that—I'm not even sure if I do.

But right now, I'm just glad I wasn't drunk enough last night to tell Mom about Miss Lange. Too much is too much. Impossible to untangle, like an old phone cord. I wipe my nose on my T-shirt, too tired to grab a tissue.

The mustard phone rings—the "kids' phone" that Dad had installed so we'd stay off the "bloody main line." For most of our lives, one phone line in the entrance foyer was all we had for thirteen kids who were dying to call out. Tying up the phone, you ran the risk of Dad's wrath. Sir John loathes a busy signal. "The telephone is for giving and receiving messages!" he'd scream, veins bursting. After years of having to call the emergency operator in order to break into our calls, he was fed up and finally put in a separate line for his children on the kitchen wall.

The ringing continues. I need to eat, not talk. I raise my wet face off the breakfast counter and head for the refrigerator, hunting for anything starchy. A pile of potato salad hides in the back underneath plastic wrap—maybe something Mom was hiding for me. Or her.

As I finger mounds of gooey chunks into my mouth, the phone begins to annoy me. Who the fuck won't take "No one's home" for an answer? Maybe it's Violet on a coffee break from returning calls to angry Kentuckians, insisting the government give them a tax break for raising Derby-bound thoroughbreds.

"Hello?" I relent.

"Hey, kid, what's up?" Margaret's voice is higher pitched than normal, sweeter.

"Nothing. Just gonna go work out," I lie.

I hear Tate in the background, begging to ride his Big Wheel.

"Feel like getting a drink later?" she says, as if we spend our days getting manicures together. I can't recall the two of us ever going out for drinks.

"I'll be at the playground till at least seven," I explain, trying to sound disappointed.

"Come on, after your practice," she insists.

I hesitate, nothing surfacing from my brain fog to offer as an excuse.

"Let's meet at the Lily at eight," she says.

"Who's taking care of Tate?"

"I don't know, but I'll get someone. All right . . . gotta get him lunch or he's gonna have a tantrum. Later, kid."

†

The Lily is actually in D.C., even though it's five minutes from our house in Maryland.

I arrive a little after eight, hair still damp from my shower after a sluggish workout. At least I didn't quit, I tell myself. At least I stayed until seven fifteen—even if the last hour was just foul shots. The lies I tell myself are getting pathetic. Really, I should be returning to Mount St. Mary's for my senior year in the best shape of my life. But lately, another basketball season and even my dream of the Olympics are no more than afterthoughts.

"Hey, kid," Margaret calls from a corner banquette.

I head over to her, thinking maybe I should have passed on the red lipstick and halter dress. The décor is modern—not as sophisticated as places in Georgetown or Dupont Circle, but a solid effort for our conservative neighborhood. Margaret gives me a once-over.

"Are you going out later?" She sounds confused, like I've already dumped her for someone else.

"No, no . . . I just . . . all my stuff is in the laundry," I lie.

What is it about my family that makes me uncomfortable standing out? Why can't I just say, "I love dressing up and I do look fucking flawless, don't I?" Someone must have sent out an unspoken message to all of us: "You are one of thirteen, so fall in line. Don't be different. Don't stand out too far." Truth is, Mom likes everything and everyone even Steven. She always has. Dad isn't against standing out, so long as it's him and only him.

"You want to eat something?" Margaret says, handing me a menu.

"Nah, just wine."

She fidgets with the fork and smooths the cloth napkin on her lap.

"Can I get you guys a drink?" our androgynous waiter sings.

It makes me happy to see something queer in this straight place.

"White wine." I forget my cover and wink at him.

"And I'll have a vodka tonic," Margaret interrupts our private exchange.

I feel Margaret's eyes on me while I pretend the other tables are extremely interesting.

"How are you liking working at the office this summer?" she asks.

"It's okay, it's money," I say.

"Dad's still talking about you taking over the business," she says, twirling her knife.

"Well, he said that to everyone," I say lightly.

Our waiter quickly returns with our drinks and grandly sets them in front of us.

I take a long sip of my chardonnay—it settles me, and I know I'll order another. The silence lingers.

"So . . . Mom called me today. She said you said some things to her last night . . . and that she thinks you're gay. Is that true?"

I take another big sip, my face heating up.

Margaret presses. "Are you?"

And before I can answer, she tears off like Tate on his Big Wheel. "Not that I care. I mean, I kind of already knew. You are, right? It's no big deal. I figured that's why you never really had a serious boyfriend."

Even after my defensive drills on the sizzling asphalt today,

I'm still not ready to guard her. She's too fast, too nimble. Before I can shut down her lane, she's breezed by me to the rim.

"Yeah . . . I am," I say.

To my surprise, my body relaxes as soon as the words fall out of my mouth into the booth. I begin to pet the black and white satin fabric beneath me. The truth is as satisfying as a hot shower after a triple overtime win. It feels so amazing, I laugh out loud.

"Why are you laughing?"

Her angry tone throws me. I shrug, feeling ashamed.

"Nothing . . . just . . . yes, I am gay." The G-word gets caught in my throat.

After so many years of careful pronouns and straight-up lies, I'm in the habit of trapping that word in my mouth.

"Is Dad gay?" she demands.

I clutch the stem of my glass. The room goes silent.

I hear someone else answer.

"Yes."

It couldn't have been me. No way. I'm the secret keeper. Luke and Simon, Miss Lange, and of course, my homosexual father's secrets, too.

"Is that why you've been spending so much time together?"

I nod, feeling an emptiness spread inside me. I polish off my wine, shocked at my words. Our waiter brings a second round.

He sweeps away, leaving us both shaky.

"Does Dad have a boyfriend?" Margaret presses.

"No, I don't think so, but he was with Harvey," I confess.

"Your godfather?! Jesus . . . he told you that?"

I nod, ashamed of having archived so much information, afraid of how much is falling out of me, suddenly impossible to contain.

"How about Father Shannon?" she presses.

"Yeah, Father Shannon . . . and Father Perry . . . maybe Father Tremaine—he's gay—but I'm not sure if they—"

"That's gross! Father Perry was always taking Philip and Luke for private confession in Mom and Dad's bedroom!"

She looks at me with a twisted face.

"I gotta use the bathroom." I rush away from the table, sprinting away and landing in the closest stall. I vomit all liquid—wine and my post-workout Gatorade—into the bowl. My breakfast was too long ago to provide a cushion. Strings of blond hair hang toward the bowl as the purging turns to dry heaves, sounding like Dad in the first-floor bathroom. I draw concern from a nearby stall.

"Are you okay?" a woman calls out.

Embarrassment and guilt are all that's left inside me.

"I'm fine," I say, unable to summon the truth in this case. I wait for the woman to leave before dragging myself out of the stall and to the sink.

My reflection scares me: thin, pale, drunk, and weak, barely able to hold myself up—looking more like Dad than ever.

20
Agony

I've been in hiding since that night with Margaret. My grand
confession. With the fall semester starting at the Mount, I simply explained that senior year with a double major and the
demands of my basketball scholarship made it impossible for
me to come home on the weekends. Other than a few dinners with Dad and Violet in D.C., I've stayed away from family.
Dad's been feeling the distance, writing letters to me at school,
bemoaning, "I haven't been out to the bars in ages." He didn't
seem to have a clue that I betrayed him, but that was weeks
ago, and now, I'm terrified that Margaret has spilled to the
family. I can't even deal with the possibility that she told Mom.
Tonight, as I drive around Chevy Chase Circle, onto West-
ern Avenue, passing Blessed Sacrament Church—the carved
doors dressed with Christmas wreaths—a wave of nausea rises
as I imagine the destruction I may have caused. Since finals
ended last week, I've been hiding out at Violet's—finding
every excuse to stay away. But Christmas Eve is tomorrow, and
not showing up for our biggest celebration of the year is as

inexcusable in the Worthington family as buying an artificial Christmas tree.

Turning Violet's Mercedes onto Irving Street, I see a trail of cars lined bumper to bumper in our driveway. The road is crowded, with only one spot left, across the street from our house. The bare oak trees under a dull winter sky add to my heavy heart. It's strange how you can long for a past that is filled with sadness. I reach for Violet's black gown in the back-seat, the dress she was going to wear if I invited her. It hurt her feelings that I didn't. But even though I told Margaret and Mom my secret, I'm still in the closet to the rest of my family. It's possible they could have told others, but no one has reached out to me, so I'm guessing my secret is safe. Before I can grab the overstuffed bag of Christmas presents from the backseat, Margaret is standing on the sidewalk—no coat, smoking, head down. Her beautiful black hair shields much of her face. I close the heavy car door and cross the street. I feel older since the last time I saw her, even though it's only been a few months, and I'm still twenty-one.

Margaret's eyes are bloodshot and swollen.

"Mom knows," she chokes.

"Everything?"

She nods and puts her arm around me as we take a slow walk toward the house.

"Helen decided we just shouldn't keep it from her anymore. Now Dad's sleeping at the office," she says.

My insides feel cold, shaky. Climbing up the front steps, my lungs feel challenged from a week of Dunhills. I stop on the porch and begin to cry. "I don't know what to say to her."

"She's stronger than we give her credit for," Margaret assures me.

I never considered Mom strong, but maybe my sister is right. After all, what weakling could have thirteen pregnancies and countless contractions? What coward could withstand a raging drunk in her face, then turn around and cook, sweep, scrub, make thirteen bologna sandwiches and place them lovingly into brown lunch bags? A weak person can't prepare a formal Christmas Eve dinner of Yorkshire pudding and roast beef for thirty-plus people, attend midnight mass, and entertain family and church friends afterward with homemade sweets, then stay up until sunrise to finish wrapping gifts and stuff thirteen stockings. Mom cared deeply that the first thing we saw upon walking into the living room on Christmas morning was our monogrammed red stockings, stuffed to the gills with Cracker Jacks, nail files, and sweat socks. It never dawned on me until right this minute that Mom might be the strongest woman in the world.

The living room sounds like group therapy—a powwow of "can you believe its" about all the missed clues and betrayals. My sisters and brothers cross-talk, trying to make some sense of their holy father's secret. Voices overlap each other like a litter of puppies.

"Dad's always acted weird around waiters and busboys."

"Father Perry gave me the creeps, taking you boys up to Mom and Dad's bedroom for private confession."

"Well, he never took ME!"

"You were too young."

"Now it's extra weird that all you boys swam naked with Dad at the YMCA."

"Hey! Everyone at the YMCA swam nude."

"That's disgusting."

"I never told anyone this, but my buddy Tommy McBride said he saw Dad once, really drunk, walking around the fountain at Dupont Circle."

"Yeah, well, what was TOMMY doing at the Dupont Circle fountain?"

"Shut up, you homo! Tommy worked down there!"

"Yeah, that's my point about Tommy!"

I sneak past our Christmas tree—not as dazzling as usual, the tinsel too clumpy this year—and drift down the hallway, avoiding the loud free-for-all in the living room.

My sister Magdalene chases me down, hugging me warmly.

"Tina, why didn't you just tell me about . . . your lifestyle? I feel really hurt that I had to hear it from Margaret."

Coming out in my family as a grade schooler, or even in high school, seemed about as safe as riptides. I wish I could say so, but even that doesn't feel safe. I shrug, not knowing how to respond to her, and to the probability that now all my siblings know my secret. I want to cover up, even though I'm fully clothed; my throat stings from the battle to contain my tears.

"I'm sorry" is all I can manage.

I need to see Mom and, hearing a low whisper, head toward the kitchen. Inside the bright yellow room, Mom sits at the breakfast bar—her back to the doorway, talking on the kids' phone. She really is just one of us, trying to survive the shocking news that the Wizard of Oz is not a wizard at all. Her shoulders have no life. A polished fingernail mindlessly scratches at the countertop.

I put my arm on her back, startling her. Pulling back, I give her a small wave.

"Hold on," she says, covering the receiver.

"I'm sorry, Mom," I blurt out.

"Let me finish my call," she says in a monotone.

There's no anger, and no love—just a flat response. As I leave the kitchen, my face is hot with shame. I feel like I have caused an oil spill. For someone so good at lying, you'd think I could have easily said no to Margaret's question. But I felt pressure to give her what she wanted. Clearly she must have already known or suspected. "Is Dad gay?" she asked me! That kind of question doesn't just fall out of a daughter's mouth without reason. But confirming this makes me no hero. Especially in a family where most of my brothers and sisters probably think being gay is wrong, even sinful.

I doubt they are interested in hearing what I have to say about Dad's secrets and lies. I've never felt that my voice—the youngest voice—was ever as important as my older siblings'. It's natural, I suppose; they are as much as fifteen years my senior—they must know better. Plus, no one is rushing to champion my coming out. Maybe they are all just too overwhelmed with the shock of what their father's been up to. I don't blame them. But I feel utterly invisible now. As I reach the third floor, the heat intensifies, radiators clanking. A large pink laundry hamper reeks from what might be a deserted towel from last summer. The smell of mildew stings my nose as I head for my old bedroom. I strip off Violet's baggy winter coat, kick off my black ankle boots, and crawl onto my bed. Assuming no one has been in here since summer, I did a lousy job making my bed. A lumpy sheet annoys the back of my legs, but I'm too lazy to smooth anything out. Pangs behind my forehead must be from the cheap table wine in Violet's fridge that I polished off, same for my dry mouth. I wonder if one day I could ever not drink. It seems impossible, although I might value not having so many headaches, upset stomachs, and blurry, lost weekends.

Arms behind my head, I examine the room, landing on the small attic door. Up there, the ceiling's so low, you can barely stand up in the unfinished room with raw beams and insulation drooping off the walls. It's there that Kate found love letters between Mom and Dad. There was the evidence that Dad was rejected from the priesthood in England. When I read them, I was shocked to hear how desperate Mom seemed for Dad to marry her, how needy. It made me see their marriage in such a different way. If this house could talk, I wonder what it would say. Would it be a good Catholic home and forgive the many sins? Or would it shake from its foundation—from all the pain and suffering and betrayals?

I throw my pillow at the clanking old radiator, wishing I could scream out loud. The heat is stifling in my room—both in the dead of winter and the middle of summer, I've never been able to breathe easy. But I can't go downstairs, either; the air is too thick down there, too. I miss Dad, but I don't know what he knows. I don't know if he's aware of what I've done. Right now, I don't know where to be.

✝

In my room, the brass desk clock reads eleven thirty. I slept through until the morning and missed any chance to connect with my siblings, or my mother, the night before. Out the French windows, the December sky is the color of a janitor's wet mop. I'm gloomy, too.

Removing yesterday's clothes, I throw on sweatpants and head for the closet, pulling out a shoebox. Inside is a shiny pair of Adidas high-tops, white with red stripes—courtesy of the University of Maryland athletic department. Scholarship players get two free pairs of sneakers per season. Without a lot of playing time, I had no use for the second pair.

On my way into the girls' bathroom, a wooden plaque catches my eye in the hallway: TODAY IS THE FIRST DAY OF THE REST OF YOUR LIFE. It's one of the many decorative items that Dad bought from priests with a knack for arts and crafts. There is one plaque I've always hated that hangs in the den: THE GREATEST GIFT A FATHER CAN GIVE HIS CHILDREN IS TO LOVE THEIR MOTHER. Dad has definitely given me and my family lots of gifts, but that sure ain't one of them.

As I hit the second-floor landing, I hear Mom's voice coming from her bedroom.

"We've been through this, John," she begs.

I inch toward their closed mahogany door, sliding slowly against the wall, ears burning. Mom weeps. I've never heard that sound from her. Whenever anyone died—including her oldest sister, Elizabeth—she would never cry in front of us, she'd retreat to her bedroom.

"What about Harvey? . . . Harvey!" Her voice is rising.

He must be giving her a heap of lies. She's on the phone, so I can only hear her side of the conversation, but I can imagine the web he is spinning.

"It's not normal, and you betrayed all of us," she continues. And then with a calm, as if the Holy Spirit has filled her, she says, "After the holidays, I'm going away for a while."

I want to run away, but I'm afraid for her.

"I'm not interested in speaking with Father Shannon! How is Father supposed to help us when he has the same problem as you?!"

I hear her blow her nose.

"John, you lied to me," she snaps.

My mother begins to cry louder. Then, finally, she says, "I'll pray for you, but I can't live with you right now."

I hear my mother walk toward the door and I hightail it away, slipping down the steps two at a time, grabbing my ball from behind the couch and hustling out the front door. Sprinting down the middle of Irving Street through the freezing December air, I pull the hood of my sweatshirt over my head, knowing I should be wearing a parka. My legs pump around the O'Neills' hedges, leaving some skin on a sharp bare branch. I ignore the sting. If I ran into traffic right now, got hit by a truck, I wonder if it would even hurt?

Like a wild animal I charge to Chevy Chase Playground. My breath pumps as I take the short cement steps two at a time, landing on the outdoor basketball court. It's empty. Most people are out doing last-minute shopping or helping their mothers bake Christmas cookies. No fools, like me, are out shooting baskets with numb fingers. Taking the court like a possessed gym rat, I sprint from baseline to baseline. I chase off extreme thoughts of divorce, our home being sold, the family torn apart. I'm scared to face my dad. If Mom told him that I'm the source, my life is over. Why didn't I just tell Margaret, "NO, DAD'S NOT GAY! HE HAS THIRTEEN CHILDREN, HOW COULD HE BE GAY?"

I grab the ball and begin full-court layups, flying from one basket to the other. His words pound into me: "Christine, I assure you, I am not going to tell your mother about your personal affairs. I am not going to tell anyone—certainly not the family. No one. This is not information that the world needs to know. But it's important that someone knows."

I ignore my queasy stomach and take ten foul shots at the peak of my exhaustion. I pant through them, hitting eight out of ten. I'm unsatisfied. Dad's cold tone keeps ringing. "Now, as for my life, I take it you will assure me the same courtesy."

I roll the ball toward the sidelines, punishing my body, pushing for more. Defensive drills are next. First, crouching into a deep squat, as if I'm sitting on a low chair, then I begin to step and slide my legs from one side of the court to the other. Hands extended as if ready to swat flies. I torture my inner thighs, knowing they deserve it after all their indiscretions. Maybe I'm just a whore. I could have told my brothers no—maybe not at nine, when I was sleeping, but later, when I let their attentions continue until I was twelve. What about the tingly feelings? That was my fault, right? Not until my relationship with Miss Lange did I begin to say no or ignore their twisted games, and sometimes even get mad at them. I notice that even now, speaking up for myself isn't easy, especially when someone does something cruel, something I don't like.

I am laser focused until my spent legs give way, sending me onto the asphalt, where I skin my knee and palm. Not feeling much, I pull out a piece of gravel, hop back up, and wipe off my dirty hands. I head toward the bushes to retrieve my ball. As I dribble back toward the hoop, a small voice in my head scolds me, "It's your punishment."

21
Wrath

Despite a house full of adults and children dressed festively and full of delicious-smelling food, from the sounds of the scene you'd never know it was Christmas Eve in the Worthington house. Yes, some aspects are the same: the roast beef with garlic and sherry is cooking in the oven, and Johnny Mathis's velvet voice does that familiar sad shaking, as if he might start crying at any second. Walking into the living room, I find my siblings talking quietly, sipping wine, nibbling on cheese and crackers and stuffed mushrooms. There isn't a whiskey sour in sight.

"Hi, kid," Margaret calls across the room, the first to notice me.

I offer hugs to my brothers and sisters. I'm bracing for some comments on my coming out of the closet, but I guess the shock of Dad takes priority. I don't mind. I hug a few of my nephews, adorable in their miniature suit jackets. I love them, and their excitement adds some much-needed pep to the room. One of my nieces plays with her doll near the fireplace. I stare at the empty space: no straw, no wise men, no baby Jesus, and of course, no need for Dad's white handkerchief.

Margaret nudges me. "It's weird not having the Nativity set up, huh?"

"Where's Dad?" I say quietly.

"He's not coming."

"But it's Christmas Eve," I say, surprised.

My heart hurts. This is really serious, and it's my fault. For as long as I can remember, Dad has always been our leader on Christmas Eve, and again on Christmas morning—the one time a year he cooks, making strange-colored scrambled eggs, into which he throws every leftover in the refrigerator. "There's no need to waste perfectly good food" is his motto.

He rarely watches us open gifts, preferring to focus on the torn and discarded wrapping paper that he compulsively stuffs into large trash bags. Dad's obsession with tidiness while raising thirteen children must have been crazy making for him. If anyone tries to give Dad a Christmas present—or a birthday present, for that matter—he refuses it. "Take it back and put the money in the mission jar for the orphans at the Home of Peace," he demands, sounding furious at the waste. Most of us don't even bother anymore. By Christmas afternoon, Dad's on his way to Rome or the Holy Land. I have no idea why he leaves us each Christmas Day to travel halfway around the world, but he does, another layer to his secrets.

I rush away from the somber mood. Desperate for a drink, I walk down the hallway toward the kitchen. On the wall hangs the large bulletin board where Dad posts his itineraries anytime he travels. He must have thumbtacked it up before Helen broke the news to Mom. I see his departure—*Dec 26th, Dulles Airport to Leonardo da Vinci, Rome*—and imagine him alone tonight, drowning in booze. I wonder what he'll do or where he will attend midnight mass. I wonder if he is as sad and confused as I am.

"Hi, Tina! Merry Christmas!"

I bump into my cousin Marianne—Mom's niece from New England—who's spending the holiday with us, her normally jolly personality blanketed. She must know, too. I hug her, getting a whiff of cigarette smoke in her tight curls.

"Merry Christmas. How long are you here?"

"Just the weekend, but don't worry, I won't take your room." She chuckles.

I peek my head into the kitchen, where a few of my sisters are preparing tonight's feast. Unwrapping dozens of French rolls, mashing an army-size portion of potatoes, dumping can after can of cranberry sauce into a lovely silver bowl, stirring the gravy while my brother-in-law Diego, in his usual sleek suit, uncorks bottles of red wine for the dinner table. Mom is nowhere to be seen.

"Marianne, where's my mom?"

My cousin points to the bathroom door.

"She's been in there awhile," she whispers.

We both know why. She's in there purging tears the way Dad would purge his dinner.

"Maybe I should knock," I say, bravely approaching the door.

"I was in there with her before. Let's give her some more time," my cousin explains softly, blocking the door.

Stepping away, I walk into the dining room and grab myself a glass of white wine. I stay tucked away, avoiding the crowd in the living room, my stomach in knots, wondering who knows what. Feeling shaky, I sneak up the back stairs, holding up Violet's loaner gown in one hand so as not to trip. I'm glad she decided to go home to Kentucky for the holidays.

As I slip up the second-floor steps, I hear Matthew talking in the foyer.

Scrunching down out of sight, I rest my head against the wooden railing, eavesdropping.

"It was in his briefcase—which was unlocked—just lying there underneath some brochures," Margaret reports.

"Are you shittin' me?" Frances rages.

"No, man, we both saw it—the gay guide to Rome," Matthew explains.

"What did you do with it?" Frances asks.

"Margaret gave it to Diego as an early Christmas present," Matthew jokes.

"Look, don't say anything to Mom right now, she doesn't need to know this," Margaret declares.

"Don't tell me what I can and can't say! He's a fucking liar and a pervert, and I'll tell Mom whatever I want to tell her," Frances blurts.

I peek through the railing and see Frances storm off. Matthew puts his arm on Margaret's shoulder.

"Mom really doesn't need to know this shit!" Margaret fumes.

"What did you do with it?" Matthew asks.

"I threw it out, what the hell do you think?" Margaret slugs Matthew in the shoulder and walks away.

†

The week after Christmas, the family grapevine has it that Mom's going to see a therapist; Dad's back from overseas, according to his itinerary on the bulletin board—probably sleeping on the cracked leather couch at his office, avoiding everyone. I found out walking home from midnight mass with Magdalene that my whole family knows about me, too. I guess they aren't dying to talk about my lifestyle any more than I am.

For now, I'm safely out of Dad's reach, since he's not calling home. And I'm not calling him. He's probably wondering why I haven't phoned him at the office, and I've already come up with excuses to tell him when we finally speak. "I thought you were still away, Dad," or "Every time I tried to call you, Mom would walk in the room." Or "Mr. Sheehan decided to cut our holiday break short for training."

No one has told me whether my parents know I'm the source, and I'm too scared to ask anyone. Tomorrow, Mom's leaving for Boston to be with relatives. Eight hours on I-95 North will be a breeze compared to this nightmare. Boston's bitter winter will surely feel warmer than sleeping alone in their lumpy bed. Margaret told me that Mom's leaving "indefinitely, 'cause she needs some time away to think."

I probably haven't had these kinds of constant anxiety pangs in my stomach since I was trying out for the Olympics. Only seventeen, I was willing to believe anything was possible back then. Now, I'm not so sure. If it weren't for my ingrained Catholic guilt, I would have found a thousand excuses for not having dinner with my mother tonight. But she cornered me this morning at breakfast, and her tone was so full of disappointment that I didn't have it in me to decline her invitation to dinner.

"Tina, you almost ready?" Mom calls up from the second-floor hallway.

I lean over the third-floor balcony, my freshly blown hair hanging like a curtain around my face.

"Coming," I say in my sweetest little girl voice.

Hopping in the passenger side of Mom's car, I find the heavy door nearly frozen and the vinyl upholstery ice cold. I wrap my winter coat tightly around the last conservative dress I own and strap myself in. Everything about my outfit, including Kate's old flats with a bow, feels wrong, but I didn't want my clothes to be the source of any tension tonight. Mom navigates herself into the lopsided driver's seat.

"Sweetie, can you do this?"

She holds out the seat belt—stretched to its limit—and waits for me to take it from her and buckle her in. Our seat belt ritual is much faster than Mom playing blindman's bluff over her stomach, trying to locate the fastener.

We mostly focus on the need for the heater to hurry up and take our chill away as we make the ten-minute drive into Bethesda. As usual, Mom's Irish luck lands us the perfect parking spot, right in front of the rustic front door. The Sir Walter Raleigh Inn—like a lot of restaurants around D.C.— has a red and black colonial décor with white tablecloths and a preppy crowd. The mostly female staff wears frilly aprons over their dresses. The hostess points out the all-you-can-eat salad bar on the way to our corner table.

"Have you dined with us before?"

"Yes, a few times," Mom assures her.

Mom and I settle into the sturdy armchairs at our table for two, reaching for the hardback menus. I know exactly what I'm ordering, but I take my time looking, since Mom doesn't know I was a regular here with Miss Lange. They had to be early dinners, since I was still in grade school. So as not to create suspicion, I'd usually make up some story about how Miss Lange's parents invited me to go out to dinner with them and then pray Miss Lange and I didn't run into any of my family. I think my fallback lie—in case of an emergency—was that her elderly mother had gotten sick, deciding to stay home at the last minute. Lies get confusing, though, when you juggle so many. Once I forgot that I told Mom I was going over to Miss Lange's to be tutored, and so when we were driving on Brookville Road coming back from lunch—out of habit—I ducked down in Miss Lange's front seat when I saw Frances's car approaching. Of course, when I got home Mom wanted to know where I'd been, because my sister had told her I wasn't in the car with Miss Lange. I lied and said I stayed at her house, studying, while Miss Lange ran out to get her mother's medicine.

"What looks good, sweetie?"

"I'm gonna have the prime rib and a side of fries."

"I think I'll go with the surf and turf."

After ordering, we take our large white plates and head for the soup and salad bar.

"I have to try a little of this clam chowder." Mom inhales deeply over the tub of white creamy soup.

"I'll get it for you, Ma. You do your salad."

Taking care of her feels as soothing as a warm facecloth. I soften from the weeks of family tension. Maybe it's my way of saying I'm sorry, but truth is, I've always taken care of Mom. Sometimes, I like being the husband she doesn't have—holding doors, helping her cross slippery sidewalks, carrying her bags, climbing up on the counter to retrieve the instant coffee that got shoved way back in the kitchen cabinet, out of her reach. I feel valuable, useful in that role.

Back at the table, I'm glad the carafe of red wine is waiting. I pour it for us as Mom slathers butter on her pumpernickel bread. The first time I drank wine from these carafes was on my thirteenth birthday, when Miss Lange and another teacher from Blessed Sacrament, Miss Ruben, brought me here to celebrate. Acting cool, I asked to have some of their red wine with my prime rib. They agreed, and we had a merry ol' time. I got drunk, practically hit on Miss Ruben in the ladies' room at the end of the night, and finally, Miss Lange had to take me to Hot Shoppes for coffee to sober me up before dropping me off at 5 East Irving Street.

"*Salute.*" I smile, clinking Mom's glass.

"You sound like your father."

It doesn't exactly sound like a compliment. But I skip over it, the way I've been taught by her—just pretend you didn't hear what you just heard.

"Have you spoken to him?" she blurts.

I shake my head, swallowing a hunk of blue cheese. The important question hangs in the air like storm clouds, dark and determined to wreak havoc. I drink and silently pray she doesn't ask me for more details about my time with Dad.

"You found the salad bar, I see." Our waitress chuckles, looking at our huge salad portions, slices of black bread hanging over the edge of Mom's plate.

"Yes, thank you, it's wonderful." Mom nods, wiping her mouth.

"It's great," I add.

Our waitress leaves and Mom finally looks me in the eye—for the first time since I arrived home for Christmas.

"Tina, you are my child . . . and I love you," she says kindly.

This is the Mom I know. The one who would make me squeal by tickling me with her pointy chin in my neck or burst out in song, a perfect imitation of the beloved Maria von Trapp.

"I love you, too, Mom." It feels so good to tell her again.

"But, sweetie, my faith is also very important to me, and I can't accept what you are doing. It's a sin and goes against my faith. I have to follow what the Church says," she explains.

Her words hurt the same way they did years ago when she mistakenly thought I took money out of her purse. I wipe my mouth on my knit sleeve, realizing what I've done only from her raised bushy eyebrows. Looks like my mom has cut me from the Holy Father's team of good Catholic girls ready to raise their pompoms and spread their legs for good Catholic boys.

The wall between us—a confessional screen shielding straight talk—angers me. *Why can't I just say what I mean and mean what I say?*

"Mom, what about Dad working for the Vatican? Isn't that wrong?" I blurt, knowing I'm avoiding the weight of her words, the hurt. I want to punish, make her see that I'm not the one to judge. Maybe she should judge Dad for all the pain he's put her through. But she's always let him off the hook, given him the benefit of the doubt at her children's expense. I think of her response after Dad slapped me for speaking up in her defense once. "He didn't hit you that hard," she said: a bigger betrayal than his hard hand across my face.

Mom clears her throat. I bite into a cucumber, knowing I've tested her. I bury my anger, allowing only guilt and hurt to surface.

"That's an awfully strange thing to say. Who said your father works for the Vatican?" She's not asking me as much as telling me I'm wrong, mistaken.

Mom ends it right there. Whether she's in denial or not, I can't be sure. But I do know my fears about tonight were way off base. Not a word about Dad and his lifetime of secrets, cruelty, and cheating. No snooping for his dirt, asking questions about our disco nights.

Nope, she's worried I'm going to hell for licking pussy. Enough has been said for one night. Maybe a lifetime. She's made herself clear: doctrine first, daughter second. Maybe she needs time. And maybe I need to get the fuck out of this steak joint. Her disapproving, flushed face considers the one remaining crouton on her plate, then she says, "I just wish you would at least be with someone your own age."

There seems to be no air in my stomach, nothing but a frozen head on top of slumping shoulders. Since it's not okay to be mad at her, everything goes tense. I'm holding back my rage with the force of riot police. *What does she mean? Why does she care how old my girlfriend is? Does age difference make the sin bigger?* I imagine, if I walked into church with Mom right now, she'd suggest I head straight for the confessional. To hell with that. No matter how much I love her, and how much I wish she would just scoop me up in her arms, I can't be different for her. And I won't.

†

Dad stands as I enter the restaurant, wiping his purple-stained lips with a white cloth napkin—a habit he has, even when he's not eating.

"Well, I nearly forgot what you looked like, my dear." He

kisses my lips and immediately helps me with my coat, then calls for the waiter to check it for me.

"Thank you, young man. Danny has been taking good care of me over the holidays," Dad says playfully.

Danny smiles, taking my coat. "Always a pleasure, Sir John."

"And let's get my daughter a glass of red wine. I'll have another . . . and a partridge in a pear tree," Dad teases.

Despite Dad's nearly full wineglass, he always prefers a backlog of alcohol lined up, never leaving a dry moment to chance. I wipe my sweaty palms on my dress pants, eager to take the edge off. No sooner had Mom left for Boston than I heard from him, insisting we have dinner the next night. I've been in complete dread, worried that Mom may have implicated me. But so far, so good; his love for me seems intact, his mood surprisingly upbeat.

"When is Violet back?"

"Thursday."

"Well, let's dine this weekend at the University Club and then hit the bars!" he says, as if everything is normal. As if his wife of nearly forty years hadn't just learned he's been screwing around with men, as if she didn't just pack her bags and leave her home to have some space and time to think. I look around, hoping something will distract me from losing my cool, coughing up the confession I am so desperate to give. Dad catches me in a thousand-mile stare.

"Where are you, love?"

"It's nice here," I cover, continuing to look around, avoiding his eyes.

The brightly lit Hannihan's is much more casual than the typical fine dining restaurants that Dad and I frequent. The large room is quiet, with a few families, some kids, a fat couple sharing some sort of gigantic gooey pie, all surrounded by droopy holiday decorations ready to come down. The thin paper menu feels almost awkward in my hand, as does the list of appetizers: potato skins, popcorn shrimp, and nachos.

"You seem hungry. Shall I order us some appetizers?"

"Sure, Dad," I say, keeping my head down.

Thankfully, Danny's back with our giant goblets of merlot.

"There's our Danny Boy—you're too young to know that song!"

Our waiter smiles, clearly used to Dad's alcohol-laced banter. I wonder if he's hit on him yet.

"Anything else?" Danny asks, holding the serving tray under his thick arm, white dress shirt tight around his biceps.

"Yes . . . why don't you bring us an order of the popcorn shrimp and an order of the potato skins?"

"That's a lot, Dad," I interrupt, still bloated from a week of holiday stuffing.

"And will you be having the Sir John Omelet for your main course?"

"Now, young man, we are going to be taking our time, so don't rush us, we are not ready to order, nor will we be for a very long time. We have a lot of catching up to do. Later— much later—I will in fact be having my usual. In the meantime, just keep a lookout for our wineglasses and make sure there isn't a hole in the bottom."

Dad whacks Danny with his napkin.

After our waiter leaves, I can't help but ask, "The Sir John Omelet?"

"They have put it into the computer, as I've been here nearly every day for my meals. I like that I can walk over from the office. By the way, you should take my car back to the Mount with you so you can get home to see me more often this semester. I don't need it. I'll take the Metro if I need to get somewhere."

I shift the conversation quickly. "How was Rome? Did you see Archbishop Magni?"

"Yes, a good meeting with Magni—although the archbishop's been having some health problems, but I was able to fit in some other Vatican meetings as well."

"With who?" I press.

"Whom," Dad corrects me.

He wipes his mouth and takes a long pause, ignoring my question.

"I trust your mother got off to Boston okay?" he asks, eyes down.

Is that shame?

"She left early yesterday, wanted to beat the rush-hour traffic."

There's a long silence. We drink our wine, then Dad leans in toward me with a half smile.

"What is the family saying about me?"

I shrug, shake my head, my nerves rising. *This is absolutely not going to end well if I don't keep my cool,* I tell myself.

"Nothing," I lie.

"I was glad not to be there for Christmas," Dad says defiantly. "I'm sure the family has sided with your mother, so to hell with them."

I grab my glass, wishing the lights could be dropped along with this topic.

"I'm sure they are talking. Have you heard anything?"

"No . . ."

I feel his eyes on me. He wants something.

I throw him a bone. "Well, everyone knows, of course, but . . . I haven't heard anything else."

He takes a long sip, giving me time to steady my uneven breath.

"I still can't figure out how your mother learned these things." He shakes his head, repositioning his wineglass.

I feel a wave of nausea, afraid of what's coming next.

"Did you know, someone went into my private office and rummaged through my things?"

"Really?" I overact being shocked.

He leans in, as if not wanting our place settings to overhear.

"I will bloody well find out, and whoever did it will be sorry! Those are my private things, and they had no right!"

I nod my head in solidarity.

He goes silent, watching a different waiter deliver food to a nearby table. My head goes light from fear. Dad picks a piece of lint off his navy blazer, his double-faced watch exposed.

"Who do you think did it?" he presses.

A hot flash of panic rises through me, and my palms get sweaty. *Why does he think I know?* I shake my head, smoothing the white tablecloth, trying to get a grip. His tapping finger plays in rhythm with my pounding temples. A heavy weight seems to pin me behind this round table.

"Popcorn shrimp!" Danny announces as if it were as thrilling as a blazing Baked Alaska.

"Thank you. Danny, please do bring us two more glasses of wine," Dad says flatly.

Danny leaves, his black trousers snug around his ass, a white apron string nearly hanging in his crack. I polish off the rest of my wine, and Dad turns the platter closer to me.

"So someone went through your things at the office?" I probe innocently.

Dad nods.

"I had gone up to New York for some meetings with Alitalia, and when I returned my desk and papers were a mess, and someone had the bloody nerve to go through my briefcase."

"Really? Did they take anything?" My voice cracks from the strain of acting.

Dad looks around the room, then leans into the table.

"They took my gay guide to Rome," he whispers.

"Why would she take that?" I react.

From the shock on his face—which must be mirroring mine—I know I have blown it, I have derailed. His eyes blow steam as powerfully as the Orient Express. My face heats up.

"Who's *she*?"

He waits like a death squad, ready to shoot, no matter the answer.

"And don't lie to me!" He slams the table.

Crumbling, I stammer, "Well, I overheard that Margaret and Matthew might have gone to your office to see if they could find proof . . . after she told Mom, I guess."

"You guess? And how did Margaret come to tell your mother ANYTHING?"

I take a giant breath. Fuck.

"I told Mom I was gay . . . and then Margaret started asking me questions."

"What type of questions?"

"Just stuff . . . She asked if you were gay."

He pauses, still as a predator.

"And you said . . . ?" he whispers.

". . . Yes."

He looks around, as if contemplating whether to kill me.

"Did you tell her about your godfather?"

I can't look at him, tears dropping like raindrops near my shrimp.

"I couldn't lie."

He bangs the table, knocking over his wineglass, yelling, "YOU COULDN'T LIE?! YOU COULDN'T LIE?! YOU'VE BEEN LYING YOUR ENTIRE LIFE!"

"Why should we be ashamed?"

"DON'T YOU DARE TALK TO ME ABOUT SHAME, YOUNG LADY. SHAME CAN BE QUITE THE DISCIPLINE!"

"Dad, times have changed!" I cry out.

"NO, DEAR, TIMES HAVE NOT CHANGED. YOU MAY HAVE CHANGED, BUT TIMES HAVE NOT!"

I catch Danny out of the corner of my eye, approaching us. Rubberneckers from surrounding tables stare at our scene.

"Sir John?"

"Not now, Danny!" He waves him off.

Dad leans inches from my face, whispering, "Now, if you choose to discuss your personal affairs, that's your prerogative, but you don't discuss mine!"

"Why did you even marry Mom?!"

His hand rises like in the old days, and I duck, expecting it might land across my face. "IT'S NONE OF YOUR BUSINESS WHY I MARRIED YOUR MOTHER!"

My hands tremble, but still I want to help all of us. Him, me, Mom, my brothers and sisters. Our lives are so horribly tangled.

"Dad, maybe you can go talk to Mom's therapist," I plead, considering for the first time that I might need to lie down on someone's couch, too.

He pounds his clenched fist onto the table.

"Christine, I didn't ask you to dinner TO HAVE A BLOODY PSYCHOLOGICAL EVALUATION!!"

Danny returns with an older man wearing a suit. But before they can speak, Dad turns on them. "I'M LEAVING!" He rises quickly.

Straightening the hem of his blazer as if punishing it, he walks around the table and stands over me. He bends down toward my ear like a vampire preparing to dehumanize me.

"Never speak to me about this again," he threatens.

A chill weaves down my back, as if Charles Manson himself had issued the warning. He marches out. And now all eyes are on me.

22
Baptism

I should pack. But I can't seem to move from my desk, sad and heavy from the August heat. I used to be able to push the chair in without my knees banging the top of the desk. Sitting on the green cushion—faded and worn thin from its years of offering me comfort in grade school—I feel like a stranger in my own bedroom. Once upon a time, I'd sit here, repetitively writing Miss Lange's and my initials inside my denim binder where no one could see. And then in high school I hunched over the oak desk, cramming for Latin exams and writing English papers on *Macbeth* and Keats's "Ode on a Grecian Urn."

"Beauty is truth, truth beauty,—that is all / Ye know on earth, and all ye need to know."

I open my drawer, maybe needing some proof that truth can be beautiful, and pull out Dad's letters and postcards to me. I sort through images from religious sites all over the world—the flip sides written in his left-handed slant, with various airmail stamps. His envelopes feature the Order of the Holy Sepulchre's red crusader cross logo. Their Latin motto reads *Deus Lo Vult*—God Wills It. At the bottom of the drawer is a large manila envelope with my old family Christmas letters in random order. Not surprisingly, neither Mom nor Dad wanted to create a Worthington Wonderland this year. "Dear Friends in Christ, 1984 was a year for the record books. John came out as gay and Anne has begun therapy . . . the end." It would have been the shortest family letter to date. Smart to shelve it.

I'm glad Violet's picking me up soon to go to the beach. Last night, over Ethiopian food, she insisted I needed to get out of town and stop worrying about my parents. She's right. After Mom came back from her sabbatical up north, she moved out of 5 East Irving Street and into her own garden apartment in Bethesda, and I went back to school for the winter semester, with anxiety that's been hanging on like a bad cold.

It was decided that before someone hammers a For Sale sign on our front lawn, Luke will do some renovations, a couple of rooms at a time, so my parents can get more money for the house. Luke's never renovated a house, and from the way he's attacking the walls, I wonder if he's held a lifelong grudge against 5 East Irving Street.

Dad was living here part-time for a while but now spends most nights at the office. Since graduation, I've been here part-time, too, preferring most nights to stay with Violet while I get ready to begin my M.B.A. in the fall.

Between the renovations and a volcano erupting in the family over his behavior, Dad's been traveling even more than usual. I learned from my siblings that a few months ago Dad—with the place to himself—had an out-of-town guest staying here, when one of my sisters showed up in the middle of the day and discovered Dad and his friend wrapped in nothing but towels, as if they had just stepped out of the showers. Or shower. There was no proof of any hanky-panky, but the serious circumstantial evidence blew through the family like a California wildfire.

In case anyone in the family wasn't angry enough at Dad, the outrage was then officially full throttle. *What was he thinking? Even if it was innocent, why didn't he just have the guy stay at the University Club?* I'm afraid to ask, and he hasn't mentioned it. I avoided Dad for much of the semester, and Mom, too, although I made sure to visit her new apartment soon after she moved in to help out and make sure she wasn't feeling lonely. I helped her grocery shop, hang some pictures, and then, like so many times before, she made my lunch. I think making a kid's lunch is one of the nicest things a mom can do. As we scarfed up our tuna on rye with lettuce and tomato, she reached over to a small buffet table and picked up her Bible. And began to read a passage out loud. It was the first time she'd ever read to me from the Bible, and even though I wondered about her motives, I decided to just listen.

I hold on to the corners of my desk, resisting the urge to lay my head down and never get up. Tensing doesn't keep tears from plopping onto my torn, worn blotter, messy from years of doodling. On the paneled wall in front of me hangs my gold medal from the U.S. Youth Games—the red, white, and blue ribbon still tacked securely. Feeling like a loser, I walk across the creaky floor to my dresser. I finish off the bottle of wine I bought on my way home from working out and head for the bathroom.

The pink Formica countertop is covered with trash: old tissues with blotted lipstick, loose blond hair, Q-tips, and blackened cotton balls. Turning on the old faucet, I wish I could just splash away the past. The filth around me is making me sick to my stomach. There's not even a clean towel. In the mirror, a wet and disappointed face stares back. It wants to tell me something, but I'd rather plug in my curling iron and get packing.

Standing in my closet, I sweep through the hangers. I decide my Rehoboth Beach weekend getaway with Violet should be glamorous. There's no reason I can't bring a little bit of fashion to the Eastern Shore. I hold up a peach chiffon brides-maid's gown that I wore in Margaret's wedding, considering its potential. Flipping through my clothes, one of Kate's hand-me-downs—purple psychedelic pants—seems an interesting option. I dash from one sister's bedroom to another, digging through their closets for potential gems. A sixties silk scarf—fallen and forgotten—lies on the floor of Helen's closet. I yank a white wraparound miniskirt off a hanger. The practically invisible stain will be easily hidden with a dab of white nail polish. I scoop up all the finds and take them back to my room, spreading them on my bed. I feel a little lighter, know-ing there is potential for an outrageously stylish weekend far away from Sir John.

†

The cursive red letters, reading DOLLES, tower over the small beach town's main strip. If my eyes were closed and I stuck my head out of Violet's car, I'd know instantly from the smell of fresh caramel popcorn and the salt water beyond that I was in Rehoboth Beach, Delaware. Towns, like people, have their own scent. Dolles and its famous buckets of sweets sit on the edge of the sun-beaten boardwalk, right next door to the shack that's been selling vinegar hand-cut french fries since I learned how to say "french fries."

The Rehoboth boardwalk, sans bumper cars and blaring arcades, is the civilized man's getaway, the place where mon-eyed Washingtonians lather on powerful sunscreen and sip daiquiris on the miles of wide white sandy beaches. Every hot and humid D.C. summer, 120 miles from the steps of Capitol Hill, the Beltway crowd is furloughed here, exchanging their conservative suits for Bermuda shorts and polo shirts. Expen-sive, maybe. Trendy, never.

Violet pulls her car into an extremely narrow parking spot on the main drag—thanks to the self-centered driver of the hunter green truck who thinks it's his or her God-given right to park outside the lines. My mother's fresh-from-the-box Hermès scarf—a guilt-ridden gift from one of Dad's overseas trips—is wrapped around my head, trailing down my back, Cleopatra style. I pop out of the car with an oversized mesh purse I found in Kate's chest of drawers and sashay up to the Dolles walk-up window.

"What would you like, sugar?" A middle-aged local eyes me, like he's got a chance.

"*Grande* caramel popcorn, *monsieur*." I pull my oversized black Ray-Bans down.

My French confuses him. The local gets busy with my order. With my back up against the counter, I check out the crowd, looking for the free spirits. There ain't no way in hell I'd spend the end of summer in this preppy factory if this weren't also a secret gay haven. It started a few years ago with affluent homosexuals from around Dupont Circle and Foggy Bottom who snatched up waterfront beach homes and brought their interior designers along. The "gay beach" is all the way at the end of the boardwalk, as far away from the center of town as possible without being in another zip code. Separate, and not equal.

"Tina!" a woman's voice calls out.

I turn toward the boardwalk, where Miss Lange is waving happily with her same-age girlfriend. Their all-white matching beach garb makes me cringe. I've never understood why some lesbians think it's an expression of true love to dress alike, when in fact it's an expression of horrible taste.

"Hi, Miss . . . hey there, missy," I mumble, at a loss for what to call her.

Missy was reserved for the bedroom, and Miss Lange for whenever we had our clothes on. But I'm now a woman who's sailed the Nile, not a kid carrying no. 2 pencils.

"How are you, Jane?" I finally manage.

I kiss each of her deeply tanned cheeks, aware of her

bad skin and her prematurely gray and dated hairstyle, still sprayed to death, despite the casual environment. She laughs at my new way with her. Her familiar L'Air du Temps perfume reels me in.

"I don't think you two have met. Tina, this is Ingrid. Ingrid, Tina. Tina was—"

"Yes, I know who she is!" Ingrid snaps.

We stand awkwardly in a triangle, halfway between their leisurely walk and my sugar rush. I'm struck by how unattractive Miss Lange is compared to Nic, and Violet, and all the others since her. I wonder if something happened to her face, or was I just blind?

"I never hear from you anymore. Rumor has it you tried out for the Olympics . . . how was it?" Miss Lange places her hand on my arm. Her genuine interest in me switches on an old light, a need to be smart and give her the right answer.

"I didn't make it, but . . . everyone else was much older and more experienced."

"You should be used to that," Ingrid says with a laugh.

"Only when they seduce me." I rub it in her thirty-three-year-old face.

"You wear scarves now?" Miss Lange touches the silk train falling down my back.

"I bought it in Cairo," I lie.

"CAIRO!? You didn't tell me you were going to EGYPT!?"

Her full mouth hangs open the way it might if I forgot to tell her I was getting married.

"I didn't know I had to check in with you before I left the country," I say, my sarcasm as harsh as when she left me at thirteen.

My directness stuns her. And me. I slip my shades back on and glance at the Dolles window to check on my sweets. I can feel my armor melting off in this heat. That twelve-year-old girl-lover still lives behind this grown-up-looking exterior, but I refuse to let Miss Lange know this.

"Well, see ya." I turn to the carry-out window, displaying the biggest bill I have. Sadly, it's only a twenty—not that impressive to the over-thirty crowd.

"All right, munchkin." She kisses my head from behind. I feel her inhale purposefully. My stomach jumps—maybe out of habit, maybe out of muscle memory. I don't know. I withhold a direct good-bye to Ingrid, as punishment for being so unnecessarily rude.

"Thanks," I say, turning to find Violet, rushing to forget the past.

†

Walking down Baltimore Avenue—a quaint neighborhood street with a mix of small shops and well-maintained pastel beach houses—you could walk right past the Blue Moon, a classy cocktail bar, figuring it was another hangout for the heterosexuals who dominate Rehoboth. But a longer look inside the wide French doors would surprise the average Joe. The patrons are almost all gay men, along with a few lesbians and some nonjudgmental straight people.

At first blush, the posh black-and-white floral wallpaper, small colored glass chandeliers, and spotless canary yellow bar stools are a bit shocking for those of us used to entering dirty gay bars through dark alleys, stepping over heroin needles just to enjoy a screwdriver or dance with one another. Violet and I are overdressed, in almost formal attire, having heard the rumors about the sophisticated clientele. One of the things I love about Violet is that she—like me—loves to make an entrance. Earlier, over a bottle of Pouilly-Fuissé from the local wine store, we sat on our balcony at the Windy Sea Motel and got creative with my chiffon gown. First, Violet had to pin the dress, since I'm thinner than I was when I wore it in Margaret's wedding as a teenager.

"I need more of a Jean-Paul Gaultier look," I insisted.

Despite the cheap fabric, and not being black, the gown, thanks to Violet's knack for sewing and my knack for ripping shit up, could now be mistaken for real fashion under the dim Blue Moon lighting. As we arrive, Violet's fitted striped cotton blazer shows enough cleavage to catch the eye of a bunch of queens as we glide hand in hand toward the bar. We make a stir.

"Love your threads," a tall guy oohs as we pass through a pack of sun-kissed boys bopping to Boy George.

Violet sings along loudly.

"Two vodka tonics, *s'il vous plaît*," I say to the buff bartender.

"*Oui*." He smiles.

If I were to guess, I'd say half the guys in this place get their checks from the federal government: lawyers for the Justice Department, or civil servants, or congressional aides, like Violet. And now that I know what I know, I would guarantee there is a priest here—having left his collar and his conscience on a motel dresser nearby. As my mother likes to say, "Only God will judge." I wish she'd said that to me after she learned my secret.

"Cheers, Miss Thing." Violet taps my glass, and we both suck vodka through straws.

The jolt of the vodka, on top of our five o'clock cocktail hour, sets my hands free to roam her ass, as we stand side by side against the bar. My eyes scan Violet's bare legs crossed at the ankles—her open-toe pumps displaying her scarlet nails. Feeling horny, I pull her face toward mine and kiss her passionately. I hold her tongue prisoner in my mouth, while my hand finds the inside of her blazer.

"Ladies, this isn't that kind of place," I hear, as I'm squeezing her nipple.

Busted by an authoritative voice, I turn around, ready to fight for my sexual defiance. A tall, handsome, middle-aged man wearing a bamboo Panama hat giggles. Only his girlish laughter belies his masculine presence.

"My friend and I saw you two girls carrying on over here, and I said, 'Those are my kind of ladies,'" he titters. "I'm Charles," he continues. "This is Billy."

Billy is in his mid-twenties, dark, short, and slim.

"I'm Violet, and this is my sex toy, Tina," she jokes, with an exaggerated drawl.

The guys howl.

"Can I get a Stoli on the rocks, a Heineken, and whatever these ladies are drinking, please?" Charles calls to the bartender. I watch him gracefully pull out an expensive brown wallet from the breast pocket of his dinner jacket.

"Where are you guys from?" I ask Billy.

"Maryland. I live in Bethesda and Charles lives in Chevy Chase."

"No way!" I touch Charles's shoulder. "I'm from Chevy Chase!"

"Where?" he says incredulously, assessing my gown.

"East Irving Street—right around the corner from Blessed Sacrament."

"B.S. is my parish!" Charles laughs.

"You go to mass?!"

"I have a lot to repent for," he says dryly. "But Saint Augustine said, 'Love the sinner, hate the sin' . . . so I guess there's even hope for me."

†

"Can I have two beach chairs and an umbrella, please?" I ask the acned teen manning the wooden shack in the middle of the "family beach."

"Let me carry something." Violet looks sexy and helpless, holding one hand on her sun hat as a hot gust blows.

"Why can't they put the rental shack closer to the gay beach?" I bitch, still nauseous from closing down the Blue Moon last night.

The four of us were barely hanging on to our bar stools when the hot bartender had enough. Charles had been bribing him for an hour—after closing—throwing fifty-dollar bills at him to let us stay. I toyed with him, kissing his tan neck, and tried to playfully seduce him. "Come on, George Michael, let us stay." At 4 A.M., he turned every single light on in the place and tossed us, despite Violet's final wild and drunken appeal—exposing her breasts to him—which delighted Charles and Billy, but not so much the barman. Me, I'm always happy to see them.

The midday heat and my pounding headache irritate me as much as the long trudge through the deep hot sand, avoiding oily teenagers and their rich parents reading political thrillers beneath their umbrellas. There's fifty yards' worth of empty clean sand between the end of the family beach and the rambunctious and preening "boys," who dominate the gay territory. It's as if both groups need time to wipe their feet, or kick up their heels, before entering their private zones.

"Hey, girls!" Charles rushes over, his long, toned legs deeply tan. We learned last night that he's a wealthy lobbyist who spends most weekends at his summer home here.

Billy laughs from a nearby blanket. "How ya feeling, ladies?"

Lying on his stomach, he arches his chest up, keeping his middle firmly planted, like a beached seal. Charles carries our gear to a clear space next to theirs, with the drive of a man who refuses to take no for an answer.

"My wife here made enough lobster rolls to feed all these fags," Charles jokes.

"Too bad, I was hoping for tuna fish," Violet dishes.

"What, you didn't get any of that last night?" Charles teases.

We settle under our umbrella, tossing a ball of dry humor around our foursome, recapping the previous night's wild highlights, and filling each other in on blacked-out moments. We all seem to love sarcasm and sex talk.

"How about Miss Violet showing her hornets for Mr. Barmaid?" Charles giggles.

"WHAT? I did NOT!" Violet screams with indignation.

"The bartender was at a total loss—'Uh, what do I do with THOSE?!' " I imitate.

"Billy, why don't you ever flash your hornets?"

Charles stands over his young lover, nudging his foot toward his crotch. Billy's greasy hands protect his packed Speedo from Charles's hairy toes. My girl relaxes on her colorful striped beach chair, occasionally tucking in what she wants in and pushing up what she wants out. One dip in the Atlantic and we will all get to see what's on the other side of Violet's white bathing suit. As I rub suntan lotion onto her back, I feel Charles's eyes on me.

"Tina, you don't have an ounce of fat on you."

"My baby's all muscle." Violet lets out an exaggerated moan as I rub her shoulders.

"Billy, see what you're missing?" Charles teases.

"Oh, honey, you enjoy it and tell me about it later," he says, yawning.

Now, facedown on my turquoise beach towel, I untie my bathing suit top and slip it out from under me.

"All right, enough of this laying around. Who's getting in the water?" Charles demands.

"You must be kidding, darling, those waves could knock a Thoroughbred over," Violet says, lighting up a Dunhill.

"Let's go." I jump off my towel toward Charles, who eyes my bare chest.

"Like that?! You're going to get a ticket."

"Fuck it. What's the crime? Small breasts?" I shout back, strutting down to the shore.

"Come on, wild thing." He throws his arm around my waist, dragging me into the ocean.

The waves crash hard as we dive, avoiding a wipeout. The

undertow sucks at my legs, pulling me from shore. Surfacing next to Charles, I let out an exuberant scream, and he joins me. He's forty-five but has more energy than most of the young soda crackers on this beach. I'm thrilled I met him.

"Your nipples look as cold as mine," he says, snickering like a nervous schoolboy.

Through aggressive waves, we are hysterical, barely able to keep our heads above water, as we critique everything from a bad toupee to a guy having an impossible time getting out of the water without losing his inner-tube-size shorts. Eventually, Charles and I wobble out of the salt water. As we climb between uneven rows of beach towels, sunken beach chairs, and coolers, Charles grabs my hand, stopping a short distance from our chairs.

"Your body is just like my ex-wife's," he says seriously.

"Is that why you left her?"

"You are too much!" He laughs.

"Seriously, why did you separate?"

"Divorce. Because she's impervious, and all she cared about was her credit line at Neiman Marcus."

"And all you cared about was guys," I scold him.

"I tried not to act on it until we were through . . . but, honey, I like coming in the back door, what can I say."

"Why do you go to mass?"

"I love the Gospels, the Eucharist . . ."

His sincere love of the Church sets my mind off. Maybe I need to atone for outing Dad to Margaret. For ripping my parents' marriage apart. Perhaps there is a way I can escape my overwhelming guilt?

"You have to meet my dad," I tell Charles as we grab our towels.

But my lip quivers at the mention of him. Images around me blur as a thick cover of tears instantly forms. And then my heart sinks. Embarrassed, I try to shake it off and straighten up long enough to collapse into Charles—nothing between our bare flat chests. His cool strong arms wrap me up. I breathe in the smell of coconut and sea salt on his skin.

"It's okay," Charles assures me as Violet rushes over.

"Darlin', what happened? Oh, baby, what is it?"

I bawl, and I bury myself into this stranger who reminds me too much of my father—if Dad had ever held me in the midst of a crying fit. Charles's palm cradles the back of my head. Suddenly aware of my nose running all over Charles's chest, I step back, wiping it away.

Despite my shame, I'm too weak to fight. Violet places me on the blanket while Charles slips his white button-down shirt around me. Billy has even risen from the dead to gawk at my suffering. Violet kneels at my pruned feet, gently cleaning off the sticky grains of sand. I wipe my eyes with the back of my hand, forcing a laugh at my pathetic self.

"I'm sorry . . . I'm fine. I just need a walk."

"Come on, we'll all go," Violet cheers.

"No, no . . . I'll be right back," I assure their worried faces.

Charles extends his hand, lifting me off the sand, and stands close to me while I turn myself into Garbo: floppy hat, black shades, and his long white men's shirt.

The sun has sunk toward the horizon, while the late-afternoon breeze sends chills through me, offering a wake-up call: I have a sunburned face. Walking toward the straight beach, I leave behind the hyper boys and their older, richer caretakers—who are responsibly planning Blue Moon cocktails at seven, followed by dinner at eight. The same full itinerary that Charles has kindly organized for us tonight.

The shoreline shifts from lithe young men in colorful little suits to giddy young girls in bright bikinis. Shockingly, my eyes don't wander. I only want to walk. And walk. If the shore would continue uninterrupted, I'll bet I could walk to New York. Or if I were Jesus, I would walk east across the sparkling diamond ocean—back to Egypt, then across the Red Sea.

Ducking behind a few fishermen throwing out their lines, I

notice the beach has emptied, the day's intense heat now gone. The straight beachgoers have the ease of a life lived well. Not stuffed into a straitjacket of lies.

I imagine a new day—Monday, arriving home.

Kissing Violet good-bye and heading inside 5 East Irving Street, where Dad sits alone at the dining room table. White tapers burning in our special-occasion candelabra; silver tray with chateaubriand for two with new potatoes; his famous alcohol-drenched brown gravy awaiting in a china boat; and a bottle of Châteauneuf-du-Pape breathing easily for hours—like him.

"My dear, come sit," he will say to me.

Slightly uncertain, I will drift to his end of the table, looking tanned and rested in my white sundress.

"You look like Katharine Hepburn, sporty and tan," Dad'll say with great pride, then take my hand and peck it, and hold it against his freshly shaven cheek.

"I have been praying each day since the family found out about me for our Lord to show me how to be a better father and a better husband." His voice will sound sorrowful as he weeps with regret.

"I love you and beg your forgiveness . . . Christine."

An angry wave bangs into me, sending me and my wishful thinking into the tumultuous water. As I sit soaked in the stirred-up ocean, Charles's shirt floating around me, I see her. On the beach. Miss Lange is reading under a large royal blue umbrella—probably her favorite, D. H. Lawrence.

As if I'm back at my grade school desk while she lectures from her fire-engine-red teacher's podium—the one I painted for her—Miss Lange licks the tip of her polished index finger and turns the page. I scan the beach looking for Ingrid. I imagine Ingrid putting her foot down in the sand. "Jane, this is crazy! We came to Rehoboth where there are gay people like us, and you insist on sitting here on the straight beach. I'm tired of living in the closet with you!" Or some such thing.

I wonder if she'll ever step out of the closet? Tell her parents? Stop hiding?

Floating in the suddenly dead sea, I take in my first love until I am full. On the distant horizon, the last of the light tap-dances—a final glow of day, before falling off into the unknown. I consider my life: basketball, sex, booze. Something's missing. I watch the water drip from the hem of my soaked garment, wondering what it is.

23
Cross

Maybe I shouldn't have, but I agreed to cocktails with Dad at the Four Seasons in Georgetown not long after I got back from Rehoboth. I've never been able to say no to him. Or most adults in my life. Saying no isn't popular in my family. Someone will be mad at you, or you'll hurt their feelings, or you will be accused of being selfish.

Being selfish in our house is a mortal sin. Mom—if she ever says no—takes an eternity to do it, hemming and hawing, taking time to render her decision, or apologizing in advance for what might be a "no." I can't recall her ever saying no to Dad, always at his beck and call. I hate this trait in myself. Why am I on my way to drinks with my father, when part of me absolutely wishes I weren't? Am I still burdened by guilt? Do I think this five-star hotel can add a little shine to this messy phase we're in? So far, my betrayal of Dad has created distance, discomfort, but not an end to our relationship.

I leave Violet's car with the valet, having insisted to her that I do tonight with Dad alone, and click my way through the marble lobby. The hotel air-conditioning brings a twenty-degree drop from the sticky D.C. night. The cold feels good, soothing the mild throbbing in my temples. *Here we go.* I enter the lounge, to the left of the front desk area. It's mostly empty except for a small midweek after-work crowd that has formed around the large horseshoe bar. A pianist at a baby grand plays a soft, jazzy rendition of "The Girl from Ipanema." Dad sits by the floor-to-ceiling window, the smirk on his face telling me that he spotted me long before I found him. He stands, looking fresh in a beige summer suit, sport shirt, and no tie, and greets me, as relaxed as I've seen him in a long time. Maybe it's the wine; he doesn't seem drunk, but the edge is off for sure. Maybe it's being newly single.

"On time for a change," he teases. "You must need a drink!"

We kiss on the lips, the scent of his cologne musky but almost sweet.

"You smell good." I smile.

"Paco Rabanne. I quite like it, too. I also picked up a few bottles of perfume on my trip. You should stop by the office and take what you like."

"Thanks, Dad, I will," I say, grateful that we are off to such a calm and civilized start.

"Now, let's get you a cocktail. It's bloody hot out there," he says, pulling out the awning-striped armchair for me.

A middle-aged waiter arrives out of nowhere.

"Good evening, madam. What can I get you this evening?"

"What would you like, dear?" Dad waits as I glance at the cocktail menu.

"I'll have a glass of Moët, please."

Dad turns to our waiter.

"And you can bring me another white wine while you're up," he says playfully.

The waiter walks away as I take in the serene surroundings, trying to think of something to say.

"I don't think we've ever been here together, have we, Dad?"

"Well, it sounds to me like you frequent the place and never invited me."

"No, no, Dad, I'm just saying . . ."

"I know what you're saying, my dear. I'm only joking with you. But it has been too long since I've seen you. I can't tell you the last time I've been out to the bars."

"You can always take a cab," I state with more chill than I meant.

He looks away, tracking down our waiter with his eyes, as if to say, let's drink first. Dad's never been a selfish drinker; he's always equally concerned that you have your drink as much as that he has his. Our waiter arrives and I await Dad's toast.

"Here's to the gods. We won't save any libations for them tonight. They can buy their own bloody drinks," he declares defiantly. "Now, tell me how you have been and what trouble you've gotten yourself into lately."

I shake my head. "Not much. Violet and I went to Rehoboth for a few days, and I'm just trying to get back in shape before preseason practice starts up in September."

"When do you start classes?"

"There's a short orientation for all the M.B.A. students on August 30th, and then classes begin the next week."

"So, you have a little time. Maybe we should plan a trip. Get out of town ourselves. Violet can join us, perhaps, fly over to Greece. I can spend a few days with you girls and then head on to Rome."

"I don't think I can, with everything going on . . ."

"Everything? What's everything?"

I drink my champagne, wondering if I should share what happened at the beach. Would he just dismiss it as weak, or something six thirty mass or a tea dance could shake off? I'm not him. Whatever happened to me on that beach has left me shaky and wondering if I need help.

"I've been thinking about going to therapy," I confess, unable to look at him.

"Oh God, not you too! My dear, there is nothing wrong with you. Has your mother talked you into this?"

His anger is palpable as he wipes his mouth with the cocktail napkin in disgust.

"No, no, not at all. I don't know . . . I was just thinking that maybe, you know, talking about stuff . . ."

"What *stuff*?"

I hesitate. My jaw tightens, clamping down on the ugliest secret. Persistent, that dark voice commands: *Say it.*

"Dad, there's something that happened in the family . . ."

"Oh, let them talk, Christine, it's none of their damn business. I don't regret one single thing. And you shouldn't either."

"That's not what I mean." My voice is shaky. "When I was little—nine, ten, eleven—Luke and Simon used to bother me."

I swallow hard, hoping the burn in my throat will disappear. "They abused me."

I hate that word. It's the most uncomfortable-sounding word in the universe. A word that, when spoken, nearly always causes someone's face to pinch, or clench, or nearly gag with disgust.

But Dad's face is hard to read. He puts his glass down. He bites down on his cheek, maybe at a loss for words. Or maybe clamping down on some emotion. Is that a smirk I see, or pain?

"Why didn't you tell me?"

My body trembles as if it can't sustain the intensity, or the enormity, of the answer to that question. I feel a swell of anger toward him for his absence and terrifying dominance. I decide in a nanosecond that this isn't the time to explain that he was the scariest person on the planet to me as a little girl. That as a rebellious teenager, I still walked on eggshells, with shoulders hunched and squeezed, as if tension might have a shot at protecting me from the avalanche of his daily rage. An angry voice barks in my head: *Are you now telling me I had an out and I didn't take it?* I can't tell if the little demon is angry at me or him.

"I don't know why," I eke out.

"Does your mother know?"

I shake my head.

"I wish you had told me. I would have beat the living hell out of them," Dad boasts angrily.

Ah, maybe that's one reason I didn't tell him. I heard about the beatings Dad used to give Luke when I was still a baby. He'd take Luke into the basement and beat him with a belt. No one has ever explained why, other than suggesting possible theories: Dad did what was probably done to him as a kid. Luke must have reminded Dad of himself. I don't need therapy to tell me that Dad was the last person I was going to tell back then. Strange, then, that he's the first family member I've told.

"I beat Faid when I heard what he did to your sister Helen, and sent him back to Jerusalem to live. And I would have damn well knocked the hell out of those boys, had I known."

I sit speechless, considering his reaction, rockets of memories firing. I never met Faid, the Palestinian boy Mom and Dad adopted from Jerusalem. He became part of the family until he molested Helen, and then Dad sent him packing, after a good beating. Luke and Simon were over eighteen and well over six feet tall when they started abusing me, so there's no way in hell Dad was going to beat them, although it's a nice thought. I look for our waiter, hoping another flute of champagne will flush this moment out of my system. Dad notices and gives him a wave. I watch the pianist settle back at the glistening ebony piano after a short break.

"Do you have a request?" I ask Dad, attempting to avoid another Rehoboth-like meltdown. My watery eyes stay fixed on the elegant piano scene. I feel desperate to get up and walk around, to flex my legs. I feel like kicking off these sandals and running barefoot through Rock Creek Park all the way home. Dad looks at me with a sorrowful expression on his face. Reaching across the table, he takes my hand.

"'Look at me. I'm as helpless as a kitten up a tree,'" he sings softly and beautifully, as uncontrollable tears plop down my face.

Dad digs into his breast pocket, pulls out a white hand-kerchief, and hands it to me. As I wipe my eyes, the smell of him is overwhelming. There's an antiseptic quality to all of Dad's scents: Listerine, white wine, cologne, Binaca mouth spray, aftershave lotion, and multivitamins. A manufactured cleanliness consistently pours out of him and lingers on his linen handkerchief. It's impossible to be this close to him and not be enveloped.

I take my hand back. Still wanting to make a request of the tuxedoed pianist, I need to walk away from him. Take a moment. Take a breath. Something has changed, as if I've been wearing the tightest suit ever designed, and a few buttons just popped. Now there's breathing room. As I glance back at him gulping his wine, I can't pretend anymore that he's not the real problem, the seed that started this mess.

†

After a few weeks at Violet's, I decide to slip home while Dad is still out of town to pack up the last of my things. Next week, I'll be starting my master's degree courses and any minute now Luke might knock down every wall in the house. Mom cleared out her favorite religious icons from the dining room ledge and even her portrait above the fireplace, the one of her dressed in her black Knights of the Holy Sepulchre cape and black veil over her coiffed hair.

Only Dad's portrait remains, way left of center. Climbing down the third-floor steps, I carry a recent postcard from Dad that someone—probably Luke—left on my chest of drawers. The fact that my brother was in my room stirs a soup of anger.

The glossy picture on the postcard is San Pietro in Vincoli—

St. Peter in Chains, a Roman basilica, home of Michelangelo's *Moses*. I'm pretty sure—if my decade of religion classes serve me—it went something like this: Peter, the head of the church, got thrown in the slammer by Herod and bound in chains. Then an angel came to him in the night, tapped him on the shoulder, and the shackles fell off, doors opened, and voilà, Peter escaped. I flip the postcard over:

> *My Dear Christine,*
>   *My love, prayers, and special blessings are with you always in the Joy, Happiness, and Peace you seek in Life—be not afraid. God's love for you is far greater than mine could ever be. Remember always "Love isn't Love 'til you give it away." So keep giving!*
>   *The Lord Bless you and keep you. The Lord make His Face shine upon you. The Lord give you His Peace.*
>   *In my prayers for you today,*
>   *Dad*

His Catholic gibberish bullshit—"Bless" this and "Lord" that, "peace," "love," and "joy"—pisses me off, and I toss the card down on the stairs.

In the second-floor hallway, the air is still sweltering, and I stop to wipe a trickle of sweat off my face with my shoulder. On the paneled wall, Dad's favorite wooden crucifix hangs crooked above the light switch just outside Simon's room. The hypocrisy infuriates me. The sight of Christ's splayed and abused body—half naked, oozing pain—ignites a pilot light within me. A swell of rage rises in my legs, and my hands fill with heat. I drop my oversized gym bag and suitcase and swing at the cross, which falls to the carpet with a quiet thud. I yank Simon's bedroom door closed, not feeling like looking in there right now.

The knots in my stomach twist tighter as I'm pulled toward my parents' bedroom. The bottom of my high-top sneaker meets the middle of their partly open door, and with one ka-rate kick, I take the room as if I'm facing my opponent after a flagrant foul.

The smell of Dad's vitamins is nauseating, fueling my disgust with him. I fling open his closet door and shove his elegant suits up against the wall. I can feel the silk pulling against the rough skin on my fingers. Hanging in the corner, a clear plastic bag covers his Knights of the Holy Sepulchre cloak.

"I don't give a shit the pope knighted you. No one is infal-lible," I mumble, slamming the closet door.

Mom forgot to pack her powder blue slippers, the once fluffy heels now worn down flat. A dried-up pink facecloth rests on an old *Ladies' Home Journal,* the cover now warped. I imagine her packing, fast and silent, and a dull ache climbs into the back of my throat. *Was she really shocked when she heard the news? Did she escape from this nightmare in shock or did it only confirm what a woman must feel when her husband is constantly cheating? Didn't Mom notice him flirting with all those waiters and priests and my godfather, for God's sake!?* If I weren't so worried about hurting her feelings, I would ask her: "Mom, were you really that clueless?" Fact is, she missed all kinds of evidence. But, no more. Mom can't pretend not to know the truth about her husband.

I turn toward Dad's side of the room. His immaculately laid-out rosary beads would be the perfect thing to strangle him with. Unless I wanted to crack his skull with the alabaster icon of Francis of Assisi standing guard next to his lamp.

His prized wooden kneeler, with permanent imprints of his knees, begs to be cast out the back window straight into the pool. I jerk open his bedside drawer. *The Loneliness of the Long-Distance Runner* is bookmarked with the Lord's Prayer. I toss the prayer card into the drawer.

On Dad's tall Danish dresser with small silver knobs sits the mission jar—the oversized ocher jar that used to sit on the dining room table, awaiting our pennies, now filled with hundred-dollar bills. Wishing he were here to witness my defiance, I stuff a few into my denim shorts.

"Where does all the money come from, Dad?"

With a swing of my forearm, I clear the dresser of everything. The ceramic bowl that Nic and I brought him from Santorini breaks against the wall, and sparkling cuff links and loose change fly across the room.

"FUCKER!" I shout, ripping pastel shirts—custom made in Bangkok—out of a drawer, flinging them around the room, pulling at their seams. My chest and shoulders strain and shake as I tear at a sleeve. I grunt as I shot-put a summer sweater into the spreading disarray. I could give a shit that my elbow burns from a bad throw. Even if my right hand were hanging broken and limp from my wrist, I'd smack him in his clean-shaven, hypocritical face right now.

Peeling strands of hair off my sweaty face, I pause before yanking his top drawer out of the dresser, heaving the entire teak box across the room. The sound of cracking satisfies something in me. The broken drawer lies beside his kneeler, a splinter jutting out. It would make the perfect spike if one were going to nail someone to a cross. Blood trickles from the side of my hand. I suck on it, catching my breath.

"Maybe you shouldn't have dumped your secrets on me," I hiss to his phantom presence.

Moving toward the door, I nearly step on the plastic container packed with everyone's baby teeth that Dad's been saving since the first one came loose. He became obsessed with every shaky tooth, compulsively checking our mouths to see if one was ready to pull. Assuming none got lost over the years, there must be 260 little fangs enmeshed in there.

I hate myself for putting up with him, for biting my tongue my whole life, for agreeing to be his confidant . . .

I kick the plastic chamber, sending the rotting enamel nubs flying, and a shocking red passport catches my eye, peeking out from the overturned drawer. The cover has a familiar gold-embossed coat of arms. Inside is a Vatican passport. *Who the fuck do you have to sleep with in St. Peter's Square to get one of these?* Hands shaking, I turn over page after page, all filled with crammed ink stamps—barely room for another trip. I turn to go, but find my foot connecting hard with the fallen drawer in the center of the room, splaying white handkerchiefs, undershirts, and more passports.

Jordan. My head spins. That's where he met the infamous Omar.

I paw through his meticulously pressed boxer shorts and catch a flash of another passport, then his native British passport, and an American passport on the bottom. Panicky, I flip them open, scurrying through the pages until I see his picture. Despite minor age differences in the photos, his clear skin and flattop are consistent. Staring at his image, I wonder what he does in all these countries. Does his secret work for the Vatican allow him to sweep through customs with a wave of his red handkerchief? His blank green eyes looking back at me bring a swell of pain into my chest. My body collapses into the carpet; I tip to my side and roll into a ball. Tears fall despite a bellyful of anger at all that he withheld from me. And all that he didn't.

Climbing to my knees, I pick up an unopened box of white handkerchiefs—a gift I gave him for Christmas the year we began our secret life together. Despite Dad's strict refusal of gifts, he accepted mine. I open the chic black box, pull out the fine linen, and clean up my face, then throw it into the pile of shit and walk out. My hand drips blood as I shut my parents' door, out of breath. I want to go. But the entrances to Luke's and Simon's rooms stop me. I can't remember every detail of every single time. There were so many encounters throughout the house with both Luke and Simon. But way too many are perfectly clear.

Standing breathless in the hallway, spent, I could run a marathon. Move to the other side of the world. Walk across the country. Get a fake passport and disappear. Kill someone.

"It's time to leave," a voice inside commands.

My adrenaline wants more fighting, more revenge, but I listen to the stillness instead.

"Leave, now."

I hate being told what to do, even by me. Whoever this me is.

I walk past my parents' door, giving it a final look. On the hall floor is the crucifix, looking sad and raw. It wasn't Christ's fault he was abused and nailed to a piece of wood. Staring at his nearly naked body, I wonder if Christ ever felt ashamed of being so exposed, so helpless. The Gospels preach forgiveness. Not sure I'm ready for all that, though.

I place the crucifix back on the wall and carry my bags down to the first floor, leaving behind bad boy behavior, and a bad marriage, and all the pain it leaked into our family. My baggage is heavy enough without taking theirs with me.

Landing in the foyer, I plunk down my bags. Reaching into my jean pocket, I pull out the house key, dangling from a silver basketball chain, and place it on the china cabinet next to Dad's leather gloves—his only winter outerwear. "Real men don't wear coats," Dad would brag as he'd step out into frigid air in a sport coat and these gloves.

Our house, which had once vibrated with energy morning, noon, and night, now has no pulse, like the Roman catacombs, only a few signs of Christianity remaining. I linger on the only female statue left in the place—a sculpture of the Virgin Mary resting on an alabaster pedestal.

I open the front door, pausing, bags balanced like a giant scale. Then I step out.

Click.

Standing outside on our blue-gray porch, I see the edges peeling, the dust underneath the railings piled high from intrusive carpenter bees. Climbing down the front steps, I see the initials of all my siblings faintly etched in the cement from many moons ago.

Sitting on one of my suitcases on the redbrick sidewalk, awaiting Violet's arrival, I am happy that the high humidity is a thing of the past, that the summer has ended, and that I am no longer the last one home. I've been protecting adults since I was a child. It's time to grow up, time to face their ugly truths. And mine.

24
Purification

2005

Clutching crumpled, disintegrating wet tissues in my warm fist, I try to get a grip. I'm stuffed up beyond being able to smell the floating incense. It's taken me until now—in my early forties—to stop faking the words to prayers that I don't know. Uninterested, I don't even bother opening the mass book. Instead, I stare at shreds of my Kleenex lying on the ancient stone floor by my high heels. The three-inch black stilettos look out of place inside the modest Church of the Pater Noster on the Mount of Olives, where Jesus—probably barefoot or in sensible sandals—prayed to his father. To my right, Peter, my devoutly Catholic nephew, puts his hand on my shaking shoulder, then hunts down more tissues from family members sitting in the pews behind us.

From the front row, I breathe in the echoing sounds of my siblings' sniffles and soft cries, which ricochet off the hard surfaces of the church. The lone piece of fabric—a lace altar cloth that lies underneath Mom and Dad's urns—doesn't have a prayer of absorbing the heavy sounds of our loss. The thick stone chapel walls protect us from Jerusalem's hot November sun but not the pain of having lost our parents, whose ashes we will leave on this holy ground—arguably the most sacred place on earth. Dad had said for years that he would be buried in Jerusalem, but we have no idea how he secured a place in this fourth-century church—behind gates, where the founder of the church is the only other person buried— and for our mother, too. To be laid to rest on the Mount of Olives, somebody at the top must have had to pull some serious strings. This is where Jesus taught the Lord's Prayer to his disciples, after all.

As the Worthington clan and a small group of mourners conclude the hymn, and my longtime partner, Gina, gracefully mills around, capturing the service on our mini camcorder, a thought grips me: I'm an orphan. Death may close a door, but burials lock it. No way, nohow, no matter. It's over. They are gone. I may have spent much of my life acting as if I was on my own, but now it's real. Thank God for Gina's ease with me, my family, my past, my edge. She's supported my healing while exploring her own. I guess what has kept us together for so long is the deep acceptance of each other. We first met while we were still in our early twenties, neither ready for a commitment. But then, as if we were acting out the final scene from a Nora Ephron movie, we bumped into each other six years later on a tree-lined West Village street and learned we lived on the same block. We had never stopped thinking about each other. Within a month, we were cohabitating in my co-op. She became my number-one fan when I decided I should throw away a six-figure fashion job to begin an acting career. Her kindness, ease, and goodness are a balm to my deep scars. Her artistic, take-it-as-it-comes vibe and head-turning Mediterranean beauty a constant pull.

Mom passed first—in 2000—then Dad five years later. The doctors were right when they found the large mass on her pancreas and told her, "You have about six months to live." In L.A., pursuing a brand-new acting career and a healthy lifestyle by then, I received a call from Margaret with the bad news. Gina took the message while I was at class. When I walked into our apartment, I saw that she had absentmindedly doodled the word *cancer,* along with other strange words, on scrap paper next to the phone.

I knew instantly it was Mom.

For the past six years, since moving to the West Coast, I'd been distant with both of my parents—taking space in order to heal. Soon after arriving I stopped drinking and made a vow not to be in Dad's presence when he was drunk—a sort of atonement to myself. I'd travel home from L.A. but avoid him, turning down his invitations to dinner or lunch because I knew they meant booze. I was starving for sober relationships, despite their intense awkwardness, after so many years of equating socializing with lots of alcohol.

He would say, "Would you like to go out for a drink?"

I'd say, "No, Dad, I don't drink."

He'd look at me like I'd just broken his heart.

I stayed away from Mom, too, finding it hard to accept her decision in 1995 to get back together with Dad. He was having some heart issues, had blown through most of his money from his half of the sale of 5 East Irving Street, and had been calling Mom for years with his intoxicated serenading of "Edelweiss." She finally succumbed to his sound of music, and they moved into a modest rental in Kensington—the poor man's Chevy Chase, albeit a sweet upscale neighborhood. He moved Holy Pilgrimages into the basement of the brick rambler to save on rent. Mom insisted they have separate bedrooms, yet he still treated her too often like his verbal punching bag. From my siblings, I knew she'd learned to have her own busy and fulfilling life, separate from Dad's, and even set boundaries when he got ugly. Knowing I disapproved and was deeply immersed in therapy and a new acting career—both of which I was getting a very late start on—Mom trod lightly with me, sending loving cards but never pressuring me to come home. She tried to soften my judgment of their reconciliation, explaining that she and Dad shared a deep faith and prayed the rosary regularly; but mostly, she believed in the sacrament of marriage, her vow of for better or worse.

Their relationship didn't belong to me; it was none of my business, really, but I still struggled with both of them for different reasons. I blamed her for not protecting me, him for everything else. To her credit, a year before her diagnosis, she flew to California and spent Christmas with Gina and me—an incredibly loving gesture. I think it was her way of trying to make things right. To my credit, I stayed away while I cleaned up my act, doing my best not to lash out at either of them, trying to learn how to see them as people and not just my parents. But, no matter, I never stopped adoring Mom.

Dad, as always, was more complicated.

My two brothers are another story. Suffice it to say, I not only told my father about the abuse, but I also released my anger on them via letters. Maybe I hadn't told my dad when he was still in a position to do something about it because I knew he would have made good on his threat to "beat the living hell out of them." And even in the pain of it all, I didn't want that. They were my family. And frankly, they'd paid more attention to me than he ever had when I was a kid. In other words, it was all too complicated to solve with a simple beating.

Apologies were forthcoming from Mom, and from my brothers, who admitted to witnessing and experiencing the abusive behaviors they had emulated. Confronting and discussing the dirty laundry wasn't easy—it never is—but exposing the truth removed the poison. And then the rest was up to me. I've devoted more than two decades to healing what, frankly, some said could have killed me or at least left me in a dire emotional hole. And it's been worth it. I climbed out and away from the dark, musty world of secrets.

†

During the final six months of Mom's life, I went home frequently, mostly alone, and for the first time since leaving 5 East Irving Street, I stayed at my parents' home. My way, I guess, to start making things right—despite the gut-wrenching sadness and longing I felt being in that strange new house, with the windowless basement echoing with the sounds of Dad's short temper and a placating secretary, the one business phone ringing periodically, and an occasional fax sputtering through—a long way from his Dupont Circle office and his formerly large staff. He did keep traveling, though, mostly to Rome and Jerusalem, but no longer jet-setting and fine dining. Archbishop Magni had retired and the money, from what I could see, had stopped flowing, although the alcohol never did.

Gina and I flew home for Mom's last Christmas, staying at Helen's and cooking the Christmas meal for my parents. I even attempted a chocolate soufflé. Their age and Mom's sickness changed everything—well, most everything. Dad still was requesting that he and I go to dinner—code for "let's go out and party." I finally got annoyed and reminded him, "Dad, I don't drink anymore." There was tension with him, but with Mom, all had to be forgiven—the end was drawing near.

One day as she sat in her recliner in the tiny, always overheated den alongside Dad's matching chair, I had an almost obsessive-compulsive need to wash Mom's feet. I have no idea why. But I had to.

Kneeling at the foot of her chair, I took off her worn slippers and placed her tired, callused feet into the rubber foot basin and washed them with Dad's hard English soap, then clipped her toenails.

Silently, she sat upright—for a change—in her upholstered chair, accepting my love. It may have been the closest I'd ever felt to her, the most grown-up, the most generous.

"This is real service," Mom said appreciatively as I lathered on lavender lotion—her favorite.

I smiled, lost in the ritual.

"It's not every day your baby washes you," she choked out, a single tear running down her cheek. I squeezed everything inside, doing my damnedest not to fall apart, not to let her see how awful it was for me that she was dying. I clenched my teeth, forcing a half laugh, pathetically. Then all at once, I fell onto her lap, my face on her soft middle, a river of tears dripping onto her pink floral nightgown. Her arthritic hand petted my long hair.

"I'm always going to be right in your heart," she promised.

We stayed connected—my head to her belly button—the way we began. I didn't want to move. Ever.

"Tina, underneath my chair is a box of coffee Nips. Would you like one?"

I knew she did, so I nodded against her stomach and lifted my head. She wiped my tears.

I reached my arm underneath the recliner, pulled out the tin box, and offered her one, but she shook her head. "It is really too bad . . . now that I can eat anything I want, I have no appetite."

Cancer had thinned her out, even her legs, but they were still raw from decades of being on them while she carried thirteen babies, peeled countless potatoes, did endless laundry, and cleaned house.

As the end neared, there must have been more than fifty people holding vigil, crammed around her bed and down the narrow hallway—her children, grandchildren, Dad—praying the rosary at all hours of the day and night.

In a brief moment alone with her, Gina and I sat in silence, other than Enya playing softly in the background. I held her hand while the morphine dripped and whispered, "Jesus loves you, Mom," still desperate to comfort her, saying anything that might take away her pain.

Out of nowhere, Dad burst into the room—as if he were arriving at the Lost and Found—and grabbed her feet, roughhousing, tickling, and teasing her. "You aren't sleeping, Mother. Come on, it's time to wake up, wake up!"

If not for the utter shock of his behavior, I might have strangled him with my bare hands.

"Dad, she's sleeping!" I begged.

Decades had passed, and even with so many years of therapy, there I was once again trying to protect Mom from him, as if I were still that kid at 5 East Irving Street. Still mediating their relationship, as I had when I was the last one living at home.

Death is the ultimate neutralizer of resentment. I forgave them and myself.

†

Dad, now in his eighties, stayed in the rental house in Kensington after Mom died, traveling despite getting weaker and unable to hold the liquor that he refused to give up. Still in Los Angeles, I called him weekly, and soon after Mom's passing, made a trip home, agreeing to stay with him at the house. The first night, Dad was weak with a chest cold, and as he sat in his recliner in the den, we ate a simple dinner I'd made of meat loaf and mashed potatoes. His hand shook, his fork unable to find his mouth without massive effort.

"Dad, let me help you," I said.

He relented without any argument. As he accepted my feeding, we remained quiet, the familiar nightly news playing in the background.

"Dad, did you really work for the Vatican?" I questioned gently.

His full mouth worked the potatoes as his eyes came to life—a sparkle like I hadn't seen in twenty years.

"Yes, my dear," he said, as if it were as obvious as his wrinkled skin.

I nodded, offering him another forkful.

" 'Edelweiss, Edelweiss, every morning you greet me,' " Dad sang.

And that was as far as we went. His body language, as much as his failing health, put me on my heels. I was afraid of upsetting him by asking too many questions. My love for him grew deeper, but my fear of his disapproval never left. There was an unspoken rule between us: we only revealed what we wanted to reveal and neither ever pressed the other for more. He always did value discretion as much as he did table manners and gracious living.

After a couple of days, Dad took a turn, and it started getting weird like *The Twilight Zone*. He began hallucinating and seemed to be suffering from dementia—often lying on the couch, thinking one of the grandchildren was a nun, despite not wearing a habit or even a hat. Dad would believe he was at the Vatican—attending mass at St. Peter's Basilica, meeting one of the popes—despite being in his plaid robe. He got out of control, leaving the house, insisting his nurse stop following him, and eventually she had to call the police, and they had to bring him home.

Two years after Mom passed, Dad's twenty-four-hour care became too expensive. Not one of his children offered to take him in. We decided to put him into assisted living, at Saint Gabriel's Home, where he was put on an antipsychotic medication. Surprisingly, that turned him into a very sweet old man—most of the time.

On his final trip to Lourdes, to celebrate the fiftieth anniversary of his Pilgrimage for the Disabled, Gina and I decided to go along, with a number of my siblings, to honor the tireless work he had done for those less fortunate.

We had a wheelchair for him, which he refused, except one night when Helen, Gina, and I convinced him to let us push him to a family dinner my oldest brother was hosting for all of us. We came to a steep incline, and he insisted he would walk as it would be too hard for us to push him up the hill. We argued.

"Dad, sit down!" I finally yelled.

And he left the chair as if he were twenty-one, not eighty-one, and marched up the hill, leaving the three of us and the wheelchair behind. We followed him like spies, from a distance, still unsure how to handle him. He was not headed in the direction of the restaurant.

"Gina, you go talk to him," Helen said. "Maybe he'll listen to you since you aren't one of his children."

Gina chased after him, and when she finally joined us at the restaurant, we were all relieved that Dad was with her. Sitting at the long table, I leaned in to speak quietly.

"What happened?" I asked her.

"He didn't want to come to dinner. He told me, 'My children don't care about me, that's why they put me in a bloody home. They never would have put their mother in a home,'" Gina reported.

He was right that we would never have put Mom in assisted living; we would probably have been fighting over who she would live with. But the rest Dad was wrong about. Despite a lifetime of cruelty to and betrayals of all of us, Mom particularly, his family did care for him and loved him in whatever ways we could. No, not always with tenderness, but with kindness. The way he taught all of us to treat the sick, the poor, and the less fortunate. He got in return what he once wrote to me in a letter: "Love isn't love until you give it away."

I made a trip home to be with him the following summer and took him for a few weeks to Helen and her husband Mike's new home. One day we sunbathed by the glistening freshwater pool, stretched on lounge chairs in our suits, Dad still working his usual Speedo. We were finally at peace together. I'd for-given him and was grateful for this time together. He was old enough, and medicated enough, and finally grateful enough, having known real loneliness in his life.

"Do you want to go for a swim?" I said, smiling.

His eyes got wide, like a child.

"I thought you'd never ask, my dear," he teased.

We went together, hand in hand, to the pool steps and slowly descended into the cold water. I was nervous he might have a heart attack, or just be too frail to stay afloat. So I stayed close, allowing him to be free but remaining vigilant.

"Let's stay in the shallow end, Dad," I encouraged.

"Now what fun would that be?" he insisted, and began kicking toward the deep end.

I chased him down, doing my best to check my fear and just let him be. As he trod water in the middle of the deep end, he laughed and gasped for more breath, clearly exhila-rated by the cold water.

"I can't believe it, I truly can't believe it, this is marvelous, I just can't believe it. I'm in the water," he exclaimed with a euphoria that I had never witnessed before.

Dad became weaker, with more dementia, over the next few years, finally having a stroke. There were so many close calls and false alarms that I nearly missed saying good-bye. His eyes never opened, but he squirmed and moaned when I whispered into his ear. He knew I had come. Thank God.

It was five years after Mom that Dad passed.

And now we have brought their ashes together, to be bur-ied side by side.

Four priests in white robes walk onto the altar from a side door. Their black dress shoes smack loudly, like a film clap-per, until they settle around the altar stone—a rectangular slab where a large Bible rests along with two glowing church candles in wooden holders. A single floral arrangement at the foot of the altar includes fronds from a palm tree—flora native to Jerusalem and my backyard in Hollywood. Tears cloud my sight again over the memory of thirteen children carrying fronds home from church on Palm Sunday, then slipping them behind the religious paintings that hung throughout our house. Easter was a sacred holiday in the Worthington house: Dad was obsessed with the Crucifixion; Mom was passionate about both the Resurrection and making sure she tossed equal amounts of pastel-colored malted milk balls in everyone's Easter basket.

"Aunt Tina, it's awesome the patriarch of Jerusalem is saying mass, huh?" my nephew whispers.

"Who's the patriarch?"

"Like the most powerful Catholic in the world—next to the pope," he explains.

I look up at the priest standing in the center, finally noticing he's wearing a red skullcap. The olive-skinned patriarch is also a cardinal. *Who requested him to say the mass? The pope? Someone in the Holy Land? Did Dad know the patriarch? Did he run secret missions for him, too?* When it comes to my father, there are always more questions than answers.

"We are here to pray for the souls of John and Anne Worthington," the patriarch says. His Arabic accent brings back memories of Dad's ties to the Middle East—constant comings and goings to the Holy Land; our trip to Amman, just the two of us. And all my bad behavior in those years. There's so much I should have asked him. Things that no one had the nerve to question—even me, his partner in crime.

As I stare at the two wooden boxes containing my parents, I consider all the mysteries locked inside. Tears stream, dripping onto my black blazer. We are a family that trades in secrets. And like my father, I was a world-class champion. But now, I want answers. I want people in this Church of Our Father to stand up and say what they know about Sir John. The Arab men sitting in the back. Longtime friends? Associates? A Vatican connection? I don't see anyone who looks like Hassan. If that's even his real name. Would I even recognize him? If I were to speak my truth, tell my story about all that Dad and I did together, I might be crucified. Called a liar, a traitor, Judas. How dare I? Many standing before me would prefer to bury the whole truth along with those boxes, deep in the ground. Just tell part of the story. But I can't. I'm tired of the partial tales.

My father, despite his many flaws, deserves to be all of himself in death, since he couldn't be all of himself in life. I told his secret once. Someday, maybe I'll finish the story.

Epilogue

A few years ago, I stopped being so polite, and careful, and cautious. I began asking questions, trying to piece together what Dad really did for the Vatican. I came upon my father's little black book, and I mean little—three inches by two inches, and thinner than a slice of pumpernickel. I recall he carried it inside his breast pocket at all times, along with his linen handkerchief.

I had taken the black book as a keepsake—along with a few other items. I'd been home visiting in 2002 and Margaret had been clearing out the drab basement where Dad had become a one-man shop, barely able to get out one or two pilgrimages a year. Between the toll of alcoholism and his lifelong excessive-spending habit, he and his business were both shadows of their former selves.

The Vatican connections were long gone, too. In 1986, Dad's point person at the Vatican, Archbishop Magni, retired as papal nuncio of Italy. After that, Dad's travels diminished significantly. The way Dad drank, who was going to trust him with their secrets now?

The day I helped Margaret sort papers, there were no briefcases, no stashes of money, and no foreign passports. Only remnants of his glory days of 500,000 miles a year, traveling around the globe in service of the Holy See on a Vatican passport remained. I did uncover an autographed photograph to Dad from Francisco Franco, the fascist and passionately anti-communist dictator of Spain from 1939 to 1975. At the time, I found it odd, not connecting the dots to my father's work until recently, when I began combing through his address book, where I found the names of men, mostly, from all over the world: Egypt, Athens, Bangkok, Berlin, Tokyo, Spain, Poland, and the USSR—handwritten in Dad's lefty slant.

Using the Internet, I tried to track down any leads that might connect me to Dad's hidden work. Now, Dad and his contemporaries would be in their nineties. One after another, I discovered priests and contacts, including Magni, were gone.

One day, I landed on the inside back cover, where I honed in on numbers that I had dismissed a half dozen times before, since there were no names. On closer examination I saw there were four sets of numbers with a letter in front of each, such as R4 L6 R15 L1 and L49 R10 L62 R35. I realized they must be combinations. *L* for left, *R* for right. The wall safe? Briefcases? Something that Dad needed to lock. I'd probably never know.

Still searching the little black book, I called my godfather, Harvey, now in his late eighties and still living in San Francisco, to see what he might know. After we had exchanged some small talk, I plowed ahead. "I'm not sure if you know that my father confided in me about his life, including the fact that he was with you."

There was a long silence.

"Well, you know I am a man of Christ and take communion every day," he said. "I've been celibate for over thirty years. I'm old now, Tina, and I need to be studying for my finals."

He went on to say that Dad was the one who had convinced him to convert to Catholicism when they were lovers in Germany in the late fifties and early sixties. It gives new meaning to the word *irony*—an active homosexual converting other homosexuals to devote themselves to a religion that rejected them.

"Did you know that my father worked for the Vatican?" I asked my godfather.

"Yes, he told me he was working for them, but he never told me what he did," Harvey said.

Not fully believing him, I pressed a bit, but he quickly changed the subject. I have tried to reach Harvey again—calling no less than ten times over the past year. Unfortunately, he doesn't answer the phone, nor has he returned my calls. I called Yusuf, Dad's longtime Palestinian friend, who was at the funeral mass and whom I had met briefly in his souvenir shop in the West Bank. He gushed about Dad's goodness, his generosity—Dad having put many impoverished Palestinians through college, unbeknownst to me—and his devotion to the Church. Then, sadly, he described the deep pain Dad felt over what he interpreted as his family's lack of love for him. Rather than paint a picture for Yusuf that might explain my family's side of things, I listened to his broken English. "Your father drank not because he like the drink, but to forget. Only to forget. He didn't feel the family loved him. He hurt deeply."

On the one hand, I felt sorry for my father. But on the other, I was happy that at least Dad had someone with whom he could to share his pain. When I asked Yusuf about Dad's work for the Vatican, he claimed he didn't know details but revealed this: "Your father had many connections at the Vatican, but it had nothing to do with the travel agency." No wonder the Vatican employed his services—he was a closed book, trustworthy till the end with their secrets.

I then started making bolder requests. I eventually found my way into meetings and conversations with the UN ambassador to the Holy See, the UN ambassador to Jordan, the former patriarch to Jerusalem, the editor of a respected Vatican publication, the lieutenancy of the Holy Sepulchre in New York City, and the office of the grand master of the Holy Sepulchre Archives at the Vatican. In most of these meetings I found my interviewees careful, cautious, and tight-lipped when it came to my questions.

However, most agreed, in light of the facts I had shared, that my father was most certainly doing missions—secret assignments for the Church. In my meetings with the UN ambassadors to Jordan and the Holy See, they confirmed the use of trustworthy laypeople to carry out political missions on behalf of the pope. It is not a well-kept secret that the Catholic Church has a vested interest in world politics, such as their active commitment to end communism after World War II. It has also been widely reported that the Church has often worked behind the scenes to support overthrowing regimes or getting rid of dictators—like Stalin—that prevented freedom of religion, or worse, persecuted Catholics. When it comes to the Vatican, politics and faithfulness are intertwined.

One Church source assured me that she would help in any way possible, promising meetings with lower-level Church figures who she said were my best bet.

"You can't go too high up the food chain because they will not tell you," she warned.

After our first meeting, I never heard from her again. When I asked the UN ambassador of Jordan how my father could have a Jordanian passport, she reminded me that the Vatican and Jordan have very close ties, stating, "If the Vatican had requested a passport for your father, the Jordanian government would have certainly issued it. I have no way of knowing, but it sounds like your father was definitely doing missions for the Holy See."

She also explained that the Vatican army was trained by Jordanian special forces. She ended our meeting with "The Church does a lot of good around the world." I think this was her way of telling me that Dad's missions may have been secret, but that didn't mean they were dishonorable. Then she suggested I speak with the ambassador to the Holy See. And so it went.

A bit frustrated, I went back to the annual Christmas letters, the Worthington Wonderland, reviewing the fifties, when it seems most likely that his work began, during the papacy of Pope Pius XII—who served from 1939 to 1958, during World War II and the Cold War that followed. The most inexplicable fact that slipped into the family letters was that Dad traveled to two communist countries—to the USSR in November 1958, and Yugoslavia in May of the same year. Catholicism and communism go together about as well as disco in Appalachia. Under a communist regime, people are not free to worship. And even worse for the Church, there was open persecution of Catholics in these two countries. Fascism may not have been ideal in the fifties and sixties, from a moral standpoint, but it sure was good for the collection basket when a totalitarian regime insists that the state religion is Catholicism—as was the case with Franco in Spain.

It was this type of investment in anticommunism, and the need to appear nonpolitical, that made couriers invaluable to Pope Pius XII and the popes that followed. I believe my father was a Vatican courier, making stops all over the world to promote the political will of the Catholic Church.

According to Mark Riebling's book *Church of Spies: The Pope's Secret War Against Hitler,* Pius ran the first spy service and skimmed from Church charities to pay covert couriers. The timing of Dad's 1958 trip—when very few Americans were traveling to Russia—is intriguing. Dad's trip coincides with a major shift in relations between the USSR and the Holy See. According to Alberto Giovannetti's *Pius XII Speaks to the Church of Silence,* published in January 1958, the Soviet foreign minister, Andrei Gromyko, announced the USSR's interest in establishing formal relations with the Vatican at this time. Pope Pius XII did not respond officially, and records will not be available until 2028, when the Vatican archives open access to all documents of his reign.

Dad also had claimed to have a wealth of information on

the former head of the Vatican Bank, Archbishop Marcinkus, who was indicted for alleged ties to the 1970s counterfeit-bond scheme involving the Vatican and the Mafia, as well as accused of being an accomplice—according to journalist David Yallop—in the alleged murder of Pope John Paul I. Marcinkus was famous for saying, "You can't run the Church on Hail Marys."

My research has led me to believe that Dad was acting as a secret servant, doing special assignments for the Vatican in political negotiations and financial dealings where the Church wanted to appear neutral in world affairs, focused on being the shepherd to its flock and not on foreign governments. Under the guise of his travel business, Dad covered inexplicable miles around the world, making mostly one-day stops—the trait of a courier on a mission. He was likely carrying highly sensitive documents, or cash, while holding a Vatican passport that let him move through customs—as I witnessed—without being searched. Dad never, ever checked a suitcase, always traveling with an overnight bag and a briefcase, no matter how long the trip. This went on for decades.

Dad's charm, his devotion to the Church, his work ethic, his ability to speak and read Latin, his unwavering commitment to lies and keeping secrets, made him the perfect trusted servant to the most secret of institutions. And because he did his job with the utmost discretion and commitment, there is no trace. No paper trail.

I've often thought of my childhood as a microcosm of the Catholic Church, where secrets and lack of transparency ruled the day. Where dark secrets—from the Nazis to the Vatican Bank scandals to clergy abuse—were kept to save face, protect the mask of morality. The culture of secrecy existed in my home, as it clearly exists in the Catholic Church. Dad's secrets may never be fully uncovered. I, too, traded in secrets, and like father like daughter, I was a champion secret keeper. But I'm through with all that. Today, I don't hide out anymore.

Dad was a charismatic romantic who appreciated living well, and yet devoted his life to serving the needs of the poor and handicapped. It's where he shined, working endless hours in the baths at Lourdes, assisting the sick and disabled. Today, his legacy continues, thanks to my devoted sister, Margaret, who is carrying on Dad's work.

I've spent decades immersed in my own healing waters—from therapy to acting—all in service of taking ownership of my life without shame or guilt. Using Dad's mantra of "There is nothing you cannot do if you put your mind to it," I have embraced my past. I think in order for me to get around the wreckage, I had to take myself on as a sort of project, an experiment in transformation. Find a way to be of service. Like Dad. But different.

is nothing you cannot do if you put your mind to it and that love isn't love until you give it away. To my one and only diamond, Gina Raphaela, you are pure heart wrapped up in a breathtaking package, who has championed my truth-telling since day one. I love and thank you all wholeheartedly.

Acknowledgments

To my magnificent publisher, HarperCollins, especially Lynn Grady and my fearless and whip-smart editor, Carrie Thornton, whose guidance and support have been priceless. To the entire team at HarperCollins, for their keen attention and care, especially Sean Newcott, Greg Villepique, Danielle Bartlett, Ben Steinberg, Kyran Cassidy, Rick Harris, and Katie Ostrowka. Thank you also to my rock-solid creative team: Susan Batson, Joel Gotler, Intellectual Property Group, Sarah Tomlinson, and Murray Weiss. And to all those who supported the early incarnations of this story across many platforms, especially Mark Lee, Daniella Vitale, Jim Fugitte, Tracy Goss, Andrea Quinn, Sandra Seacat, Wendy Spiller, Alexis Gargagliano, Kim Gillingham, and Vicky Pynchon. To my great big Catholic family—most especially my twelve siblings—for their love and support and their fierce commitment to serving others. My greatest love and gratitude to my mother—"the saint"—for her kindness and constant modeling of unconditional love and forgiveness. And to my partner in crime, my father—Sir John—who taught me there